ROYAL INSTITUTE OF PHILOSOPHY LECTURES

VOLUME ONE · 1966–1967

THE HUMAN AGENT

ROYAL INSTITUTE OF PHILOSOPHY LECTURES
VOLUME ONE · 1966–1967

THE HUMAN AGENT

MACMILLAN
LONDON · MELBOURNE · TORONTO
ST MARTIN'S PRESS
NEW YORK
1968

MACMILLAN & CO LTD
Little Essex Street London WC2
and also at Bombay Calcutta and Madras
Macmillan South Africa (Publishers) Pty Ltd Johannesburg
The Macmillan Company of Australia Pty Ltd Melbourne
The Macmillan Company of Canada Ltd Toronto
St Martin's Press Inc New York

Library of Congress catalog card no. 68-10755

Printed in Great Britain by
ROBERT MACLEHOSE AND CO LTD
The University Press, Glasgow

24268

CONTENTS

FOREWORD

On Friday evenings in the winter months London members
of the Royal Institute of Philosophy and their friends meet in
a small hall in Bloomsbury – 14 Gordon Square, London,
W.C.1 – to listen to, and discuss, lectures by foremost British,
and visiting, philosophers. The Institute has a quarterly journal,
Philosophy, edited by Professor H. B. Acton, in which wide-
ranging philosophical issues are debated in as lucid and non-
technical a manner as the subject-matter permits. Such are the
demands on the space of this journal, however, that no more
than two or three of each year's lectures can be reproduced in
it. In response to requests by members of the Institute living too
far from London to attend the lectures (the Institute has a
world-wide membership) arrangements have been made for a
limited number of them to be recorded for broadcasting by the
B.B.C., and for all of them to be published in a yearly volume,
which is for sale to members of the general public as well as to
members of the Institute. This is the first such volume, containing lectures delivered during the winter of 1966–7.

The lectures in a particular session are on more or less
closely related topics. In 1967–8, for instance, nearly all of
them will be on issues in the philosophy of religion. Some of
them will be by people whose teaching has contributed to the
re-examination of traditional views about God that is a
feature of contemporary professional, and popular, theology.

The lectures reproduced in this first volume are concerned,
not with God, but with man: man as an agent, a being who
acts and reflects on his actions. Even the very concept of man
as a free agent is questioned. In what does his experience of
being free consist? Can man be free and yet his actions be
predictable? How is a man's own explanation of what he does
related to the scientist's account of what goes on in his brain

and nervous system? Are his 'deliberations' and 'decisions' really nothing but his brain processes as they are subjectively apprehended? And what are we to understand by the notion of man as a moral agent? Can studies of how people use words to persuade and prescribe reveal the nature of morality, or do they leave out what is essential – reference to the grounds of moral judgment? Do they favour an unduly individualistic account of morality? How is the concept of being moral related to that of playing a role in society? These are but a few of the questions to which answers are sought in this volume.

The lectures are by G. P. Henderson, Professor of Philosophy at Queen's College, Dundee; Aurel Kolnai, Visiting Lecturer at Bedford College, London; Bernard Mayo, Reader in Philosophy at the University of Birmingham; Alan R. White, Ferens Professor of Philosophy at the University of Hull; David Pears, Student of Christ Church, Oxford; C. H. Whiteley, Reader in Philosophy at the University of Birmingham; The Earl of Halsbury, President of the Royal Institute of Philosophy; G. N. A. Vesey, Reader in Philosophy at King's College, London; R. J. Hirst, Professor of Logic at the University of Glasgow; C. K. Grant, Professor of Philospohy at the University of Durham; G. J. Warnock, Fellow of Magdalen College, Oxford; Gilbert Ryle, Waynflete Professor of Metaphysical Philosophy at Oxford University; and Richard Wollheim, Grote Professor of Mind and Logic at University College, London.

G. N. A. VESEY
Honorary Director,
The Royal Institute of Philosophy

1

PREDICTABILITY IN HUMAN AFFAIRS

G. P. Henderson

I WANT to talk about a strong sense of the terms 'predict', 'prediction', 'predictability', and so on; to take up the question whether a social science may aspire to predict in the strong sense; and to consider some bearings of this question on the free-will problem.

There are ways and ways of saying how the future, in some respect, is going to turn out. In so saying we may base our words on evidence, or we may not, and we may be more or less committed by them. Thus, there is prophecy, prognostication, precognition, clairvoyance, expressing a hunch, forecasting, making an estimate and predicting. I do not propose here and now to judge the question whether there is or can be some distinction in meaning between any pair of these expressions that you may take. My immediate interest is in only two of them, namely 'making an estimate' and 'predicting': let us approach the notion of a prediction (eventually, of a 'strong' prediction) through that of an estimate. Imagine, therefore, the following situation:

A large, powerful and sophisticated modern state, Galenia, has as one of its neighbours a small but hostile country, Sphekia, which it regards as a constant danger to itself. Sphekia is under the authoritarian rule of a certain Agrio, a man who has been well trained in un-Galenian political doctrine, but also a complex character who does not always play the political game according to the book. The Galenian government, there-

fore, appoints a psychologist to do nothing but study and report
on him. Such action by a government is not, in these days,
incredible; and the example may suggest some familiar differences in the expectations that people have as to its results.
What would be the psychologist's general brief? Obviously his
task would be to study Agrio's history on every side and to form
conclusions about how Agrio behaves and acts in different
circumstances. His objective would be to supply the Galenian
government with what we may call, in a low key, estimates;
anticipations, good enough to act on, of Agrio's responses and
initiatives in any future situation where they matter. Such
situations would vary, of course, and any one of them could be
to some degree unprecedented, but the psychologist's estimates
ought to be on the right lines at least. They should save the
government from having either no policy as regards Agrio or
else the wrong one. In the first instance they should lessen the
fear of being taken by surprise: in the second they should be
adaptable, capable of being corrected instead of abandoned if
conditions to some extent new should arise.

In thus describing what might be expected of the Galenian
psychologist I have used the weak term 'estimates'. The term
'predictions' might have been used, in a loose way, for the same
purpose, but also it might have indicated expectations that
were too high. An estimate is an approximate judgment. It is
reflective, that is, it depends on evidence, but it is not logically
entailed by the evidence and does not purport to be.[1] Anyone
who means what he says when he calls some judgment of his
about the future 'an estimate' is prepared to have things not
turn out accordingly. This can be conveyed in, for example, a
portentous or ceremonious use of the verb 'estimate': 'I estimate that Agrio will decide to attack Limani eleven months
hence.' It has to be emphasised that an estimate of this kind
about the future might quite readily and naturally, in an
unreflective use of terms, be called a prediction. Very frequently
we do use the term 'prediction' of what we are prepared to see
falsified. But sometimes, with some consciousness of a contrast
between estimates and predictions, we do not. On this side of

[1] An estimate in this respect is like a certain well-known kind of forecast,
namely weather-forecasts.

the coin, an estimate about the future is not a prediction. In 'estimating' that Agrio will still be in power a year hence I may well convey, by my use of that word, that I am unwilling to go so far as prediction. I should thus be trading, I think, on a strong sense of the latter term. How is this sense to be explained?

We are working, it appears, towards a sense of 'prediction' according to which a prediction depends on evidence, but depends on it in some more satisfactory way than does an estimate. Even in this sense, a prediction cannot be logically entailed, any more than an estimate, by the evidence available. But a prediction, most strongly regarded, is a judgment made both as if the evidence available were all that is required and as if precisely it were what the evidence entailed. The point comes out, again, in ceremonious usage. Someone who means what he says when he calls some judgment of his about the future a prediction is not prepared not to have things turn out accordingly. Take, for example, 'I am prepared to predict that there will be no settlement with Rhodesia during the next three months.' Here prediction is – as nearly as can be – purporting to foretell, purporting to say what will or will not happen, in effect providing the world with a fixed point. When I say, deliberately, 'I am prepared to predict that the trade gap in November will be at least 20 per cent. smaller than June's' I am expressing only slightly less complete commitment: at any rate the greatest confidence attainable in these matters. By contrast, when I say 'I estimate that the gap will be at least 20 per cent. smaller' I am expressing assurance in some degree, but one which falls perceptibly short of certainty or near-certainty. A prediction in the strong sense is to an estimate as a firm belief is to an opinion. Neither strong prediction nor firm belief is completely unrelative: as my examples may have suggested, there are strong predictions and strongish predictions: but of strong predictions, as of firm beliefs, we have familiar enough examples.

Suppose that our Galenian psychologist has been asked for predictions rather than estimates. If he has, his government's expectations of him are pitched high. And one can quite easily imagine some official as saying: 'I don't want "estimates" from

you, I want to know for sure what the fellow will do.' Here
predictions, in the strong sense, are being asked for, and the
demand may well be premature. On the other hand it may not
be premature in some circumstances.

There may be scientific and there may be unscientific prediction, both in the strong sense of the term. Often when someone says, ceremoniously, 'I predict . . .', what he has to say is
of autobiographical interest only. All that is happening is that
an individual is making the strongest possible claim for what
he is saying about the future, namely that what he is saying is
true, and he conveys his confidence by means of the words 'I
predict . . .'. 'A prediction', correspondingly, would be a statement as to the future made strongly, but under mainly personal auspices. However, there can be better auspices than
these. Such auspices are taken for granted, for example, by the
official who (misguidedly it may be) calls on the Galenian
psychologist to produce predictions and not just estimates of
what Agrio will do. There are predictions expressive not merely
of confidence but of justified confidence. I mean, justified not
solely in the sight of God but in the sense that the confidence
can be made good in human terms. A prediction of this kind
is one which derives its authority exclusively from the theory
in terms of which it is made, and not at all from the individuality
of the individual who makes it. That there are such predictions seems clear. Thus, a scientist at the Royal Observatory
'predicts' that a satellite will be visible in such-and-such a
position at such-and-such a time, granted such-and-such
weather conditions. He does so not on his own authority, but
in the name of the astronomy, physics and meteorology whose
mouthpiece he is.

When is a science strong enough to have 'strong' predictions
made in its name? There is no precise answer to this question.
One can only try to point out the sort of general conditions that
would have to be satisfied. One might safely suggest three.
First, the science would have to have a well-established
theoretical apparatus, namely a recognised technical language
or notation, together with logically satisfactory procedures for
connecting its accepted principles together and for deriving
new ones (independently of experiment). These conditions

would be satisfied by the mathematical theory or theories appropriate to some physical science; for example the geometry of a four-dimensional space–time manifold involved in the theory of general relativity. Secondly, the science would have to possess a relatively long and varied case-history. One can only say 'relatively': what I have in mind is a case-history that has passed its critical stage, so to speak. (It is hardly necessary to say that experimental physics provides a case in point. It is perhaps more interesting in this connection to mention the situation of psychiatry. Psychiatry for some time past has been supporting itself to a very large extent on accumulated case-history. It lacks the sort of theoretical framework that physics possesses, but its case-history is sufficient to furnish what Mill called Empirical Laws, and these, though they may want 'the causal laws which explain them',[1] are sufficient in turn to let the science work and progress. Whether this means that psychiatry's case-history is near, at, or beyond its critical stage I need not attempt to say: but it does convey the idea that a stage in the elaboration and elucidation of case-history is reached, after which, but not before, the science concerned may be said to operate with some confidence.) There remains a third condition to be satisfied by a science strong enough to have 'strong' predictions made in its name. This is that the science would have to have well-recognised ways of interpreting its case-history in terms of its theoretical apparatus. I am thinking of what Mill, following Bacon, called *axiomata media*: mediating principles like the various ways that exist in physical science of establishing connections between different geometrical schemes and the distribution of masses in some spatial region. (Whether Mill is right as against Bacon in thinking that these are got deductively and not inductively is of no consequence here.) In general, what I want to suggest is that many of our older 'natural' sciences, organic as well as inorganic, satisfy the three conditions mentioned, at least over large stretches of their more familiar subject-matter. In other terms, many are in a position to make 'strong' predictions in a great variety of circumstances.

Take a familiar example in which, given some natural or

[1] *Logic*, Bk. VI, ch. V.

contrived event as a starting-point, we know in what sort of sequence it will, characteristically, be an item. The oxidation of oil on the fibres of rags or waste, in a sufficiently confined space, can be counted on to result in combustion. We have to do here with a pattern of sequence, and we are at no loss how to refer this pattern to 'laws'. Thus, we know that the combustion of oily waste in the circumstances described is an instance of the generation of heat faster than it can be dissipated. Explanation and prediction are interwoven here. In explaining some present event we commit ourselves not only as regards its background, temporally regarded, but also to viewing nature, in respects suggested by the occurrence of this event, as repeating itself. The event, in its setting, tells us what laws are involved, and the laws tell us about other events, whether past, contemporary or future, besides this one. To enlarge the horizon: it would be pedantic and ridiculous for an astronomer, who had given his mind to computing accurately the present phase of the moon, to affect not to be sure when some other phase will be due but to offer, on reflection, only an 'estimate'. He is fully entitled to predict, in the strongest sense of the term.

The astronomer's confidence, his right to predict, presupposes that the course of nature in relevant respects is and will be uniform. Of course we can, if we are so minded, apply to his predictions a classic scepticism about inductive reasoning. We can affirm that in some ultimate sense of 'validation' they can no more be validated than can their contraries. With this particular problem, however, I am not concerned here. What does concern me is that for vital purposes we grant the exact scientist the prerogative of knowing, within a broad field, how things are and will be. Indeed we rely on him to have this knowledge. We do not expect it to issue in a (strongly) predictive answer to any and every specific question about the future which we may put to him within his field. Often enough we shall be satisfied with an estimate at best. But sometimes we do expect, and we receive, predictions. The question to which I want to turn now is the question whether the ability to rise to prediction, in the strong sense of the term, must be confined to the classic, hitherto more 'exact' sciences. Still setting aside the problem of induction, we may ask: is there some reason of principle – and not just the degree of 'exactness' achieved hitherto – why the newer, 'social' sciences should not have the same ability? In the field of human nature can we know how things are and will be, so that we are entitled, on occasion, to offer predictions and not estimates of what people, even most thinkingly, will do? And is there some intellectual confusion behind the dislike which some people undoubtedly have for this prospect?

Let us try to keep clear what a reason of principle would be. You hear it said often enough that the circumstances in which individual human beings act are such as to make the prediction of anyone's actions always presumptuous. What does this mean? It may mean that such circumstances just are very complex, and too involved ever to get hold of properly. This, I think, would not be a reason of principle; though I shall return to establish the point later. Or it may mean – and this would be one – that amongst the circumstances is some one which simply, of its nature, escapes prediction; and that you cannot normally ignore the possibility of its being there. It could be some circumstance which had a necessary bearing on the action which you were trying to predict, but it itself would be a sheer quintessential variable, as impossible to pin down as a blob of quicksilver. I have in mind free will understood in an indeterminist sense: a will which bears on action but which is a law unto itself, and which ensures that there will be an eternal gap between any system of principles, general or mediating, which we may construct for prediction, and the human actions to which they are to be applied.

Who holds such a view of freedom? I propose to name no names, but simply to observe that an 'indeterminist' notion is not unknown, taken as a fixed point from which to survey and co-ordinate the whole remaining field of moral notions. What excuse can I have then for dismissing it from consideration, as I propose to do? Simply that in speculation on the present scale about the possibility of prediction in the social sciences, one cannot treat this beleaguered philosophical notion as a stopper. Notoriously, it is a matter of dispute how successfully it does co-ordinate moral notions: and, to go further back, its very intelligibility is in question. We cannot therefore cite it as an essentially variable condition which, without more ado, rules out prediction, in the strong sense, of human action. If we want to be less question-begging about the conditions which pose a difficulty for such prediction, we must concentrate on alternative objections.

One alternative which does not presuppose any particular analysis of *freedom* is this. We are commonly reminded that human beings, and human beings alone amongst possible objects of scientific study, have the power actively to falsify predictions about themselves. The power depends upon knowing what a particular prediction is, so that then one can set oneself to upset the prediction, perhaps just for the heck of it. Worse than this: it is logically possible to upset even a prediction which allows for one's desire to upset predictions. Perversity can be erected into a policy, and so the predictability of human actions can never be guaranteed.

This line of thought is engaging, but I am inclined to disparage it, for the following reasons:

1. Not all predictions need be known by those to whom they refer, so that at least some predictions can ignore the kind of mischief-making just described.

2. The desire to upset predictions merely for the sake of doing so is a recherché one and could be self-sacrificial. Other predictions, therefore, provided they took this fact into account, could be redeemed: that is, we could allow for the fact that with some people the desire to upset predictions about themselves is not a sufficient motive for upsetting certain of those predictions.

3. I can of course say to someone, for whom the desire referred to is a sufficient and predominant motive, 'You will do the opposite of whatever I predict', and be correct at this level – provided always that 'predict' is not used here in its strong sense. Apparently, however, I cannot specify what such a person will do. The moment I specify what he 'will' do, he will do the opposite. Keeping my ultimate corrected prediction about him secret from him is the only way of catching him out, as it were.

In principle this difficulty must be admitted, but we should keep it in proportion. It is only where agent and predictor are in a position to continue their dialectic indefinitely – so long as, for one thing, the agent's policy does not break down in psychosis – that there can be no prediction of what the agent will do. The situation thus imagined is in any case artificial; but even if it were not, the exercise of anti-scientific zeal in this particular way is unlikely to take place on a large scale.

4. The lurking enemy here is perhaps not so much the person who tries to be madly consistent, as the person who keeps the possibility of upsetting predictions in his pocket, as a threat that may be pulled out at any time; but when, we do not know. What hope is there of 'strong' prediction about this man – who might be any one of us?

The question when a certain person *A* will set himself to upset a particular prediction about him is itself a question of social scientific interest. Why should he do it at one particular time rather than another? If questions of this sort can be answered (and I assume that in principle they can), then we can use the knowledge so gained to revise and correct our prediction of what *A* will in fact do: but only so long as we keep this prediction secret from *A*. One would only defeat oneself if one said: 'I predict that you will do *x* and not *y*, and in predicting this I am taking into account the consequences of telling you that that is what you will do.' If *A*'s policy is simply to spring a nasty surprise as and when opportunity offers, then here is just as good an opportunity as any, and there is no hope of disarming him or browbeating him by professing to have taken care of whatever he does in the light of one's 'prediction'. Once again it seems as if a determined enemy could rule out the possibility of 'strong' prediction regarding himself, when one of the conditions of the prediction's being made is that he shall know of it.

But consider once again what this concession amounts to. *A*'s cat-and-mouse version of anti-predictionism was made intimidating because *A* was represented as a person 'who might be any one of us'. And of course he might, but any one of us, in order to play the game described, would have to be in a rather special position: he would have to have predictions about himself communicated faithfully to him over an indefinitely

long period of time, and he would have to be strongly motivated
against the idea of strong prediction applied to himself, in order
to find the game worth playing or worth persevering with.
And of course it is only predictions of what he individually will
do that are affected. As a factor in the community, when we
are interested in what the community will do, he can be
allowed for.

I must now consider a second alternative objection that
might confront the exponent of prediction. I have already noted
it briefly, and dismissed it provisionally as not involving a
matter of principle. However, there might well be argument
over this point. The objection runs that a human being's actions
are too many and too complex ever to allow of authoritative
prediction on a scientific basis. The difficulty of prediction, it
is pointed out, mounts the more we try to be definite and specific
in saying what people, taken either generally or severally, will
be doing at some particular time or place. To put it rhetori-
cally, how can we know enough about someone's (or some
group's) material and spiritual (or 'cultural') conditions –
wealth, health, education, social ties, ambitions, tastes, beliefs
and values, as they interplay in some particular setting – to let
us predict what he or they will do: predict, that is to say, with
anything remotely like the precision and the authority with
which a physicist or a chemist may speak, even with regard to
changes destined to happen at times and in places far removed
from the present?

The problem of complex circumstances, it seems to me,
remains an empirical problem in the sense that, no matter how
impressively stated, it implies no actual incoherence in the
supposition that we can know enough about the laws and
conditions of human action to predict with scientific confidence
what people will do. But if one observes that the difficulties
just described are purely practical, the reply is apt to come that
difference in quantity here turns into one of quality. The
practical difficulty is of such a degree that it *is* a difficulty of
principle. Overcoming it is not something that we can envisage.

Clearly, to dispute whether a matter of principle is involved
here is partly to engage in a battle of words. That is, if we
accept the implication that the ideal of predictability in social

science is a practically hopeless one; and if we can comfort
ourselves only with the reminder that, nevertheless, the difficulty is such as could logically be overcome, then it matters
little whether we call this a defeat in principle or not. But is the
prospect in fact as hopeless as all that? Rightly or wrongly we
do envisage overcoming the problem of complex circumstances,
in special fields intensively studied. For example, we are only
at the beginning of our knowledge how to deal with young
people sent to remand centres or approved schools. It is not
unrealistic to think that some day we may know very well how
to deal with them. We hope to predict the cure of their disturb-
ances as confidently as we predict, say, recoveries from
operations for appendicitis. In this connection we are liable to
be browbeaten by an *a priori* scepticism about what we are
trying to do.

But knowing enough about the laws and conditions of human
action – what is this? (Let us return to meet the general
challenge.) Is there any limit to such possible knowledge, so
that on some occasions at least we can be sure that we know
all that is relevant? That is to say, is there such a fixed set of
principles ('laws') of human action, that on some given
occasion we do not need to worry ourselves with the prospect
that a hitherto unformulated law may be needed: and is there
any limitation upon the circumstances which might call for the
introduction of some such law?

These questions are general, and my reply has to be equally
general. There *may* turn out to be a fixed set of principles,
comparable with those which certain sciences have used
successfully in explanation (and prediction) hitherto: the
contrary of this, I suggest, has not been shown. And we *may*
come to know what circumstances are relevant, because this
too can be a function of our scientific experience. Any science
has to make its own decisions about economy and relevance,
and the question what counts as 'enough' in our knowledge
about laws and conditions is a scientific question, the answer
to which is competently given in terms of the history and
methodology of the science concerned. The trend of my
remarks hitherto has been that an *a priori* case has not been
made out against social science's ever laying claim to such

competence. Rather it seems reasonable to wait and see whether
one or more of the social sciences may not feel strong enough to
make predictions in a strong sense of the term.

When you come to think of it, the complacency with which
the objection just considered is often made is of a rather
interesting kind: suggesting that the objection registers some
sort of safeguard of our freedom. Human nature and its scene
of action are too complex to allow of scientific prediction,
therefore we are assured against determinism. As if the knowledge involved in scientific prediction bound the future, or
actually constituted the pattern of things to come: as if it were
not a case of things having to be known as they are, but of
things having to be as they are known to be. The problem is
the old theological problem of God's foreknowledge, feared as
making what will be inescapable, but with the social sciences
cast in the role of Gods-presumptive.

Scientific prediction is not the same as prophecy or pre-
vision; and if it is foreknowledge then it is foreknowledge of a
quite particular kind. It is preparedness to say what will be on
the basis of what is or has been. It is built on explanation, on
the ability to give an account of how things of a certain kind
are, or have been, and its prediction consists of an extrapolation, as it were, from past and present. No bond is put on the
future thereby. Nothing is made to come about merely because
science says that it will turn out thus and so.

No, but is not science in a position to say this only because
things are made to come about in the way it says? Allowing that
knowledge does not constitute a bond on the future, are we any
better off? If what is worrying us is the idea that whatever we
do we must do, then would not the success of social science be
at least a sign of a completely freedomless universe?

By this route we have arrived at what I think is the heart of
the problem of free will. The worry that I have just been
speaking about is associated explicitly or implicitly with a
certain view of knowledge, which could be expressed in the
slogan 'Knowledge is of what must be'. The slogan trades on a
somewhat arbitrary stipulation about 'knowledge', but one
which has an ancient history in philosophy and has been
influential. 'Knowledge can only be of necessary truths', we

might put it, formally. And so anything that aspires to be knowledge, as the propositions of science do, would have to claim to express necessity in some sense. Not that all those philosophers who have held most strongly to this view of knowledge would have recognised the claim of what we now call science to aspire to 'knowledge': but some would. For these the necessification of science has been an ideal to be aimed at, if very far indeed from being achieved. Few would now deny that to think of science as consisting, ideally, of necessary truths, on the model of pure mathematics, is misguided. But, still, the feeling that a well-proved scientific proposition must express necessity in some way has outlived the critical destruction of the rationalist necessitarian view. In some minds causal necessity (a *revenant* from 1738) has satisfied the feeling, in others a quite crude mechanism, in others the forces of nature (again understood very vaguely, but in the biological sciences taking such forms as natural selection, the *élan vital* and even economic determinism). The idea has persisted, anyhow, that anything which science proves to exist or to act in such-and-such ways must exist or, in those ways, act.

Let us try the effect of dropping the 'must'. Let us say that science shows us how things are, how things happen and how things are to be done. The 'are' and the 'happen' are untensed, because science is not history, not even contemporary history. It tells us, amongst other matters, how we act and how we are motivated, the ways in which we develop and satisfy desires, form and fulfil intentions, and so on, always in some special set of terms, those of physiology, for example, or some branch of psychology, or sociology. In doing so it does not obliterate but rather it takes up the distinction between acting freely and acting under compulsion and makes of it what it can. A science tells us in its own terms how a certain action takes place. But there are free actions, in the sense of actions done because of a preference for one course over another and done for an explicit reason, after greater or lesser deliberation. Science tells us about such actions amongst others by showing us what general 'laws' they satisfy, or, to use a more innocuous terminology, of what general ways of working they are instances. A preference, for example, may be understood in scientific as in other terms by being typified, in science by being shown to be a more or less special instance of a general kind with which, scientifically, we are familiar. A reason given for some action may be understood (say because it adverts to values of some sort, or obligations, or custom, or fashion, or a role to be played, all of which can be studied in general), be thus referred to more or less familiar general principles, and become intelligible, in or out of science, accordingly. And if acting freely and acting under compulsion are the same from a certain point of view, for example if both can be represented as ways in which energy is transferred from one set of cells to another set of cells, this indicates merely a general basis which they share. No number of discoveries that they both satisfy this, that and the next general scientific law, that is, that they may be explained to the satisfaction of a particular science by means of a common technical vocabulary which represents them as instances of a common way of working – no amount of success in this direction should be thought to drain away the distinction between acting freely and being compelled. What it comes to is rather that a science is competent to tell us, in its own terms, how we act when we are acting freely; just as it can tell us how we act when we are acting under compulsion.

Of course there are limitations on human action, and science will have its own way of describing what these are. Flesh and blood can do only so much, and experience can teach us only so much. All of our freedom is freedom within limits, physical, mental and social. But determinists often speak as if this conception of limit could be extended inwards, as it were: as if the limits to our freedom which we all recognise were merely a conventional boundary: as if under a clear scrutiny this boundary retreated inwards and shrank, leaving less and less and finally nothing at all to be encompassed as free action. Such an extension of the notion of limits on action is a misconception. To say that 'free' action, within its natural limitations, satisfies 'laws' or principles is not to say that that action is limited all along the line in that same natural way that we have recognised. It is to say that it is limited in a different way or not at all. And there is little to be said for retaining the word 'limited' in this connection, considering that what we are drawing attention to in treating free human action scientifically is regularity, the peculiar sort of regularity that free human action does have. To say that free action, like other action, satisfies laws is to use language which may be convenient in some respects. But it is very misleading. 'Laws' here are general principles, and these express regularities, patterns of co-existence and sequence the discovery of which *is* making intelligible, according to scientific canons, the subject-matter so co-ordinated. Free action is not action which is quintessentially irregular. This is a point that science is making, and I cannot see that in making it science is really destroying what it contrives to explain.

Such, then, is the effect of giving up the narrow view of knowledge as of 'what must be'. And the effect, it seems to me, is beneficial. The antithesis of freedom and determinism remains irreconcilable if we shift that narrow view into the scientific field and join with it the view that science can produce 'knowledge' in whatever is to be the best and most respectable sense of the term. The effect of doing this is to suppose that whatever is true of human beings, amongst other subjects of scientific study, must needs be true. So that what, in fact, is to be also must needs be. If it is in fact the case that I am going to make such-and-such slip of the tongue half an hour hence, then I cannot not make that slip of the tongue. If it is true that X is going to commit a crime of violence fourteen years hence, then X cannot not commit that crime. As is notorious, there is a carry-over here from one kind of 'cannot' (proper to 'What is true cannot be false') to another, the 'cannot' of natural or human inability. Whatever may be known about me or about X (in the sense that it may be accurately predicted on good grounds), this of its very nature is not something that constrains or compels us. And equally, the knowledge does not depend on there being a constraining or compulsive factor in whatever we do. The truth of a scientific prediction is not tantamount to our being at the mercy of anything, to our proceeding into the future like more or less well-engined automobiles, or to our being highly-programmed logical machines.

It is a curious paradox, is it not, that we should resent the prospect of successful prediction in human affairs only when the predicting is done most carefully? Is it not odd that we should regard predictability at one level only – the scientific as distinct from the common – as blowing the gaff on our 'freedom'? For on the common level predictability is, on the whole, something that we all value. To get along we must know what people are going to do, individually and together: common relationships like friendship, business affairs and any kind of social organisation all require at least some such knowledge. Why then the nervousness about probing more deeply into what we ordinarily accept with equanimity?

It must seem apparent that at this point I am asking what is strictly a psychological or sociological question rather than a philosophical one; but what I want to argue is that the roots of the question lie in philosophical confusion, so that, no matter the auspices under which it is asked, the answer to it cannot do without philosophical explication. I think, then, that the reason for our nervousness is twofold: first, the idea that psycho-analytic and other scientific theories, or more heterogeneous theories like Marxism, purport to tell us how we 'really' behave and act, and that thereby they do away with the 'validity' of our reasons and the 'worth' of our motives for what we do: secondly, and possibly connected with this first idea, comes the idea that science's arcane knowledge allows of control, and that in a bad sense; to wit, the manipulation of individual human beings in the interests of plans and values other than their own.

Consider the sayings, 'All our values are functions – in a complex way – of our material, economic conditions' and 'All action is compulsive – like kleptomaniac behaviour or a check-ing complex – only more or less subtly so'. These are examples of a kind of universal statement which may sound chilly and depressing and may even inhibit people from taking proper account of such evidence as does underwrite them. In fact, each of those statements is a metaphysical exaggeration: in other terms, each expresses a metaphysics of 'latent' versus 'manifest' content, according to which the only or the real significance of what somebody says when, for example, he offers a reason for something that he has done, is more or less latent, and is subject to no such justification as he may claim for it in operating on the 'fictional' level of our normal thought. Consider especially the second of these sayings, which is the more relevant to the present theme. 'All action is (fundamentally) compulsive. . . .' It seems to mean either that the notion of freedom makes no sense or that, even if it can be defined after a fashion, it applies to nothing. In neither of these interpretations, I suggest, should the statement be allowed.

To begin with, the understanding of 'compulsiveness' itself is bound up with the understanding of 'freedom' (at any rate in some sense of this term). And to go on with, *freedom* is not one of those technical or theoretical concepts with regard to which it is an open question whether it applies to anything or not. On the contrary, the notion of freedom has grown up in – or, if you like, is at home in – a context of action. It is as silly to say 'We can't be sure that any action is really free' as it is to say 'We can't be sure that anything we see is real'. The distinction between free action and compelled is, quite simply, a reflection of human experience. What theorists do with the distinction is another matter. Amongst traditional determinists it is admittedly common to speak as if the distinction as such is improper. But many so-called determinists (Spinoza, for example) have really been interpreting or re-construing the distinction, not abolishing it: which I take to be a reflection of the fact that *freedom* is not a concept, some one concept, belonging to an *a priori* theoretical system for which we have to look around to discover possible applications; the *freedom* about which we may be concerned when we try to assess the notion of social science is a concept or perhaps a family of concepts, which is essential to the way in which we handle our experience in a day-to-day, common-sense fashion: it is completely at home in that setting, completely native to it. There is no question of doing without it. And within this same context it is absurd to say that there are really no such things as good reasons for making some choice, or a valid defence of one action as preferred to another, or worthy as opposed to unworthy motives for doing things. Moreover, this context is one to which we all belong some of the time. It is not merely that of common sense in its brute, unreflective aspect, but is also that of common sense 'methodised and corrected', of much of our educated, critical thinking.

What freedom, valid reasons and worthy motives may look like when, along with compulsion, invalid reasons and unworthy motives, they become part of the subject-matter of some science is that science's business – and of general human concern inasmuch as sciences tend to overflow their banks. Here is a main source of the sort of apprehension about social science which I have been discussing. I may have been speaking as if common sense (critical or not) and the sciences were isolated conceptual systems. But theorists of the various sciences make sure that this is not so. And it is certainly true that various psycho-analytic theories, for example, have modified in many ways our views of freedom, of valid reasons for action and of the worth of motives. There has been a change in our recognition of what in particular counts as acting freely, or as having valid reasons or worthy motives for what we choose to do. This change is proper. What is not proper is the abnegation of the concepts *freedom, validity* and *worth*. These concepts may be no part of the theoretical apparatus of some special science. To say unrestrictedly, therefore, that they are empty concepts is no better than to say unrestrictedly that there are no such things as tables because the most successful physics recognises only atoms and the void. Acting reasonably remains different from acting unreasonably, choosing after deliberation from a panic plunge, having, in the old-fashioned sense, a philosophy of life from being a mass of prejudices, and so on. In various ways (to sum this up) there remains a distinction between freedom and unfreedom.

The understanding of human action and behaviour which a social science may achieve is not, it should be remembered, a revelation of the ultimate human essence. A scientific account of human action and behaviour is less than social philosophy just as physics is less than natural philosophy. I do not mean that there is a subject called social philosophy which on its own disengages the essence of humanity; but there is a way of being conscious, critically conscious, of the linkage, the interrelationship of accounts which may be given of 'humanity', and this is in a sense more than any specific science. The account which any specific science may give is integrated with practice. It attempts to understand nature only through special kinds of observation, change and control of nature. Its language is operational, peculiarly adapted to the science's interference with its subject-matter in more or less set, formal ways. This applies, with due reservations, to the scientific study of human action and human behaviour *inter alia*. That study is limited in the general way just indicated, and is not (or at any rate ought not to be) essentialist in its outlook.

There remains the second source of apprehension to which I referred: 'Science's arcane knowledge allows of control, and that in a bad sense.' When the knowledge is direct knowledge of human nature, then the control of individual human beings in the interest of the scientifically stronger can be correspondingly direct. This fear may simply be a continuation of the one which I have described already: resting on the misconception that unless we are able to think in terms of some science or other we really don't understand ourselves at all, so that it is always up to science to say what should become of us and what is to be done with us. This fear may be unrealistic or it may not: it all depends how generally held is the misconception just mentioned. But there is another way of looking at our nervousness about science's power to control. Fear may rest not so much on anyone's misunderstandings as on the cynical misuse of science by persons who may be scientists themselves or may not. This fear, however, is both realistic and salutary.

Science, it must be admitted, knows how to prevent us from acting freely, but it knows also how to secure the conditions of free action, or at any rate many of them. Its ability to do these things is the operational side of a knowledge which permits, or foreshadows, prediction; of what we do freely as well as of what, in one way and another, we are compelled to do. I cannot see that this power to predict is offensive to human dignity, any more than did Leibniz, who was preoccupied with much the same problem when he said: 'Everybody agrees that future contingents are assured, since God foresees them; but for all that, it is not admitted that they are necessary.'

2

AGENCY AND FREEDOM

Aurel Kolnai

I. FREEDOM OF ACTION BY CHOICE AND FREE CHOICE

MOORE in *Ethics* (1912), ch. vii, writes – if I understand him
right – that our basic experience of free-will resides in our
certain feeling, in regard to our past actions, that we could have
acted differently if we had so chosen; more exactly, that we
should have acted differently if we had so chosen, which
precisely means that we could have acted differently. He adds
the qualifying adverb 'sometimes'; I think we may well say
always, keeping in mind, of course, (i) that we are only concerned here with 'actions' proper, as contrasted with involuntary movements, twitchings, starts, fits, etc., and also with
wholly habitual, routine-like movements or manipulations
performed without any attention and without the slightest
deliberation, and (ii) that only such actions are meant here as
are within our range of physical or psycho-physical power,
which is anyhow implicit in the concept of choice: there is no
sense in my saying that I might here and now 'choose' to carry
this building on my back to Paris, to dismiss the present
Government or to continue writing in impeccable Japanese.
However, Moore is aware of the clearly meaningful objection
that 'acting as we choose' (within those obvious limits) would
not establish the fact of free-will unless it were also the case
that our choice itself is (often) free, in other words that we not
only choose to act so instead of acting differently but also
choose to choose so instead of choosing differently. He argues

20

that this too is indeed (often) the case, emphasising in this context our experience of the unpredictability, even by ourselves, of our future choices (or of many or most of them). He concludes, though, on a note of doubt which shows that he is not quite sure in his own mind to have definitively disposed of the objection.

It is here that I propose to take up the thread again, suggesting a re-examination of Moore's proper starting-point, the experience of 'doing what we choose' – rather than going on to ask whether we really 'choose to choose what we choose' and challenging the determinist to predict our (or again, his own) future choices. My tentative contention is that the concept of 'choosing to choose, etc.' is apt to lead us into a maze of infinite regress and that a discussion of predictability,[1] though certainly not devoid of interest, may well prove (as Moore himself seems to have found it) to be inconclusive, whereas the incontestable fact that we act by choice may itself furnish the key to our focal experience of free-will – an experience that perhaps has something illusory about it but cannot, in common sense, repose on mere illusion or misinterpretation.

Suppose I am confronted with a classic situation of practical choice, e.g. two offers mutually exclusive, each of them involving obvious advantages but also some drawbacks, while to turn down both offers would land me in dire difficulties without any substantial advantage to balance them, and after weighing the respective pros and cons ('deliberation') I decide in favour of one of these offers as against the other: that is, I choose *A* discarding *B*; I choose to accept *A* and, correspondingly, to reject *B*. I then proceed to act according to my choice, on the lines of the policy implied by my acceptance of *A* and rejection of *B*. Now, on being asked the question why I do (and omit) the various things I do (and omit) in following up my choice, I may meaningfully answer by pointing out the main advantages and disadvantages in question and explain how, in my estimate, 'on balance' *A* has emerged as the more advantageous

---

[1] That freedom, 'an intrinsic characteristic of the agent', should not be based on 'unpredictability' (which is 'extrinsic to the agent') is forcefully argued by A. R. Lacey, 'Free Will and Responsibility', *Proceedings of the Aristotelian Society* (October 1957), p. 32.

of the two alternative courses. This is indeed what my inter-
locutor, or perhaps I myself in surveying *après coup* the reason-
ableness of my decision, probably wished to know (or to test
once more). But the purport of the question, and accordingly
the relevancy of my answer – no matter how far it, that is to
say my choice itself, may be materially correct – is not unam-
biguous. So far as the 'Why' of the question is a causal 'Why'
and refers, not to the justification of my choice, but to the
explanation of my doing such and such things, rather than other
things, in the sequel, the proper answer is not that I do them
on the grounds listed nor because they satisfy this or that urge,
inclination, interest or aspiration of mine, but that I do them
because I have chosen to do them. In all exquisite choice
situations, a case might be made out just as plausibly for not
doing these things but on the contrary to embark on the
alternative course of action; this is implicit in the fact that I
was carefully weighing the respective pros and cons before
taking my decision. And my acting is my carrying out that
decision, i.e. my execution or 'making valid' of that choice;
not, as it were, the unfolding or the continuing operation of
what has commended or commanded or perhaps 'determined'
my choice. In order that I may act in the sense so desired
or urged or suggested or postulated, I must choose or decide
to act thus.[1] (Between 'choice' and 'decision' I can see
no distinction other than that of contrast-emphasis: my

---

[1] See the discussion about whether actions must be preceded by decisions
(acts of will) between D. F. Pears, J. F. Thomson and M. Warnock in
Freedom and the Will, ed. by Pears (London, 1963), esp. pp. 19–26. Professor
Ryle's 'infinite regress' argument against the necessity of decision – acts of
will being themselves actions, every act of will would have to be preceded
by another act of will, this again by another, and so on – is countered by
M.W. with the suggestion that not every act may have to be thus preceded
and that acts of will may constitute a particular class exempt from this
necessity; J.F.T. rejects this distinction as subversive of the model of 'action
based on decision' as a whole; D.P. seems to argue (more in keeping with
M.W.) that between initial thinking and planning on the one hand and
overt action on the other an express act of decision and 'effort of the will'
may or may not intervene. Cf. A. C. Ewing, 'May Can-Statements be
Analysed Deterministically?', *P.A.S.* (1964), p. 172: Some voluntary acts
are preceded by specific acts of volition. My own contention is that decisions
('acts of will') are not in themselves actions at all (as are 'overt' or physical

'choice' of A as against B is at the same time my 'decision' which puts an end to my previous state of hesitation or 'indecision'.)

I am aware of the two standard objections to this description of the phenomenon of agency, and shall presently deal with them; but let me first state more explicitly what the point of the description is. It purports, as it were, a positive rather than a negative interpretation of free-will. It emphasises a special – and very definite – mode of determination rather than a lack of determination. It suggests an experiential account of free-will in terms of a positive and indispensable 'decree' or 'fiat'[1] as distinct from the argument that the causal machinery of the determination of our actions has only been insisted upon as a scientific requirement but never actually demonstrated. But, admittedly, freedom is a primarily negative concept; and the view I am here proffering of agency has its essential negative aspects. If choice is the unique and sovereign author of action (or policy) which must intervene between its (let us say) determinant motives and the actual execution of action, then those motives or springs are not properly the determinants of the action – in much the same way, if a crude simile be permitted, in which we call John's father his 'maker' ('l'auteur de ses jours', 'sein Erzeuger') but do not so call his paternal grandfather, i.e. his maker's maker, nor of course his more remote male ascendants on his father's side. What strikes us as a salient trait in full-fledged action is precisely this feature of 'saliency': the sharp break in the agent's behaviour, the

---

but also purely internal actions such as deliberately fixing one's attention to some object or contemplating the virtues of a person one dislikes) and are not of course preceded by 'decisions' to make this decision, though they invariably have their intellectual and emotive-volitive prehistory including all sorts of decisions (our choices being partly determined by previous events: Ewing, op. cit., p. 170); with Pears's account I would agree so far that acts of choice or decision can indeed be casual, unemphatic and toned-down to the point of being difficult to locate and all but imperceptible, but I would make the reservation that his vague concept of '(practical) thinking and planning' obviously already includes preliminary choices and identifiable decision-like acts.

[1] The expressive term *fiat*, in this context, originates to my knowledge from William James.

discontinuity between the action itself or the launching of the action and the multiplex of the desires, concerns, regards, etc. which – really and truly, or apparently – motivate it. That point of discontinuity is the locus of 'free choice', 'decision', 'decree', 'making one's mind up', 'resolve' or whatever we may preferably call it in the context; and it is here that we touch on the nerve of 'free-will', the differentia of agency proper as contrasted with mere 'behaviour'. In other words, action is not a 'resultant' of psychic urges, pressures, yearnings, cravings, attractions and repulsions, forces or bents, not an emergent product of motives relevant to its content; rather, it is the execution of a decree[1] issued by something like a unitary 'self' or 'ego' or 'sovereign ruler' who consults those motives and is influenced ('inclined', 'pressured', 'urged', 'instigated' or 'coaxed') by them but who in its turn is in control of motility and directs its workings.

Kant, in this respect closely echoed by N. Hartmann, emphasises the nature of Will thus understood in saying that, while physical events are universally subject to a pattern of mechanistic determinism governed by causal laws, the so-called 'intelligible ego' has the power of initiating new chains of causation and thus intervenes in the mechanism of world events without upsetting or invalidating it. To whatever other objections this schematic picture may be open, Kant bungles it hopelessly by arbitrarily placing on it a peculiarly moral construction:[2] in his view, the 'intelligible ego' enacts its autonomous new departures by obeying the dictates of 'practical reason', i.e. of a 'moral law' unrelated to the natural law of causal mechanism; from which it would ensue both that morally right action was free action and morally wrong, unfree action, and that morally neutral, in particular random, choice did not exist but was in reality either evil or in some way yet determined by reverence for the moral law, i.e. a farrago of

[1] The scholastic concept of *actus imperatus a voluntate* is endorsed as 'the right metaphor' by A. Kenny, *Action, Emotion and Will* (London, 1963), p. 238.

[2] Lacey, op. cit., p. 27, justly writes: 'I am surely as free in non-moral situations as in moral ones' and '. . . it would be odd if conscientious action were alone in being unaffected by the agent's background'.

absurdities. None the less, Kant rightly saw the essence of free action in its being performed at the 'dictate' of the will over and above the interplay, the confluence and antagonism, of fluctuating 'inclinations' and even of rationally fixed and formulated 'interests'.

In a sense, indeed, free agency is more conspicuously brought out by random choice, 'liberum arbitrium indifferentiae', than by the example of moral self-control, for the latter might be described by determinists as an instance of the stronger desire subduing the weaker – seeing that our desire to 'be moral' may sometimes happen to be 'more intense' than the sensuous desire with which it is incompatible. When we freely delegate our choice to an alien will (e.g. agree to accompany our friend to the cinema and ask him to choose the picture at his pleasure) or entrust it to sheer randomness (e.g. by tossing a coin or submitting to the blind 'decision' of a roulette ball), we shall be doing something mediately 'determined' by ourselves, but totally cut off from the flux and mechanism of our psychical forces or our physical constitution and condition. We have, as R. C. Skinner[1] puts it, chosen to choose in this way, but the issue (the content) of our choice is absolutely independent of any 'determinants' within our soul (or body). This, however, only constitutes the extreme limiting case of free choice and agency as such. Even in the more normal case of deliberative and reasoned choice, my decision is an act in its own right – an act of 'sanctioning' a policy as against others, of 'setting a stamp' (of validation) on one alternative possibility, of 'self-commitment' to one selection of aims and desirabilities – quite different to the calculable resultant from a parallelogram of forces or the calculated result of a problem of commensuration with its implied additions and subtractions. I may, but need not, try to work out a 'wise' choice, and I may even deliberately choose what appears to me to be the less 'wise' (e.g. an utterly risky) course; more important perhaps, in the case of the so-called wise choice itself I may tentatively come to scale *ad hoc* my relevant preferences or re-assess and alter my established

[1] R. C. Skinner, 'Freedom of Choice', *Mind* (October 1963), p. 476. There are, I think, few attempts to defend the libertarian doctrine as admirable as Skinner's.

H.A.

grading of them, and the inchoate choice thus formed may in its turn intervene as an autonomous factor in the shaping of my definitive decision. Practical choice proper is unlike the 'choosing', i.e. picking up, of the heaviest or the lightest out of a given set of weights, or the writing of the correct sum under a column of addenda; for in the business of life we are not in general pursuing one determinate and insulated 'end' but have to keep our eye on an indefinite manifoldness of mutually conspiring and competing concerns.[1] Except for limiting cases of preferring the obviously better to the obviously worse with no balancing counter-aspects whatsoever (and even the un-equivocal simplicity of such types of situations may be deceptive), an element of randomness and sheer arbitrary self-causality will slip into the play of our deliberation so as to enable us to lay down our volitive position, to trace our line of conduct and to maintain ourself at the level of agency. Reason, that is the organ of cognition and vehicle of 'compulsive evidence', never 'commands' the will as Aristotle in his Greek or Platonic intellectual snobbery, and his pious commentator, Aquinas, would have it; against them, Duns Scotus – in this respect, a nobler precursor of Hume – justly insists on the full practical sovereignty of the will which reason merely enlightens and informs as to the possibilities and the limits of its action, placing before it the facts which as such are independent of it and which may fall within or without its range of efficacy.

I will now turn to the two standard objections hinted at above and in the sequel try to confront some more objections to which I may have laid myself open in my further elaboration of the original thesis.

2 (a). THE PROBLEM OF AGENTIAL CAUSALITY

The position I have been trying to set out might be para-phrased thus: Free-will means, primarily, not so much free choice as free action (not only externally uncompelled, that is, but intrinsically free); and free action means, not uncaused

[1] Cf. my paper 'Deliberation is of Ends' in *P.A.S.* (March 1962), esp. p. 272.

action but action caused, in any direct sense of the word, by the agent's choice or decision alone, not by a machinery of psychic 'determinants' – regardless of how far the 'motives' conducing to that decision may operate in the mode of necessary determination. To such a view, the objection may first of all be made that, as has sometimes been suggested, the underlying decision is not properly a 'cause' of the action at all[1] but, rather, its beginning or first phase, its initial aspect or the agent's accompanying experience of his entering upon it. A decision not followed by any corresponding action, not carried at all into execution, is indeed not a true decision but merely something like a velleity, a wish or a temptation, an un-serious and illusory mood such as that of a man muttering desperately 'Unless this ends within five minutes I shall instantly kill myself' or 'If that happens I shall kill X and Y and Z', yet in fact far removed from being resolved on suicide or multiple murder if the abhorred condition should come true. The decision, then, seems to be an inseparable part rather than the cause of the

---

[1] The case against decisional or volitive causality in action has probably been argued most subtly and insistently by A. I. Melden in his book *Free Action* (London, 1961 and 1964), esp. ch. v ('By Willing, One Does . . .'), pp. 43–55. The gist of his argument appears to be that volition cannot be the cause of action since it cannot be neatly separated from the action it is supposed to cause, i.e. individuated as an event distinct and independent of the event constituted by the action to which it necessarily refers. My objection to this, as set out in my text, is that decision, though not logically independent of the action decided upon, is *de facto* sufficiently distinct from it to form another event preceding it and – in what manner is indeed an obscure question – bringing it about. I suggest that if Melden's argument were sound, the odd implication would hold that whereas a stroke of lightning setting a house on fire could be called the cause of the house's being on fire, an incendiary's act of arson could not be so called, for 'setting fire to a house' and 'that house being on fire' are somehow contained in each other or fused together. Cf. Ewing, op. cit., p. 171: 'I cannot see any good reason for saying that choice as part of a mental state may not be a cause of a physical action'. I do not, however, deny the tendency of volition to 'fuse into' action, significantly revealed by the English idiom 'I will . . .' which Fowler describes as the 'first-person coloured future'. This meaning of 'I will . . .' (I intend or am resolved to . . ., and shall do it) is also, less often, similarly expressed in German (*Ich will . . .*, and particularly *Wir wollen . . .*, in the sense of 'It is fit, or best, for us to . . ., and so that is what we are going to do forthwith').

action; to imply or entail and at best introduce the action rather than engender it as a consequence – similarly as wars are caused by developing clashes of interests or national aspirations, by threats to national security, etc., and not by declarations of war or by suddenly provoked frontier incidents and so on.

The objection cannot be lightly dismissed, but I propose a twofold reply to it. First, it is not clear to me that to call a man's decision the 'cause' of his ensuing action is incorrect language just because some decision-like acts are sham decisions or because some conspicuous indents or junctures or points of articulation in our behaviour are in the nature of formalities rather than of effective decisions. I may well – as an instance, intended to serve as an argument – now conceive and proclaim my intention to take a sip of water three minutes hence, go on doing nothing of the kind and make no preparations for it during that interval and then do it at the end of three minutes sharp; or likewise, decide now to ring or visit my friend X tomorrow at 3 o'clock and execute my decision tomorrow, having done nothing connected with it (not even reflected on the matter) until the said hour, though not having done meanwhile anything incompatible with it either, e.g. made another engagement for the said time: in all similar – quite common – cases, it would appear unnatural to me to deny that the decision has been the cause of the action. A cause of a somewhat peculiar kind, to be sure, inasmuch as the decision does not of infallible necessity compel or conjure up the action. The water now available may no longer be available in three minutes, and by 3 p.m. tomorrow my friend or myself may be dead, for one thing; for another, I may reconsider and revoke the decision I have taken. So that the causality in question may operate, a certain relevant substratum of factual circumstances must endure; and so must my resolution: in other words, my decision has to be maintained, or to vary the expression once more, my 'will' has to remain fixed in its established position, placed towards the chosen objective. But if this is the case, it is correct to say that I do the action because I have so decided. Secondly, even though it may equally well be said that the motives that have elicited my decision – induced me to take that decision – are also the springs of my corresponding action (for, should

anything happen or any consideration occur to me in the meantime which is apt materially to alter my scheme of motivation,
I may revoke my decision and omit the action contemplated),
it still remains true that deliberate action is never simply
'caused' by its 'motives' and their prevalence over contrary
motives but necessarily starts from the germinal act of decision
and is performed as if it were the execution of a decree which
endures in the shape of a 'sustained will'. A feeling of 'I could
have chosen otherwise' characteristically attaches to it – 'I am
doing this for such and such reasons and from such and such
motives, but I could have accorded greater (decisive) weight
to countervailing or inhibitory reasons, and actualised a
different set of motives' – and often, though by no means
always, there is also present an express consciousness of my
doing this, as opposed to something else, 'just' because I have
so decided rather than because I am solidly convinced that this
is plainly the more expedient, the wiser or the better or 'the'
right thing to do. In the solution of every practical, as contrasted with a theoretical, problem the arbitrary gesture of
Alexander's 'cutting the Gordian knot' intervenes at least
virtually, sometimes conspicuously and perhaps dramatically
as the characteristic act of volition as touching off, discharging
and 'commanding' action – somehow comparably to the god
committed to the Federal and anti-slavery cause who 'hath
loosed the fateful lightning of his terrible swift sword' and 'is
trampling out the vintage where the grapes of wrath are
stored'.[1] The 'sword' of decision has to be 'loosed' as the final
determination of the indeterminate state of things which
inexorably demands a settlement by the agent; the 'stored
grapes of wrath' may be translated into the language of
tensions accumulated between competing desires, concerns and
claims; and action is 'marching on'.

Free-will, I would argue, is not so much a gift or quality or
power which man might or might not be 'endowed' with, as a
logical postulate of Practice with its inherent incertitude and
opaqueness on the one hand, its unevadable factual pressure on
the other which connotes a logical necessity of its own. The
'compulsive evidence' of cognition is matched here by a com-

[1] Julia Ward Howe, *Battle-Hymn of the Republic*.

pulsion to choice, implacably non-compulsive (i.e. withholding compulsive evidence) as to the question which choice: whether to choose this or that or that other action in the given context, including possibly the choice of 'inaction' as an alternative to some positive action 'proper' in the descriptive physical sense of the word. A theoretical problem will indefinitely tolerate a 'modal' answer, a reservation in the form of 'conceivably', 'probably', 'to the best of my knowledge' or 'so far it would appear that', etc., any more complete and definitive answer being disingenuous so long as sufficient 'compulsive evidence' for it is lacking. Not so, practical problems. These, while sometimes susceptible of a delayed or again of a compromise solution, are in principle intolerant of any enduring answer couched in terms of probability or the like: I cannot 'probably' choose this drink or that if I am here and now offered a choice of drinks but only take actually one of them (or none); I cannot 'probably' go to a specified lecture next Monday night, once next Monday night has arrived, but only actually go or not go. The decisive factor has to be my decision, which can be manifoldly influenced, guided, grounded or goaded, yet for which no other factor can be substituted. (Whenever we use the verb 'decide' in its improper, theoretical sense, e.g. 'the doctor decided it was a case of perforated appendix', we mean 'I find that this assumption, though not indubitably true, is more probable than others I can think of, and so decide to act upon it'.) The point is that action in the marked sense of the term cannot but be set off by decision and that the agent alone can make the decision – either, which is the normal primary form, deciding directly and intrinsically, or else, which is a derivative form but conspicuously throws free-will into an even bolder relief, deciding mediately and non-contentually, in that he decides to entrust or delegate or 'farm out' the practical problem on hand to the decision of somebody else or even to blind chance.

2 (*b*). FREE-WILL AND AGENTIAL POWER

Yet, once more, a critic of the Moorian starting-point might object that the crucial part which the act of choice plays in action performed or policy carried out, however significant, fails to argue for the freedom of the act of choice itself. The action, dependent on choice, may indeed be of formidable amplitude and consequence; but the amount or indeed the range of power exercised is irrelevant to the freedom underlying its exercise. A 1000 h.p. engine acts no more freely than a 100 h.p. engine; a man ten times as powerful as I am in the sense of muscular strength, of financial means, of intellectual capabilities or of social prestige has not for that reason a ten times freer will than I have; and a paralysis of my limbs does not deprive me of free choice within the limits in which I can make it effective or at least express or indicate it, nor do I regain it by recovering the use of my limbs.

The last example, however, sounds a little less convincing than the previous ones. Evidently free-will does not mean power and, so far as it may admit of degrees (which is doubtless not plainly and straightforwardly the case, as it is with physical and mental power in their various forms or again with so-called 'inner freedom', a distinctive moral quality),[1] it is not proportionate to the powers possessed by a person. Yet, would it make sense to attribute free-will to a person completely inert, i.e. deprived of all power of action? (Including such purely intra-

---

[1] Professor B. A. O. Williams in his Postscript to *Freedom and the Will*, ed. by Pears (quoted above), p. 124, emphasises the degrees and limitations of freedom of choice, particularly as dependent on the agent's true and false beliefs concerning the courses of action open to him. Light is thrown thereby on the relations, not to say transitions, between the concept of free-will as a status or constitutive attribute of man and that of 'inner freedom' as a distinctive quality or 'virtue' which quite plainly admits of an infinitude of degrees. Nevertheless, the distinction is conspicuous and ineliminable. In ordinary life, we simply assume freedom of the will, with responsibility as its corollary, in everybody not in a condition of insanity, intoxication and the like, though we may also recognise its being perhaps abnormally circumscribed by an amount of ignorance 'extraordinary in the circumstances'. We do not praise (or in any way single out) a man for his 'unusually free will' or 'highly developed freedom of choice'. Whereas, this is precisely what we do in reference to 'inner freedom'. When we say that a man is 'responsible for what he does' and when we call a person 'highly responsible' we mean two completely different things: in the first case, that his doings are imputable to him; in the second, that he is laudably mindful of his responsibilities. 'Responsible' in the first sense is opposed to 'non-responsible'; in the second sense, to 'irresponsible'.

mental actions as turning our attention to one object of thinking as against another, or deliberating and deciding in regard to the taking of a position that for the time being we cannot in any way make effective.) Reduce agential power to zero, and free-will appears to have vanished: if I cannot act at all I cannot act freely and, a slightly less tautological further step, cannot 'choose'. What a person 'does' in a state of drunkenness or under the empire of 'overwhelming passion', i.e. when the normal control and ordinance of motility by a focal and unified 'self', set at a distance from desires and impulses, has well-nigh disappeared or is considerably upset and interfered with, will be 'attributed' or 'imputed to him' in a problematic and diminished sense only; it is in such contexts that we speak, without fear of paradoxy, of a diminished freedom and responsibility, of an impaired freedom, of (relatively) non-responsible conduct. In contrast with sleep-walking and perhaps things done in a total state of trance or under hypnotic compulsion, we for various reasons still describe what the person is doing as 'actions' but in view of the 'irresistible' invasion of motility by immediately effective spontaneous impulse or urge we hesitate to call them 'free actions' and assume the presence of a state which, in the language of moral theology, *minuit* or even *tollit voluntarium*. Thus the concept of free-will appears to be linked if not to the extraneous efficacy of the agent's choices (for he may plainly decide, in the full sense of the word, to do something that he subsequently proves altogether unable to achieve in fact) and much less to the volume and scope of that efficacy, at any rate to an intrinsic effectiveness of choice. For whatever 'reasons' and regardless of the determinist assumption of a mechanism of 'causes' – reflected or not in those reasons – which in the mode of an occult background activity 'compel' my decision, I 'coolly', in full possession of 'reason' or rather of 'my wits', but certainly not as a logical 'conclusion' from my reasons, decide to displace this object from the right to the left side of the table and forthwith do so displace it: here is the basic model of free-will and of conduct informed by it. The very fact that my decision is not only the starter but itself already part of my action contributes to my experience of freedom, in that my sense of continuity between choice and action (virtually contained in it) heightens my sense of discontinuity between choice and its psychical antecedents and physical preconditions.

While on the one hand 'sustained will', i.e. the carrying out of a policy pre-decided in a possibly distant past, expresses emphatically the continuity and self-governance of the person, on the other hand it is choice directly effective, decree manifestly and in a 'lightning-like' fashion transposed into terms of reality, which lays bare the very core of free-will and exhibits the indestructible nucleus of freedom as the centre of a human life inalterably embedded in a network of fore-given facts, conditions, causal machineries and constricting limitations. In a sense, all our long-term decisions with their delayed-motion efficacy drawn out in time and subject to all sorts of reservations, reverses and unforeseen reactions are only hypothetical decisions, and continue to be exposed to the pressure of our psychic 'determinants' and waxing-and-waning rival motivations; and any action decided long in advance requires for its actual performance a set of renewed and revised, confirming and modifying, acts of choice as well as of sub-decisions, so to say, for its 'application' to the emergent circumstances of the concrete situation in which it is to take place.[1] It is, on the contrary, in choice directly issuing into action – in action decided *sur-le-champ* – that freedom bursts forth in its raw reality, over and above the mutual push and pull of intrapsychic 'forces', and presenting man as a reduced and dwarfish 'godling' and his world-shaping 'decree' as a caricature and yet somehow a likeness of divine omnipotence. Thus it comes about that man, clinging to his decisional power yet aware of its frailty and vulnerability, would often, in the case of significant choices whose execution might be obviated by formidable difficulties and demands a painful 'effort of will', fret with

[1] That is why Intention, which on the one hand tends to outrun actual performance (since this may partly or wholly fail, or even prove to be altogether impracticable), on the other hand never embraces the whole content of Action and sometimes strikingly falls short of it; and this fact also lends colour to the appearance that actions sometimes 'grow' out of antecedent desires and speculations without the intervention of true decision or willing (see p. 22, note) in a sort of haphazard rambling or vegetable continuity.

impatience to inscribe his choice immediately into the massive tissue of accomplished facts, translating it presently into some kind of outward action; that he would take vows or give pledges and undergo commitments, look for objective safeguards and artificially circumscribe the range of his freedom in order to buttress its validity and ensure its efficacy. It is said of Generalissimo Joffre that when on the eve of the Battle of the Marne, 3 September 1914, he had decided to relieve General Lanrezac of the command of the Fifth Army, he hastened to appoint unofficially General Franchet d'Esperay to that crucial post of command before visiting Lanrezac at his headquarters to inform him about his decision, lest the possible indignation and remonstrances of that great and respected but in Joffre's judgment worn-out, discordant and inopportune military leader should make him waver and perhaps go back on his decision – he 'could not' very well do so after having as it were 'embodied' that decision in Franchet d'Esperay's fierce and stocky person. Thus there is a modicum of truth in Sartre's extravagant doctrine that men seek to find reasons *ex post* for their choices already taken, or in Miss Anscombe's infelicitously argued contention that men can 'choose their motives'.[1]

3. 'DECREE' AND COMMITMENT

A further and capital objection I have now to anticipate bears on the doubtful legitimacy and merely metaphorical character of such words, used in the context of willing, as 'decree',

---

[1] See Kenny, op cit., p. 88, note 1. Anscombe misleadingly writes (*Intention*, p. 22) that Plato's example of a master refraining from beating a slave who has deserved punishment lest he should do so from anger shows that we can choose our motives. Kenny points out that we can indeed choose our actions and so far can choose between doing something from a certain motive or not doing it ('actualise' a motive or not, I would say with Sir David Ross) but, having once decided to do something (from whatever motive), we cannot then on top of it choose the motive from which to do it. I submit that if Plato's model shows anything at all it is precisely this inability of ours to choose our motives as such. The master felt that he ought to exercise an act of 'retributive justice' but, being in a dudgeon, also felt that he could not help doing it with anger and therefore could not be

'command', the *actus imperatus* of the Scholastics (meaning, a fully voluntary, deliberate and intentional mental act, preparatory or not to bodily action), or indeed 'commitment' of the will. For, on closer inspection, we fail to distinguish the author and the recipient of the 'decree' or to discern who 'commands' whom in the act of a man's deciding something and carrying out his decision. We experience something like a focal 'self', an indeterminate formal 'ego' which determines a choice between contending impulses or competing aims and thereby the movements to be performed, the utterances to be pronounced, etc., by the agent; but we cannot as it were identify, as in a social situation where these words are properly used, a person who commands and another who obeys, an authority that issues a decree and its subjects or subordinates who conform (or in part are just supposed to conform) to it. My decision to, say, raise my right arm here and now does somehow look like 'decreeing' that my arm shall be raised or 'commanding'[1] myself to raise it or again 'commanding' my right arm to rise – a command addressed to my body – and such a model of action gains in plausibility whenever an effort is needed to make the decision effective, e.g. when I am tired, and yet the action ensues in effect: it appears as if I had compelled myself to do the thing ordained, or forced my body to execute the required movement. But on a more critical examination the analogy threatens to break down. I decree, mentally or aloud: 'My arm shall be raised', but no serviceable occult forces will rush swiftly to raise it, and my arm remains still in its resting position. I command myself to raise my arm, but I cannot find any second self in me to do it, indeed such a self, being still 'myself', would again have to transmit my command to a third 'self' and so on; meanwhile, my arm stays where it is. And if I try to move my body by addressing a command to it or saying 'Right arm, rise!', once more nothing happens: my body or my arm will prove entirely disobedient

---

sure that he would not do it from anger as well (which he considered an improper motive). None the less, Anscombe has a point in so far that through deciding our conduct we can indirectly curb or, as Joffre did in the reported case, strengthen the operation of our motives.

[1] Cf. p. 24 n. 1.

and unresponsive, staying inert and heeding my command as little as the most headstrong of true-bred dachshunds would. If I really am intent on raising my right arm, I must needs raise it myself – with or without effort. What, then, has become of 'decree' or 'fiat', of command and obedience within myself, or indeed of my being in control of my body (so far as its voluntary muscles and agential movements are concerned)?[1]

But we can seldom prescind from the use of metaphors when venturing on an account of mental phenomena; what is required is only our being aware of the metaphoric character of the expressions in question – lest, by taking them literally, we should be misled into facile allegorising and arbitrary constructions – and our making sure that the metaphors actually point to significant aspects of the phenomena we are concerned with and shed some light on what we experience as palpable reality. And this, in my submission, is true of the 'decree', 'self-command', etc., language notwithstanding the pertinent criticism levelled against it. Decision is decree-like in virtue of its effectively ushering in, its enacting as it were, action – whether immediately, flagrantly and with a strong note of 'infallibility' or in a mode of action delayed, suspended and conditional as the case may be; the second type lacks the note of flagrancy and conveys a weaker suggestion of infallible efficacy, but once the effect is produced it places the power of decision over the shaping of reality in an all the more glaring light. The fact that the decree is not automatically 'obeyed' by the universe but carried out by the agent himself detracts nothing from the experiential phenomenon thus described; it only shows the indissoluble unity of action, the compenetration of decision and purposeful 'commanded' movement or system of movements. On the contrary, the reflexion in the physical action of the underlying 'motives' is merely contingent, it may or may not show forth; the action subserves some desires and interests (while it is likely at the same time to express a veto or restraint placed on others, no less real and propulsive), but the decree, not the motives favoured or concerns privileged on the occasion, is that to which it conforms and from which it proceeds with logical univocality. Further, although it is not

[1] See Melden, op. cit., ch. iv: 'How does one raise one's arm?'

literally possible that the agent should 'command himself' – he
does not harbour several 'selves', e.g. a higher and a lower self;
the promptings of moral conscience are not 'commands' but
demands, as are the stirrings of a turbulent passion, and may
or may not prevail – still there is an aspect to decision of the
agent 'commanding himself', inasmuch as he undertakes to do
a thing as opposed to another thing and then goes and does it,
thwarting the tendencies in himself to do the opposite thing
and silencing the apparatus of arguments he has tentatively
built up in himself for the service and advocacy of those
tendencies. He may, in the given case, choose the moral thing
as against the pleasant or inversely, though the second choice
may stand out in less clear outline, a veil of sham-moral
arguments being drawn over it to make it more palatable;
again, he may choose to enjoy a magnificent sight at the cost of
climbing up a steep hill, or inversely choose to rest at the cost
of renouncing enjoyment of the sight, and so forth. But even
if he chooses to do what, on some examination, he finds to be
altogether right and very pleasant and economical and good
for his health, etc., at the same time, he is likely to miss some
advantage or accept some hardship in so choosing; and even
should he 'will' to do a thing he finds to be advantageous from
every point of view he can think of, in virtue of the categorial
schema of choice and action at least a shadowy sense of contra-
dictoriness still attaches to his experience – he might, after all,
have decided otherwise, perhaps wilfully invoking a countervailing motive; he could have chosen an alternative course (but
why do so? why should he need to 'demonstrate' his free-will
by an act of gratuitous folly?).[1] Again, an aspect of self-
command and self-obedience is inherent in the agent's manifest

[1] Skinner's (op. cit., p. 468) common sense is quick to notice what un-
sound enthusiasts and misinterpreters of freedom, such as most Existen-
tialists, are apt to forget: 'that we seldom concern ourselves just with
making a choice, but almost always with making the best choice, whether
it is best from the point of view of our own comfort or pleasure, or from
the moral point of view, or from the aesthetic point of view, or from
the purely practical point of view of choosing a means to achieve some
particular end.' For the view that 'counter-suggestion' (i.e. my doing
deliberately the opposite of what I know somebody has predicted that I am
going to do) fails to prove free-will, see Pears, op. cit., p. 97.

ability to use his limbs (and to concentrate or deflect his attention). Certainly my arm does not rise by my summoning it to rise; but neither does it rise on its own, independently of my will, as the various glands in my body secrete their products: it obeys my command in the sense that I can raise it, and do raise it if I so choose, be it once or twice or ten times over again; and I can also feel a sort of muscular desire to raise it, yet (for reasons of manners, say) choose to leave it still, in which case it will not rise. Because my body is not just an object at my disposal but organically fused with myself, in some sense is also 'myself', this 'being in control of motility' peculiar to the 'ego', the bearer of choice and will and issuer of 'decrees', also means a kind of command-and-obedience relation within the agent, and it is through the instrumentality of this control that he can bring his will to bear on extraneous objects including other selves. Thus it comes about that some events in the world happen in conformity to our free decrees.

Another facet of free-will, however, is presented by what I have just called 'undertaking' or 'pledging oneself': the phenomenon of (self-)commitment. Freedom necessarily means servitude of a kind (how far Luther may vaguely have had this, too, in mind when he spoke of *servum arbitrium* I cannot say); by making a decision I am exercising and thereby of necessity consuming my freedom; in following out my decision I am operating as it were under a dictate. That 'dictate' emanates from myself and remains subject to my control until the action be accomplished or the policy carried out; yet it appears embodied, we might say 'reified', in what is no longer myself but an 'order' or 'rule' or 'law' somehow detached from myself, projected out of myself and a solidified 'power' above me to which I owe obedience although it only exists by my grace. Commitment is obviously very like a promise and yet sharply different to it: it is not a social act, not a pledge given to another self, and does not entail a highly imperative, paradigmatic moral obligation; the subtle distinction between the self '*quâ* commanding' and the self '*quâ* obeying' is only remotely analogous to the massive distinction between two distinct selves (the promiser and the promisee). But, though I can commit myself without making any promise (cf. the 'declaration of intention'), I cannot promise at all without committing myself; and, seeing the constitutively social character of man, the assumption would seem justifiable that the concept of commitment (engagement, *Sich-Festlegen*, decision, resolution, etc.) implies at any rate an oblique reference to that of promise. Similarly, 'responsibility' or 'answerability' or 'accountability' is a concept with a social connotation, indicating that I – my 'focal self', of course, not the 'forces in my soul' nor the parts of my body – owe an 'answer' or 'account', pledging my whole person so far as I am its 'master', concerning such actions of mine as have (in certain ways and degrees, at least) exercised or are apt to exercise an impact upon the interests of others. Here, once more, freedom is inseparable from subjectness to law. Sticking to one's commitments, or in other words sustained resolve or a consistent policy, is not *per se* tantamount to the fulfilment of moral obligation, much less of jural or legal, yet in a germinal sense bears within it the pattern of moral obligation and points to the basically and thematically moral character of man – not to his morally good original nature, to be sure; it is, as Aranguren puts it, a matter of *moral como estructura*, not of *moral como contenido*.[1] Man as an agent is neither morally good nor morally bad – and, I hold with Duns Scotus, any single action of his need not be either right or wrong – but man as an agent is ineluctably subject to the polarity of good and evil (involving many of his choices that must be right or wrong); and agentiality itself carries in it an adumbration of goodness while the attempt to escape from it is branded with a sign of immorality. It may be morally inconsequential, and in certain circumstances obviously even a moral duty, to go back on a decision; yet, other things being equal, abiding by one's choice or maintaining one's decision and acting upon it, i.e. 'obedience' or 'fidelity' to one's own

[1] Professor J. L. L. Aranguren, *Ética* (Madrid, 1958), pp. 62–6 and 72. He borrows this basic distinction from X. Zubiri, whose disciple he professes to be. Morality as structure is inherent in man's character as an agent, morality as content represents the moral standard and man's possible conformance to it. The distinction is obviously akin to, but not identical with, that between formal and material ethics and that between 'meta-ethics' and the descriptive analysis of moral consciousness or phenomenology of moral experience.

decree, is endowed with a *prima facie* moral privilege: constancy or perseverance is rightly looked upon as praiseworthy, flightiness and 'weakness of will' as blameworthy – if not always as guilty conduct, at any rate as a moral deficiency.[1]

It is by virtue of the constitutive division and distance within the person, between its multeity of concerns and between these and the central volitive or agential Self, that Commitment exists and is closely comparable to promise; but though it underlies morality, it is a pre-moral rather than a properly moral concept. We make promises, as we freely commit ourselves, decide, perform acts of will, etc., *quâ* 'constitutively moral' beings; we keep promises *quâ* 'actually' moral or morally 'good' or 'virtuous' beings. But we only choose freely what to promise; we do not at all choose freely promise-keeping as a standard or criterion of morality. Again we are free to keep or to break our promises; yet our moral worth resides not in that freedom but in our keeping our promises, whereas our breaking them stamps us as immoral. To talk of 'autonomous' morality or a 'morality of freedom' is thus ambiguous and misleading, and lends itself to easy misuse by votaries of various forms of immoralism. If morality presupposes freedom, so does immorality. The locus of moral evil is not the 'lower self' as prevailing over the 'rational self' or the 'will' but the will itself – in its perversion, to be sure. Nevertheless, freedom does not stand to good and evil in complete symmetry or blank neutrality; it is attracted towards the moral good as towards one pre-eminent 'good', towards evil (primarily, at least) in virtue of some non-moral 'good' attaching to it. Hence our fairly universal tendency to blur our awareness of doing wrong when or so far as we do wrong, or again to build up in our

[1] The concept of 'unpredictability' – a distinctively English idiom only translatable into other languages by some equivalent of 'inconstancy' or 'capriciousness' – bears an adverse moral sign which, however, is barely more than marginal. It plainly means something far different from 'non-predictability' which, taken descriptively, simply refers to free-will, and, taken evaluatively, would point to a rich and complex nature amply endowed with 'inner freedom'. But neither is 'unpredictability' a synonym of 'unreliability'. It is the attribute, not of a person whose promises cannot be trusted, but of a person whose presumable commitments, practical 'maxims' and policies cannot be safely built upon or expected to operate.

minds the spurious sense of acting, when we transgress, not in freedom but under a sort of irresistible compulsion. Whether 'vicious habits' tend to diminish our freedom of choice more than 'virtuous' is a complex question which cannot be argued here.

On the pre-moral practical level of Commitment, submission to objective 'given' standards of rationality (not without properly moral implications) still fills an essential place but the central postulate here is the self-limitation of freedom as a condition of its efficacy. If commitment were deprived of its force of compulsive obligation, agency and volition would vanish and the concept of freedom would sink into inane vacuity.

4. THE TWILIGHT ZONES OF FREE-WILL

It must be admitted, and has often in recent times been discussed, that the commonsensical experience of free-will is not altogether proof against philosophic criticism and indeed constitutes no wholly solid and of-a-piece datum in itself. There is some truth in the determinist contention that, whatever its basis in reality, our familiar sense of doing what we choose and thus *eo ipso* 'choosing what we choose', i.e. 'choosing freely', involves a kind of illusion. Even though Hampshire may be entirely correct in asserting that we cannot with certainty fore-tell how we shall act in a certain future situation without having hypothetically decided or deciding that we shall so act, it may well be the case that we can foretell it with a high degree of probability without being decided to act thus and perhaps without approving of our self-predicted behaviour; and this points to the probability that our sense of 'not being determined to act in a certain manner' springs, in part, simply from our incomplete knowledge of our motivation in the heat and pressure of having to decide ourself here and now. Again, looking back on some of our past choices we may feel that they may not have been so arbitrary and uncaused, so 'free' in a word, as they appeared to be at the moment of our making them, but obviously prompted by some potent and plausible 'motive' of which at that moment we were unaware or but dimly and marginally, inexplicitly aware: a motive 'sub-

D   H.A.

conscious' or 'sub-liminal' or 'semi-conscious' at the time but
unearthed and brought into the light of full consciousness since.
True, such hindsight self-interpretations are themselves far
from infallible. I would only say briefly that we are anyhow
always conscious of having motives whenever we are acting
deliberately, and that the fact of our never being fully conscious
of all of them cannot affect our certainty of there being present
'spots of indetermination' waiting for our 'own' decree to fill
them, and thus of an indestructible 'nucleus' of freedom.[1]
Moreover, our partial ignorance of what is going on in our
own soul is an argument that cuts both ways. The area of our
free choice may be more circumscribed in some ways but also
wider in other ways than we might believe. It occasionally
happens that in the end we do carry out a brave and selfless
action we have in advance decided upon *pro forma* as it were,
yet in a well-founded state of apprehension lest we should prove
unable to give effect to our decision when it comes to the point.
If there are illusions of freedom, there are also illusions of
unfreedom; and I still think that the ultimate decisiveness for
our action lies with the one 'motive' of our having taken this,
and no other, decision.

The objection concerning the oscillations and variations
intrinsic to our experience of freedom as a whole appears to me
more interesting and fruitful. Given the technical possibility,
I feel that I could choose – to freely and effectively 'will' – to,
say, kill myself, or to give away or destroy all my possessions,
or commit some heinous crime, or gratuitously insult X for
whom in fact I have the highest regard and appreciation,
though I could not desire, or by any effort of will bring myself
to desire, any of these things. But there is some curious inanity
and abstractness about this sense of 'I could choose'; only some
very forced and artificial imaginary schema of circumstances
might in a dubious and tenuous way 'give body' to such an
experience of 'real possibility'. And, if some configuration of

---

[1] The expression is Professor G. P. Henderson's (see his lecture, pp. 1–19
above), meaning, unless I have misunderstood him, the presence of free-will
which can always be felt in agency and made conspicuous in salient cases
but which is inextricably embedded in the network of psychological
determinations.

events or pressure of adverse forces really did 'compel' or 'oblige' or 'induce' me to do one of these hideous things, i.e. to 'will' to do it (for otherwise it would not be an action: if a brawny ruffian takes hold of my arm and slaps X's face with my hand, I am performing no action and thus am not insulting X), I still should not desire or want or wish to do the thing in question: hence in ordinary language we should not call that action 'voluntary' – though, on pain of not being an action, it would be 'intentional' – and some people would say that I did the action yet did it 'against my will', did 'not will it' or did not will it, choose it or do it 'freely'. Here the point in question is whether I can 'will' a thing (or 'choose' it) which I do not desire or want or wish to happen; or, rather, since that description would perhaps apply to purely random (and innocuous) decisions as well, a thing that goes against all my desires, wishes and wantings. It might be countered, however, that my 'will' to do that thing – most unwillingly, to be sure – would at any rate be in accord with my desire or wish to preserve my life or to avoid some other, even more monstrous, dishonour or disaster. In another type of case, on the contrary, it might be claimed that I do 'against my will' something which I loathe morally or emphatically reject on principle but which I happen to desire or want intensely: the case of the will faltering under the impact of passion, as when St Paul misleadingly but picturesquely speaks of 'his members' doing the opposite of what he 'willeth', or St Augustine speaking of the 'members of the body rebelling against the soul' in concupiscence (as a punishment of man for original sin), though of course if my limbs really performed any movements against my will I should be doing no action and not be responsible for the 'sin-like' event that happened, and though the soul not the body is the seat of evil inclinations and no action, sinful or not, is possible without the consent – the 'seal' or 'sanction' – of the focal self. There are more incongruities or at any rate odd features, somewhat different in various linguistic media, about the language of 'will' and 'voluntariness', to which I have no space left to advert.[1]

---

[1] Kenny's (op. cit., p. 214) proposal to use the technical term 'Volition' as a portmanteau word for all emotive strivings and tendings that may issue in 'willing' proper, and especially his bold attempt to make up for the

It seems certain to me that the domain of man's will is not purely and simply the area of *liberum arbitrium indifferentiae*, that he may in some sense not only be compelled to suffer alien power and influence which cannot be dislodged by his action as well as to endure originary inner realities (e.g. cravings and mental limitations) over which his will has only an indirect and dubious power, but even be constrained to adjust his willing to imperious quasi-necessities of the situation and to decide and act in a line that goes integrally against his grain (e.g. yield to blackmail or do something he is thoroughly ashamed of). And this aspect of the human condition, no less than the phenomenon of free-will, is very familiar to common-sense consciousness and is laid down in such idioms as 'acting against one's will', 'I don't want to do it but I have to' (where 'I want to' is almost a synonym of the technical-language 'I will to', *je veux, ich will,* etc.); 'I would but cannot' (where the 'cannot' is not rigorously but only 'quasi' or 'practically' true); or again 'he did not of course do it voluntarily, though neither did he do it involuntarily' (his action having been a real action though most unwillingly done, not an involuntary movement made inadvertently, below the level of volition and action proper). Similarly, on the positive side, with an emphasis on spontaneity, enthusiasm and eager 'willingness': 'He volunteered for the army immediately on the outbreak of war'; 'Volunteering an information'; 'He voluntarily offered double the amount of the obligatory subscription'; and most

---

absence in English of an ordinary, idiomatic form of 'to will' as it exists in most languages (ἐθέλειν, velle, vouloir, wollen, etc.) by introducing the ill-sounding technical term 'to volit', is open to manifold criticisms but reveals a deep-seated need in man to 'integrate' his being in certain 'whole-hearted dedications' comprising his free-will and his psychological infra-structures alike. Paradoxes like the Christian quasi-commandments 'Thou shalt love (God, thine enemies, etc.)', or the feeling of 'guilt' for things one is not actually responsible for, or the ancient experience of 'sin' that 'happens to' the person and yet is somehow 'sin' and 'soils' him, are of course closely relevant here. So much is certain that, while – as we have seen – freedom of choice is not as such a moral category at all, moral evaluation on the other hand, as distinct from deontic moral demands, applies to many features of character and behaviour outside the range of free choice, and moral achievement clearly depends on such factors also: e.g. to a large extent, 'fortitude' and some other classic 'virtues'.

markedly linking the 'will' to wanting and desiring, the adverb 'willingly' (the French *volontiers*) and the locution 'with all my heart' (in German, *von Herzen gern*). The focal, central, or 'decreeing' and 'sanctioning' self is not exactly, not in all rigour of the word, an 'indifferent' self; rather, it is an 'undetermined' self, set at a distance from the impulses and concerns of the personal soul and a critical arbiter placed above them yet from the outset biased in favour of them as a whole and representing them in a sovereign attitude of conspectus rather than judging them as an alien and as it were blindfolded court of justice.[1] Thus it comes about that the legal formula *placet* stands for strictly volitive, agential decree, that the pleading lawyer at court introduces a proposal with the hedonistic tail-waving words 'May it please your Lordship', and that some offenders are sentenced to detainment 'during her Majesty's pleasure'. Will is free-will but it is not only free; its element of un-predetermined random 'decree' can be compared to the impure randomness of loaded dice. While Austin Farrer has rightly said that 'free-will' is a pleonastic term since there is no such thing as a non-free will,[2] the freedom of the will is not that of an unweighted entity sauntering about aimlessly in a vacuum; and thus the expression 'free-will' is not quite so starkly tautological as, say, 'a female cow', and had, I think, better be retained by libertarians as a useful and significant

---

[1] In the discussion following the reading of this paper at the Royal Institute of Philosophy, a speaker (unknown to me) made the most interesting remark that in ordinary language an 'agent' meant somebody acting on behalf of another or of others and that something of this aspect also survived in the philosophic concept of agency. I entirely agree with that suggestion. My volitive and responsible, choosing and 'decreeing' or 'policy-making' ego is representative of the world of concerns, interests, wants, etc., compacted in my person as a whole; and in some sense also representative, in relation with these, of the macrocosmic world of facts, forces, standards, persons and institutions that surrounds me. I believe that the institutional presuppositions of 'agency' and 'will' have in fact been discovered or vaguely surmised by a number of sociologically interested authors. Cf. Mr B. Mayo's analysis of agentship in terms of 'playing a part', pp. 47–63 below.

[2] A. Farrer, *The Freedom of the Will* (London, 1958), p. 106. With several other trains of thought of this pithy but somewhat diffuse book I feel to be in substantial agreement.

reminder that ultimately and principally the will is free but that this fact is not so self-evidently and unproblematically established as to be in no need whatever of continued assertion and argument.

3

THE MORAL AGENT

Bernard Mayo

I WANT to examine how far the question 'What is it for a man to act morally?' can be answered in terms of the sociological concept of a role. Is, for example, acting as a moral agent consistent with acting in the capacity of one's role, or even identical with it if being a moral agent is acting a role? In the first part of my paper I shall examine some of the relations between morality and roles, especially from the point of view of that freedom which is always regarded as a necessary condition of a man's being a moral agent. In the second part I shall examine the concept of a role itself, not from the point of view of sociology to which it notionally belongs, but from the point of view of the philosophy of mind; this is the point of connection between my own theme and the general theme of this series of lectures. The role concept will thus be a bridging concept between ethics and the philosphy of mind. Finally I shall bring to bear on the idea of the moral agent any insights that may be yielded by the psychology of role-acting.

I

In the history of thinking about moral concepts there are two poles, to one or other of which moral philosophy has tended to gravitate. These are the ethics of rule and the ethics of character. They are respectively symbolised or exemplified by: the right act, and the good man (and their contraries); the lawgiver, and

47

the paragon; the Decalogue of the Old Testament, and the
Beatitudes of the New; the offence, and the vice. The first
member of each of these pairs has affinities with the philosophy
of law; the other with the philosophy of education; and it is a
commonplace in the history of ethics to single out two classical
works located at either pole: Kant's *Grundlegung*, and Aristotle's
Nicomachean Ethics. Kant's work is said to be about what it is
to do the right thing; Aristotle's, about what it is to be the
right sort of person.

The contrast is, of course, over-simplified. One does not just
do things; one does the sort of things one does because one is
the sort of person one is. And, as Aristotle stresses, one becomes
the sort of person one is by doing the sort of things one does.
But the attempt to state more precisely than this what are the
connections between person and act runs into many difficulties:
I will select one because it gives a sort of preview of the
psychological complexities underlying the concept of role. Is
a right act one such as a good man would do? Does right, that
is, depend on good? But what is it that we are supposing a good
man would do? Right acts, surely; we move in a circle. Well,
is a good man, then, one who does right acts? But what is a
right act? It cannot be one that has certain identifying features
of its own; for, whatever these features might be, a good man
cannot be one who merely does what as a matter of fact has
those features: he must be one who does it because it has those
features, and it will not be right without this 'because'; but it
is just because of this 'because' that he is a good man. So again
we have a circle. Kant was quite right to insist on that *because*,
but its elucidation remains one of the darkest problems in the
philosophy of mind.

I want to consider whether there is a role morality around
which, as a third pole, an ethics of role might be centred. And
it seems that there certainly is. We scarcely need books like
The Organisation Man to remind us that we are constantly
invoking rights and obligations and adopting standards of
conduct which are created and controlled by the parts we play
in a variety of more or less complex institutions, of which plain
morality is, at most, only one. There is no doubt about the
existence of role-morality; what can be questioned is only

whether it is really distinct from the other two. I am inclined to think that, rather than being distinct but intimately and puzzlingly related, as are the other two, role-morality is not distinct, though it offers a useful new approach to the other two. It is not distinct, because the demands of one's role can be represented either as more or less formalised rules – this will be the case, for instance, with professional 'ethics' – or as the requirement of certain postures, attitudes or qualities of conduct, as in the case of Sartre's waiter[1] (or even Kant's grocer), family relationships, or the military ethos.

Indeed Aristotle himself can be seen as developing an ethics of role. Many of the virtues and vices which he thinks worth singling out for special treatment are just those postures, attitudes and qualities of conduct the presence or absence of which is required by a person's role in society. The notorious absence of most of the Christian virtues is a reflection of this. Aristotle is not writing about virtues and vices which anyone can practise, as the Christian writers do, but only about those virtues and vices which are the concern of the upper classes. Courage is practised only on the battlefield, by armed gentlefolk, not on the sickbed. The ideals and shortcomings of friendship make no appeal to readers who are not familiar with the stylised homosexual relationships of the class and period.

The distinctness of rule-morality and character-morality comes out clearly in relation to the problem of freedom. It is often said that the reason why the Greeks were not bothered with the free-will problem is that they had no machinery, and so no conspicuous paradigms of fully deterministic systems. It is true that this gap left them, instead, with those conspicuous paradigms of fully purposive systems, namely, human beings; but what is important is not what they lacked, but what they had, namely a character-morality. Now what a person is, and what he wants to be, and his aspirations, ambitions and purposes generally, are all in the strongest possible sense *his*; they cannot possibly be represented as something alien, and without this possibility the traditional problem of freedom could not arise.

---

[1] *L'Être et le Nèant* (Eng. tr. Hazel E. Barnes: *Being and Nothingness*, Methuen, 1957), p. 59. Quoted in Dorothy Emmet, *Rules, Roles and Relations*, pp. 152–3.

An ethics of rules, however, faces the problem of freedom immediately; mechanism only aggravates it by adding another dimension of unfreedom. A rule necessarily restricts my freedom; so far from not being representable as something alien, a rule cannot, at least initially, be represented as anything else. Unlike my character and my purposes, a rule is an *it*. Only at the end of a long programme of conceptual reconstruction, if at all, can rules be reconciled with freedom; and it is still very questionable whether either Kant or Professor Hare have established the existence of universal imperatives, their identity with moral principles, or the possibility of self-addressed behests.

Does a role-centred morality raise a problem about freedom? That is, is a role necessarily, or typically, something alien to the person who acts it? Is a role, like a rule, but unlike a character, an *it*?

Here is an example which will both illustrate the temptation to think of a role as an alien *it*, and at the same time expose the mistake of yielding to it. Professor Smith writes from another university: 'Thank you for inviting me to be your external examiner when Jones retires. (Is there then somebody, namely the Redbridge University philosophy department's external examiner, such that Jones will stop being *he* and I shall begin being he?)'[1] To which the natural reply is, 'No, there is no such body, but there is some such thing, which now Jones, and later Smith, is'; and this could easily foster an impression of it-ness and alienation. But, of course, being the Redbridge University philosophy department's external examiner, which is certainly a role, is no more a thing than being red-haired is, or being Jones, though all three may be things that someone is. The word 'thing' here is purely syntactic.

Nevertheless, a recent speaker to the Aristotelian Society feels so strongly about the it-ness of roles that he writes as follows about the possibility of assimilating the behaviour of people and the roles they act:

> If sets of roles are conceived as persons, the social *status quo* is immediately sanctified: when roles constitute selfhood, to

---

[1] I owe this example to Professor P. T. Geach, of Leeds, who is to be the Birmingham University philosophy department's external examiner.

change society is to mangle human beings.

And he concludes:

There are theories which would engulf personality in role-playing; there are people who present themselves as so engulfed; there are institutions which foster engulfment. The propensity to engulfment must be resisted in theory and practice, because it poses a threat to the exercise of our freedom, and, ultimately, to freedom itself.[1]

Professor Dorothy Emmet, in her book *Rules, Roles and Relations*, is more cautious: in the chapter 'Persons and Personae' she, too, considers the possibility of regarding people as 'assemblages of the roles they play' or a person as the 'incumbent' of his roles, and judges that this would not leave the necessary room for a 'personal morality': and 'we shall never catch the conversation-like nuances by which role-performances are also found to be relationships between people'. She also draws attention to the frequent cases of role-conflict, calling for a personal, not role-determined, choice.

I wish to take yet another view, that a person can perfectly well be regarded as an assemblage of roles, without missing any nuances we may want to catch, much less condoning mangling and engulfment. All depends, of course, on how widely or narrowly we interpret the term 'role': a question to which Emmet devotes much, and Cohen but little, care. Are we to consider only highly formalised offices and functions; or are we to include everything down to the most intimate relations between lovers, or the most casual social contact, so that there will be roles which cannot even be named? Professor Emmet considers this question, and observes that we do have considerable licence here. We could say of someone helping a bus passenger who has stumbled, that they were acting the roles of helper and helped; but she decides that the extension of the concept to cover the most transitory social relations would make it 'so all-embracing as to lose its effectiveness as a tool of social analysis'. I do not doubt that such an attenuated concept would be of little use to sociologists, but in relation to ethics and

---

[1] G. A. Cohen, 'Beliefs and Roles', *Proc. Arist. Soc.*, 1966–7, pp. 17–34.

the philosophy of mind I shall try to show that it can still have a cutting edge. As to the place of personal morality, I want to say that any conduct that is to be distinguished from spontaneous behaviour, as Professor Emmet does distinguish personal morality, is still a matter of roles; a person can choose in what role to act, including the choice to remain in high office, the choice between conflicting role-requirements, the choice to act as helper on the bus, and even the choice to act in no role at all. In this consists his moral freedom; though to choose to act in no role at all is to choose not to act morally. This, however, will have to be substantiated in Section III.

I now proceed to what is long overdue, a critical examination of the notion of a role in my preferred wide sense.

II

The concept of role is irreducibly sociological; it cannot be reduced to elements of individual behaviour or belief. To describe someone's behaviour in terms of a role is never merely to describe, but to give a condensed explanation of his behaviour. Take, for example, the role of bus conductor. No conjunction of statements about an individual's beliefs and actions can amount to a description of what he does as a bus conductor; the qualifiers 'as', '*qua*', 'in his capacity as', are essential. And his actions *qua* bus conductor can be understood only in terms of other people in other, correlative, roles, such as passenger, driver, or manager.

Now although a role is not reducible to behaviour and belief on the part of an individual, it most certainly enters into an individual's behaviour and beliefs, especially into his beliefs about his own behaviour, his thinking about what he is doing. It is this point of contact between individual and society, how a person's knowledge of what he is doing involves knowledge of what he is doing it *as*, that is specially relevant to our enquiry into role-morality.

We can state the problem thus. Except in certain non-standard cases, a person who is acting a role knows that he is, and others know that he is. Further, he knows that the others know, and the others know that he knows they know. Etcetera. The bus conductor knows that he is a bus conductor, and the driver and passengers know this too. Further, the conductor knows that the driver knows, and the driver knows that the conductor knows that he knows. Etcetera. Before we look at the implications of (what I shall call) this infinite etceteration, let us ask, of the first item of knowledge in the series, just what it is knowledge of. What is it that a person who knows he is acting a role knows? Let us look at Professor Emmet's answer. A role, she says, is a capacity in which someone acts in relation to others. We have already agreed that. She also speaks of 'mutual reciprocal expectations' and of 'requirements'. This, too, is surely right, though I shall need to make a distinction in favour of 'expectations' as against 'requirements'. What a person knows, then, when he knows that he is acting a role, is that certain things are required or expected of him. Now requirements are made, and expectations entertained, by other people; and this seems to be as far as Professor Emmet goes. But these requirements and expectations on the part of other people do not constitute the role; they are themselves determined by the role which the other people take the first person to be playing. That is why it is not enough that the first person knows what the others expect: they must know that he knows; and even this is not enough, as we shall see.

What seems, but is not, a different way of putting this is to say that the person does what he does *because of* the requirements. But this is not a helpful way of putting it. For, as I have already said, and as Dr Kenny has written with admirable frankness, the question of what it is to do something because of something is still an unsolved problem.[1] Doing something as something – as a requirement of one's role, for instance – is a sub-class, a very large one, of the class of cases of doing something because of a consideration; and although the working out would take me too far beyond this paper, it is my hope that the critical examination of doing-as will help to solve Kenny's problem.

What is it, then, to do something as something? I shall review a number of widely different examples, reserving two

[1] *Action, Emotion and Will* (London, 1963), p. 238.

or three for treatment in some detail to bring out their common features.

1. First, an example from Professor J. L. Austin which may seem at first sight very remote from the area of roles, though in my view it is not. This passage from *How to do Things with Words* is remarkable, not for what it says but for what it does not say. Austin was a notorious turner of unturned stones, yet here is a stone which he not only failed to turn, but left sticking up in the middle of his path, italics and all:

> To say anything is . . . always to perform the act of uttering certain vocables or words, i.e. noises of certain types belonging to *and as* belonging to a certain vocabulary, in a certain construction, i.e. conforming to and as conforming to a certain grammar.[1]

Now it is clear from Austin's terminology that he thinks of language in terms of rules: the rules of vocabulary and grammar. His italics raise the problem of what it is, not merely to do something which does conform to the rules, but to do it *as* conforming to the rules. Notice the immediate resemblance to Kant's ethical problem: the problem of what it is, not merely to do something which does conform to the moral law, but to do it *as* conforming to the moral law. (The problem of the Good Will.) Both moral action, and speaking a language, are in my extended sense cases of acting a role; certainly they both require, in Emmet's phrase, mutual reciprocal expectations.

2. For my next example, consider a motorist who is pouring boiling water over his car's radiator on a frosty morning. His intention is to try to thaw the frozen radiator. But it would be incorrect to say that he is pouring the water *as* an attempt to thaw the radiator.[2] What we do say is that he pours the water *in* an attempt to thaw the radiator. The difference between the 'as' and the 'in' just is whatever does distinguish the 'as'

---

[1] Edited by J. O. Urmson and G. J. Warnock (Oxford, Clarendon Press, 1962), p. 92.

[2] It could, of course, be said that in pouring the water he thinks of the act as a way of thawing the radiator; but it certainly cannot be assumed, and I think it is certainly false, that doing something as *x* is the same as doing something and thinking of it as *x*.

case as a member of that particular sub-class of cases of doing something 'because of' a consideration. What would be a case of pouring the water as something? Well, it would be proper enough, though improbably true, to say that he pours the water as a libation to the Thaw God. He still does it in an attempt to thaw: what do we add when we say he does it *as* this other thing?

What we are doing is to place him in relation to others. His intention is no longer directed solely to a private object, but to an area of reflecting expectations. These may, in the extreme case, involve only himself and the Thaw God; at the other extreme, they may involve only the bystanders, actual or possible, before whom he enacts a ritual which is logically independent of any existence-beliefs. In between there will be an interesting variety of degrees of religious commitment which I shall return to shortly.

My next example, to be treated in still more detail, brings out the 'infinite etceteration' of the mutual reciprocal expectations.

3. What is it for a joke to have been made? – And this is not a question about the psychology of humour.

Clearly, we have, to begin with

(i) A speaker, A, utters a certain string of words, J, in the presence of a person addressed, B.

Do we have to add

(ii) B is amused by (A's uttering) J? But (ii) is not a necessary condition of a joke's being made; if it were, someone's not being amused by my joke would entail that I did not make one; in fact it entails only that I did not succeed in making one effectively.

Do we have to add, instead,

(iii) A expects to amuse B by uttering J? It might be objected that (iii) is not necessary either: for A may not be expecting to amuse B, but to embarrass him by a smutty joke, or to bore him with a polite one. But in that case it would follow that he was not joking. However, there still is an objection to (iii): not that it is not necessary, but that it is not, together with (i), sufficient: for A may be expecting to amuse B by uttering J, but knowing or suspecting that B's amusement will be occasioned by circumstantial features of the telling of the joke (grimaces, for instance), not by his actually seeing the point of it. We can try to write this in:

(iv) *A* expects to amuse *B* by uttering *J* and by *B*'s seeing the point of *J*.

(Note that *B*'s seeing the point of *J* is not itself a condition of the joke's being made, but is internal to the expectations of *A* which are conditions of this.)

But what do we mean by *B*'s 'seeing the point' of *J*? It is certainly part of the meaning of 'seeing the point' of a joke that teller and hearer should have, and get, the same point in mind; we could, without much loss, define 'point of *J*' as 'feature of *J* which both *A* and *B* find amusing'. But, as we saw under (ii), it is not enough that both *A* and *B* should as a matter of fact, and independently, find *J* amusing because of some feature *F* of *J*: for it to be the case that *A* has made a joke, *A* must have expected to amuse *B* by that feature *F* of *J* which he, *A*, finds amusing (note that to mention feature *F* within *A*'s expectations is not to imply that *A* could specify *F*.) But it now appears that *A*'s expectations with respect to *B* themselves include *B*'s expectations with regard to *A*: for it is still not enough that *A* should expect *B* to be amused by the *F* which amuses him, *A*; he must expect *B* to be amused by the *F* which he, *B*, expects *A* to be amused by; and if we ask what this is, we discover a Chinese box of expectations, and this is the box which we wrap up in the commonplace formula: *A* utters *J* as a joke. This readily implies that *A* expects *B* to take *J* as a joke, that is, as what he expects *B* to expect him to be making it as . . . Notice the intimate connection between *making as* and *taking as*.

The disclosure of this infinite etceteration of expectations within expectations is not a mere logical virtuosity. It is, partly, of course, a reminder that all illocutions – all things done *in* language – are locutions – things *of* language – and that communication is *communi*cation. Moreover, the successive elements in the Chinese boxes are not necessarily homogeneous; and the possibility of variety therein offers a way of systematising all sorts of subtle and unsystematic-looking distinctions in ordinary talk about people's social behaviour, most of which could be called the varieties of insincerity. I mention these non-standard cases of variety within the Chinese boxes because, as so often, it is the divergent and outlandish cases that throw light on the normal and central ones. Ways of going wrong – of misunderstanding, or insincerity – show what it is to understand, or to be sincere. I shall illustrate this variety with an example from the field of stylised courtesies:

4. When I as host say to you as guest, 'It's still quite early, you surely aren't going yet?', you may take this either as a hint to speed your departure, or as an invitation to dwell another hour. In the second case, of course, you took my remark as a request to stay, that is, as addressed to someone who was expected to take it as a request to stay . . ., and there is no variety here. However, I may have intended my remark as a hint to you to leave, and then there is variety as between what I in fact expected and what you took me to expect. But this is a simple misunderstanding; and in the niceties of actual social discourse there is a variety which can be contained in full understanding. It may well be, for instance, that for things to go right the following has to hold: I say 'It's still quite early . . .' and I expect you to take this remark as a request to stay uttered by one who expects his hearer to take it as a hint to leave.

A similar variety was foreshadowed in our motorist example. If he expects the Thaw God to take his act as a libation, the series is homogeneous and it is a case of full religious commitment. If he expects only the bystanders to take his act as an act which he expects the Thaw God to take as . . ., there is variety, and we have something less than full commitment, possibly total insincerity. If, in the end, he just expects the bystanders to take his act as an act which he expects the bystanders to take as . . ., and if the Thaw God never enters this series, we again have a homogeneity. Replace the Thaw God with something less primitive, and this wholly institutionalised 'religion', into which the numinous object itself never enters, could well be one or another that is actually among us.[1] But we are getting a bit off the track.

---

[1] See, for instance, J. N. Findlay, *Values and Intentions* (1961), ch. 9.

For another real-life example, compare Georg Simmel on 'the Sociology of the Sexes': 'The simple and pure form of erotic decision . . . by definition does not enter into coquetry . . . sociability appears only when the man desires nothing more than this free moving play, in which something definitely erotic lurks only as a remote symbol.' (*Grundfragen der Soziologie*, iii. 3.f.)

We are now in a position to see why the term 'expectations' conveys more of what is wanted than does the term 'requirements'. Both expectations and requirements are satisfied or unsatisfied, fulfilled or unfulfilled; but expectations, unlike requirements, are true or false: they include beliefs about their own satisfaction. They also include beliefs about other people's expectations. I can expect you to expect . . ., but I cannot require you to require . . . It is these features which enable 'expectations', but not 'requirements', to capture the inwardness of the individual's assumption of his roles.

To sum up this examination of the role concept. To describe a person's behaviour in terms of a role is to offer a condensed explanation in terms of an open-ended series of expectations by, and of, others. It is essential to keep in mind the infinite etceteration of the series; if we have in mind only the first member of it, we shall not see beyond the actual, particular demands of the actual participants in the role-situation; and this is to ignore what makes it a role-situation at all. The inward aspect of this in the life of the individual is reflected, though opaquely, in the indispensably recurrent 'as' idioms.

III

We must now return to the question, whether being a moral agent is acting a role in any useful sense. It should now be clear, though, that the features of role-situations that I have singled out are important features of moral situations. The notion of morality implies the notion of a moral consensus just as role-acting requires a consensus about what is required for a particular role; in the same way, too, this consensus must not merely exist (indeed it can, in an extreme case, fail to exist as a matter of fact): it must enter into the thinking of the individual. It does so, as I have argued at length but in quite different terms elsewhere,[1] as one of the three dimensions of universality in moral thinking.

Here I shall consider two specific cases where the features of role-situations can help to clarify some actual problems in

[1] *Ethics and the Moral Life* (Macmillan, 1958), pp. 83–92.

moral philosophy. First I consider Kant's difficulties about the
motivation of moral acts. Kant's attempt to distinguish between
moral and non-moral motives has frequently been criticised on
the ground of importing irrelevant psychological considerations
into ethics (a charge to which he was himself acutely sensitive:
witness the long footnote in chapter i[1]). What does it mean
to say that a certain action was performed 'from' inclination,
or again 'from' self-interest, and as opposed to: 'from' a sense
of duty? Does 'from' mean the same, or anything at all, in all
these three cases? Notice that we can translate all three cases
into the 'because' idiom, but only one of them into the 'as'
idiom. We can say someone did X because he wanted to, or
because it was in his interest, or because it was a matter of
moral duty; but we cannot say he did it 'as' a thing he wanted
to do, or 'as' a thing that was profitable, though we certainly
can say he did it as a moral duty. Is this sort of doing-as of the
same sort as our examples in Section II?

Before asking whether moral imperatives generally are role-
requirements, I shall stop to examine, and reject, what someone
might claim to be a short and simple way of dealing with what
I call doing-as. It might be claimed that all cases of doing-as are
reducible to cases of what Professor Ryle has called mongrel-
categoricals, in a section of the *Concept of Mind* (1949) where
he claims to deal with the problem of motive-attributions. Just
as, on the view in question, to say that someone did X from a
certain sort of inclination is to say that his doing X was doing
something which that sort of inclination is an inclination to do;
so, to say that someone did Y from a sense of duty, or from
respect for the moral law, would be to say that his doing Y was
the exercise of a disposition which just is a disposition to do
things of that sort. This kind of disposition, of course, is
different from the kind to which inclinations belong; it is more
like an Aristotelian *hexis*, something which the traditional
jargon of 'sense of duty' or 'respect for the moral law' would be
poorish attempts to characterise. Now I do not deny that this
could be a proper way of describing at least some aspects of
the moral life, notably those which we should be prepared
ordinarily to call exercises of a virtuous character-feature; but

[1] p. 69 of H. J. Paton's translation of I. Kant's *The Moral Law* (1961).

I do doubt whether it could do justice to other aspects, and in particular to those in which Kant was interested.

For if we try to interpret the motive-attributions 'on principle', 'from a sense of duty', 'as a matter of right and wrong', on the lines of the mongrel-categorical analysis, we get something like: 'His doing Y satisfied the law-like statement that whenever he finds himself in situations of type T, he does Y' – and this is indeed a possible interpretation of 'He did Y from a dutiful disposition' but not of what we wanted. What is left out here is the agent's own recognition of what he is doing or, rather, what he is doing it as.

He is acting a role. Not necessarily before witnesses, of course; but playing a part before one's own eyes, acting a role with oneself as witness, is clearly a notion parasitical on the notion of acting a role before others. To play the moral role is to recognise, and to be recognised as recognising, a system of moral expectations which is common within the interlocking recognitions. If I do Y as a matter of moral principle, then so far as witnesses are concerned I expect them not merely to note my doing Y, but to note it – again, to *take* it, *as* done in fulfilment of expectations, and moreover in the expectation of recognition as having fulfilled expectations, the expectations being shared between me and them.

For another illustration consider two more examples from J. L. Austin.[1] One crook is pretending to clean windows, another to cut a tree, in both cases to conceal their true intentions. Will their pretence be less of a pretence if they actually clean the window, or let the saw bite into the wood? It will certainly be a more effective pretence. But how can a man who is actually cleaning a window be only pretending to clean it?

The answer is, of course, that what is faulty about his performance is not what he does, but what he does it as; not the cleaning of the window or the cutting of the tree, but the being a window-cleaner or a tree-feller. He performs the act, and he even performs it because it is required by his pretended role, but he does not actually participate in any of the expectations further along the series that actually constitute the role: he

[1] *Philosophical Papers* (Oxford, Clarendon Press, 1961), ch. 9.

only pretends to do so, and his actual wiping or sawing is the substance of his pretence. The real tree-feller saws the tree as a tree-feller, that is, with expectations of others whom he sees as having expectations of him, whom in turn they see as . . . . The bogus tree-feller only saws the tree. If, and to the extent that, he does enter into the series of expectations, he becomes a tree-feller, and depending on the degree to which he enters in will be the depth of his commitment to tree-felling.

So for the moral hypocrite; and I think degrees of moral commitment, different levels of insincerity, could be distinguished in the light of our examples. To know that a person is morally insincere, it is necessary to know that some expectation is not entertained, or not recognised; but to know that a person is morally sincere, or fully committed, it is not necessary, and indeed on the foregoing analysis not possible, to know that all expectations are entertained and recognised. Moral sincerity will then be a defeasible concept.

Indeed, I think one of the strongest arguments for looking at moral action in terms of role situations is that we get a simple and persuasive solution to a second problem: the problem of moral sincerity. Kant was notoriously sceptical about getting any proof that there actually are any moral agents; it is always possible, he argued, that an outwardly 'moral' act might in fact be motivated by pure love or even pure greed.[1] And so he felt obliged to remind his readers that that part of the *Grundlegung* is analytical: it shows what would have to be the case if moral concepts have application, there being no proof that they do. It shows what it would be like for someone to act morally.

Most readers of the *Grundlegung* are inclined to regard this as an extravaganza of Cartesian doubt, while remaining uncomfortable about it. Perhaps their inclination can be justified, and their discomfort eased, by constructing a similar paradox about our bus conductor. Fred Smith goes through all the motions of handing out tickets and receiving coins, pressing the bell, and so on. Does anyone suggest that even some, let alone all, of those actions might be motivated by inclination or self-interest? (Kant, of course, did try to say just that about his

[1] Plato, of course, carried out a somewhat similar exercise in the characters of Glaucon and Adeimantus.

shopkeeper. That just shows how wrong he was about shop-keepers too.) Fred Smith does all those things because he is a bus conductor. And this does not mean that we have to invoke a special sort of motive, the bus conductor motive. We could, indeed, write an analytical treatise about the bus conductor concept, but it would be absurd to stress the hypothetical nature of the exercise by insisting that perhaps there aren't really any bus conductors.

There are two objections to the idea of role morality which I must note briefly. First, it will be said that a sociological concept cannot cover the 'inner' aspects of morality: conscience, and the freedom to resist or reject the social consensus. This objection is misconceived. It mistakes the consensus of mutual expectations, as it enters into the moral thinking of the indivi-dual, with the actual existence of a social consensus. This latter is required for the existence of morality as a social fact, but only the former is required for the 'inwardness' of the moral life. The objection is also misconceived in its assumption that resis-tance to the pressure of an actual consensus cannot itself be a role-requirement. Professor Emmet's point, that something over and above a role-morality is needed in order to decide conflicts between role requirements, makes the same mistake. Even familiar social roles often require of their incumbents the resolution of conflicts arising from other role-requirements; for example, a tribunal. There is no reason why someone who says 'Speaking not as a father, or a government employee, but from the moral point of view . . .' should not be assuming a role, though certainly a very special and important one.

Secondly, there is the claim of 'personal morality' to be exempted from role-status, and I promised earlier to substan-tiate my objection to this claim. In fact I can do little more than reiterate my puzzlement about the very existence of such a thing. Neither Professor Emmet nor anyone else has per-suaded me to alter my view that 'personal morality' is a mis-nomer for two other things, one of which is not personal and the other is not moral. One thing that might be called a personal morality is the morality of the saint, hero, missionary or prophet; someone who conceives himself to have a mission which is for him alone. But this cannot possibly be the sense of 'personal' which is contrasted with 'role-determined', for his actions certainly are decided by (what he conceives to be) his role, even if he is the only one who occupies it, and even if few or none recognise that he does. What Professor Emmet seems to have in mind is quite different: the conduct of a person in his intimate personal life with other persons. Now much of this conduct will come under the head of 'spontaneous behaviour' which no one wishes to call a morality; but once we introduce the element of reflection and consideration, the question 'What should I do?', the context of moral discussion, we have already moved beyond the purely personal situation; the morality of our decision is merely in degree more personal than the morality of deciding about abortion or Vietnam. But this, I fear, is still open to argument.

4

ON BEING OBLIGED TO ACT[1]

Alan R. White

THERE are various ways in which a person's freedom of action may be diminished or restricted. Instead of acting, he may be acted upon; or he may be unable to help doing what he does. He may suffer from some disability, have a duty imposed on him or do something because he is obliged to do it. In this essay, I wish to examine the notion of being obliged to do something. I shall investigate the differences between 'being obliged by A to do X' and 'being obliged to A for X'; between 'being obliged to do X' and 'having (or being under) an obligation to do X'; between being physically obliged and being morally, legally and logically obliged; and between saying 'X is something I am obliged to do', 'X is something I choose to do' and 'X is something I ought to do'.

1. 'OBLIGED BY' AND 'OBLIGED TO'

If I am obliged by somebody or something to do X, then he or it obliges me to do X. If, on the other hand, I am obliged to somebody, or perhaps something, for doing Y (or for Z), then he or it obliges me by doing Y (or with Z). For instance, in the first case, if I am obliged by the Vice-Chancellor, the University Regulations or the illness of a colleague, to attend a

---

[1] I am indebted to my colleagues at Hull, to H. L. A. Hart of Oxford, P. J. Fitzgerald of Leeds and A. Sloman of Sussex for criticisms of an earlier draft of this paper.

meeting, then the Vice-Chancellor, the University Regulations or the illness of a colleague, obliges me to attend a meeting. In the second case, if I am obliged to the desk clerk for (or for giving me) the required information, then he obliges me with (or by giving me) the required information.

I am not obliged *to* what I am obliged *by*, nor obliged *by* what I am obliged *to*. The person, or thing, to whom I am obliged has helped me; the person, or thing, by whom I am obliged has hindered me. The person to whom I am obliged is obliging, but not the person by whom I am obliged. An obliging person is necessarily helpful. I am obliged to someone for his doing of something, but obliged by someone only by his doing of something. I am obliged to someone because of what he has done for me, but obliged by him because of what he has done to me. I can be obliged to someone to a greater or lesser degree, but there are no degrees to which I can be obliged by someone. He to whom I am obliged simply obliges me, whereas he by whom I am obliged obliges me to do something. I can either be obliged to someone or be obliged by someone to do something, but I cannot be obliged to someone to do something.

There is, however, a basic similarity between these two cases. Whether I am obliged to someone for what he has done or obliged by him by what he has done, whether he simply obliges me, or obliges me to do something, I am obliged by his doing of something. Further, though I cannot be obliged to myself for what I myself do, I can be obliged to do so and so by what I myself do, as when I am obliged to do *X* by my having promised or contracted to do it. Finally, when what obliges me to do something is not a person at all, but e.g. a rule or a physical event or a psychological condition, then also there is something by which, though nothing to which, I am obliged. In every case of being obliged, therefore, whether I be obliged to someone or to do something, there is something, though not necessarily someone, by which I am obliged. That by which I am obliged may be called the 'obliging factor'.

Besides being obliged to or by, I can also feel obliged to or by someone or something or feel obliged to do so and so, irrespective of whether or not I am in fact obliged.

2. 'being obliged' and 'having (or being under) an obligation'

I may have (or be under) an obligation to someone or to do something. An obligation may be 'assumed' because of what I do, as when I make a promise, or 'incurred' because of what someone has done for me, as when he helps me, or 'imposed' because of what someone or something does to me, as when the law puts me under an obligation. I may 'acknowledge', 'fulfil' or 'be released from' such an obligation. I may enter into negotiations 'with' or 'without' obligation. I may receive something which 'carries' or 'is free from' obligation.

To have (or be under) an obligation is necessarily to be obliged. I am obliged to the person to whom I am under an obligation and obliged to do what I am under an obligation to do. I may, however, have an obligation or obligations – though I cannot be under an obligation – to someone according to which I am obliged to do something for him, though I am not obliged to him. Of this kind are treaty obligations, e.g. to come to the help of an ally in the event of an attack by a third power, or family obligations, e.g. to play with my children, or a doctor's obligations to his patients. I have obligations to my allies, my children and my patients, and am, therefore, obliged to do something for them; though I am not obliged to them, nor under an obligation to them.

But though to have (or be under) an obligation is necessarily to be obliged, the converse is not true. I can be obliged without having (or being under) an obligation. Neither the yachtsman who is obliged by the wind to alter course, nor the traveller who is obliged by the gunman to hand over his wallet, nor the motorist who is sentenced to a month's imprisonment without the option of a fine, has (or is under) an obligation to do what he is obliged to do.

What, then, is the difference between having (or being under) an obligation and being obliged? The difference, I suggest, is this. We may be obliged to do so and so either because of the presence of a factor of circumstances, such as the threats of a gunman or the force of a prevailing wind, or because of a position which we occupy or have assumed, such as that of promisor, debtor, contractor, parent, doctor, or treaty power. In the latter case, there will be a rule to the effect that anyone in that position must do so and so in certain circumstances. Such rules will thus impose obligations, that is, things one is obliged to do, on those who are or come to be in that position; the position comprises, amongst other things, an obligation or set of obligations. These obligations may be social, family or treaty obligations, or they may be moral or legal obligations according to the kinds of rules imposing the conduct. Anyone in such a social, moral or legal position has or is under such and such an obligation and continues to have or be under the obligation as long as he is in that position. Furthermore, though he is from the moment of coming into that position under an obligation to do X, and therefore obliged to do it, he may be obliged to do it only if and when certain circumstances arise. A nation may according to its treaty have an obligation to come to the help of its allies when attacked; a doctor is under an obligation to visit his patients when they become ill.

If, on the other hand, the obliging factor is not some rule-bound position which we assume or are put in, but some physical circumstances in which we find or get ourselves, then we are obliged, but not under an obligation, to do so and so, since in this case the obliging factor is forcing us to act forthwith and not merely if and when certain circumstances arise. Indeed, the obliging factor is the circumstance. The obliged action is called for as soon as the obliging factor comes into operation. The yachtsman is obliged, not put under an obligation, by the wind to alter course.

To say that I am now obliged to do X if and when Y happens is not the same as saying that I will be obliged to do X if and when Y happens. In the latter case the happening of Y is the obliging factor; until it comes into operation no question of being obliged arises. In the former case something other than Y is the obliging factor, in virtue of which I am from this moment under an obligation. Thus, a doctor may now be obliged, e.g. by entering into a contract, to visit a patient if and when the patient becomes ill. He is from the moment of signing the contract under an obligation to do so and so in certain circumstances. On the other hand, the doctor will perhaps be obliged, e.g. by the future throat condition of the patient, to resort to surgery, though he is not at the moment obliged. He is not under an obligation to use surgery. To specify the future circumstances in which a man is, because of some present obliging factor, now under an obligation (and hence obliged) to act is not to specify the future circumstances by which he will be obliged to act. To be obliged 'to do X when Y happens' is not to be obliged when Y happens 'to do X'.

My thesis is that whether one is obliged by circumstances or by a rule-bound position, he is obliged in one and the same sense of 'obliged'. The reason why only he who is obliged by position has or is under an obligation is that only he is subject, because of his position, to a rule about what he must do when . . .

A different explanation of the distinction between 'being obliged' and 'having (or being under) an obligation' has been offered by H. L. A. Hart (e.g. *The Concept of Law* (1961), chapter v, section 2).[1] In the first place, Hart suggests that these phrases signify two distinct notions; and, in the second place, he gives a somewhat different account from mine of the difference between the two.

The main objection to Hart's suggestion that 'being obliged' and 'having an obligation' are distinct notions is that it entails either that 'being legally or morally obliged' and 'having a legal or moral obligation' are distinct notions or that 'being legally or morally obliged' and 'being obliged by circumstances' use different notions of 'being obliged'. Now it seems clear from Hart's writings that his object is not to distinguish 'being legally obliged' from 'having a legal obligation' but only 'having a legal obligation' (or 'being legally obliged') from 'being obliged by circumstances' e.g. by a gunman.

His actual arguments, however, allege general distinctions between 'having an obligation' and 'being obliged'. Moreover, these arguments are fallacious. First, Hart asserts that the statement that a person had an obligation to do X, e.g. to report for military service, may be true irrespective of his beliefs and fears of discovery and punishment, whereas he suggests that the

---

[1] K. Baier, 'Moral Obligation', *Am. Philos. Quarterly* (1966), p. 220a, note 24, asserts that 'being obliged cannot be used to explain having an obligation'; but his assertion lacks argument.

statement that a man was obliged to do Y, e.g. hand over his money to a gunman, means that he did Y because of his beliefs and fears. But a man may truly be said to be obliged (i.e. to be legally obliged) to report for military service independent of his beliefs and fears, since what he has an obligation to do he is obliged to do. Secondly, Hart asserts that 'whereas the statement that he had this obligation is quite independent of the question whether or not he in fact reported for service, the statement that someone was obliged to do something normally carries the implication that he actually did it'. But this is not an implication of 'was obliged'; it depends on the type of factor by which one is obliged. Prosecuting counsel might well say in 1965 of a doctor who was under contract from 1960 to 1962 that he was obliged by his contract to visit the deceased when telephoned, but that he failed to do so.

It seems clear that Hart's actual arguments do not prove a distinction between 'having an obligation' and 'being obliged', but only between being obliged by one kind of factor and being obliged by a different kind. There is, of course, as I have argued, a difference between 'being obliged' and 'having an obligation'; but it is of a different sort. It is only because one kind of factor, e.g. force of circumstances, does not, while the other, e.g. a rule-bound position, does give rise to a standing obligation, that one can be said to have or be under a legal or moral obligation, but not a physical obligation.

Not only are Hart's reasons for believing that 'being obliged' and 'having an obligation' signify two distinct notions mistaken; his account of what the difference is seems to be wrong. According to him, the essential difference between 'being obliged' and 'having an obligation' is that the latter implies social rules which make certain types of behaviour a standard and bring serious social pressure to bear on deviants from the rules.

The first objection to this is that the existence of social rules and social pressures does not distinguish, e.g. 'having a legal or moral obligation' from 'being legally or morally obliged', but only 'being legally or morally obliged' from 'being obliged by circumstances'. A second objection is that it is not the idea of social pressure that distinguishes 'having an obligation' from 'being obliged', but the fact that the obliging factor in cases of obligation is a rule-bound position in virtue of which one is not merely (legally or morally) obliged but also comes to have (legal or moral) obligations.

3. 'BEING OBLIGED BY'

Having argued that common to all the uses of 'oblige' is the idea of being obliged by something, and also that having (or being under) an obligation implies being obliged, I want now to examine this notion of *being obliged by*.

When I am obliged by something, I am obliged by it either to someone or to do something. In both cases there is something I am obliged to do, but only in the latter case is this deed specified. Both the kindness of the man who opens the door for me and the inconsiderateness of the man who locks it against me (or the faulty mechanism which makes it stick) oblige me to do something, though the latter obliges me to do something which can be specified as being any alternative other than the one barred to me by the locked door, while the former obliges me only to make some unspecified return for the help given.

Though the only thing that can make me obliged to someone is a deed of his, there are many factors which can oblige me to do something specific. I can be obliged by persons, e.g. a gunman; by circumstances, e.g. a locked door or the inefficiency of a servant; by my own deed, e.g. the giving of a promise or the assertion of a thesis; by my position, e.g. as a secretary or a doctor; or by rules and regulations, e.g. of morals, the law or a club. Sometimes the obliging factor is not mentioned, but only what I am obliged to do; e.g. to give my full name and address, to offer either paper X or paper Y, if I offer paper D.

Ordinarily a person of a certain position, in certain circumstances, with certain aims and following certain rules of conduct, has some freedom of choice. There are various alternative ways in which he can behave compatible with his position, circumstances, aims and rules. Within this sphere he can do whatever he wants. A yachtsman intent on making port may have several alternative routes; there may be no agreed date on which a manufacturer has to deliver his goods, a candidate's choice of papers may be fairly unrestricted, a chess player may have several possible moves. In different circumstances, however, a factor may be present or may intervene which limits this choice by leaving him with no alternative, compatible with his general position, but to do so and so. His hands are tied. He is now obliged by this factor to do so and so. He has to do it. The wind obliges the yachtsman to alter course; his contract obliges the manufacturer to deliver his goods within a fortnight; the degree regulations oblige the student who offers paper D to choose between papers X and Y; a particular move by his opponent may oblige a chess player to move his King. As the case of the student shows, what one is obliged to do may be to choose within a restricted field rather than to take without choice. Similarly, the man who is under an obligation because of a kindness received or a promise given or who has obligations to his children or his allies is restricted, in a specified or unspecified way, in regard to his future acts. I may not be free to dine with you because I have promised to visit someone else; my country may have no choice but to go to war, if its allies are attacked.

What I am obliged to do is not something I cannot help doing or something I am unable not to do. I may sometimes quite easily not do what I am obliged to do. It is something I am unable not to do without incurring certain consequences. There is always an 'otherwise' in the offing (cf. Nowell-Smith, *Ethics* (1954), p. 202). I have to do what I am obliged to do, otherwise these consequences will follow. In legal, moral or logical obligation, this otherwise is the breaking of some rule or law. The manufacturer who is legally obliged by his contract to deliver the goods within a fortnight can only not do so at the cost of illegality. The man who promises to do X can only not do X at the cost of behaving immorally. Where the obligation is circumstantial the 'otherwise' in the offing is the loss of some specific objective. The yachtsman who is obliged to alter course can only not do so by throwing away his chance of reaching port; the traveller who is obliged to hand over his wallet to the gunman can only avoid doing so by giving up his life. It is always possible to act incompatibly with the legal, moral or logical situation or with one's objectives. But given that there is no alteration in these, one is in the stated circumstances obliged to follow a certain course. The question whether someone has a choice or not does not occur in a vacuum, but in a particular situation. The question is whether, in this situation, I am obliged to do X or whether, physically, legally, morally, logically, I have a choice between X and other alternatives. It is a different question whether I have a choice between doing X and either giving up my objective or behaving illegally, immorally, illogically. What I am circumstantially obliged to do is what, given adherence to physical conditions and to my objective, I have no option but to do. What I have a moral or legal or logical obligation to do is what, given moral or legal or logical conditions, I have no option but to do. The obliging factor narrows down what I can circumstantially, legally or morally do.

What I am obliged to do, I do; it is not something done to me. The yachtsman is obliged to alter course, he is not swept off it. The gunman obliges me to hand over my wallet, he does not snatch it from me. To be obliged to do something is quite unlike being physically compelled to do something, even when the obliging factor is a physical event such as a fall of snow on the line by which I had hoped to travel. For a physical compulsion, unlike an obliging factor, turns a deed done by me into something done to me. When I am obliged, I still have a choice and am still called upon to act, but the choice is not among alternatives at the same level as the obligatory alternative. At that level, I must take the obligatory one. The difference between what I do because I am obliged to do it and what I do because I choose to do it is not the difference between a choice and a free choice (*e.g.* Nowell-Smith, *Ethics*, p. 202; cf. Gauthier, *Practical Reasoning* (1963), p. 176) but between a choice whether or not to act inconsistently with one's general position and a choice among alternatives compatible with one's general position. If I am obliged to alter course, I do not choose to do it, though neither is it impossible for me not to do it. I alter course because, given that I do not want to be driven out to sea, I have no choice but to. The fact that I could choose to let myself be driven out to sea is irrelevant, since the original problem was whether, given that I did not want to be driven out to sea, I had any choice of course. Similarly, the manufacturer delivers the goods within a fortnight because, given that he is to act legally, he has no choice but to deliver. Hence, there is no paradox in saying that a man who is obliged to do X has no choice, even though it is physically possible for him – and perhaps quite easy – not to do X. (Cf. Nowell-Smith, *Ethics*, p. 201; Hart and Honoré, *Causation in the Law* (1959), p. 72.)

What I do thinking I am obliged to do it, I do; it is not something done to me. Yet I do not do it voluntarily. To say (e.g. Gauthier, *Practical Reasoning*, p. 176) that I was obliged voluntarily to do so and so is a contradiction. I do not do it voluntarily because I do not choose to do it in preference to another alternative; the other alternative was, I thought, closed to me by the obliging factor. What I voluntarily do is contrasted with what I do thinking I am obliged to do it and not, except by philosophers and jurisprudents, with what is done to me (e.g. Aristotle, *N.E.* III. 1; Nowell-Smith, *Ethics*, p. 201; Gauthier, *Practical Reasoning*, p. 176; Ryle, *The Concept of Mind* (1949), pp. 73–4). Even Nowell-Smith, who realises this, allows a sense of 'voluntary' in which it is contrasted with having something done to me. A trade union member may give a voluntary subscription to charity, but he is obliged to subscribe to his union fund; a man may give himself up voluntarily or because he thinks he is obliged to do so; a student may withdraw voluntarily from the University or be obliged to withdraw. Contrast answering because you were asked a direct question and volunteering the information. The contrast between a voluntary and an obligatory subscription, surrender or withdrawal is not the same as the contrast between a voluntary payment and a levy, a voluntary surrender and a capture, or a voluntary withdrawal and expulsion. For the former contrast is between two things I do, one voluntarily and the other obligatorily, while the latter contrast is between what I do and what is done to me. What I do thinking I am obliged to do it, I do not voluntarily do; since I think I have to do it. What is done to me I do not voluntarily do, since I do not do it at all.

It is these two contrasts which, it seems to me, Aristotle is struggling to distinguish in the opening sections of *N.E.* III. 1,

F   H.A.

i.e. (i) the contrast between throwing one's goods overboard to save oneself in a storm and throwing them overboard voluntarily, and (ii) the contrast between being carried out to sea by the wind and putting out to sea. He is also unclear, I think, on the difference between doing something involuntarily (or non-voluntarily) and doing it unwillingly.

Further, if what I do is unintentional, unknowing or in some respects non-attentive, it is neither voluntary nor obliged, though it is still a deed of mine. If, by a voluntary remark of mine, I quite unintentionally hurt your feelings, I did not hurt them voluntarily nor was I obliged to hurt them. If, by voluntarily handing over a letter to you, I give you a secret document by mistake, I did not voluntarily or non-voluntarily pass on secret information. What I do absent-mindedly is neither voluntary nor obliged.

The contrast between an act and happening is one way in which being obliged is different from being bound. I can only be obliged to do something, whereas I can be bound either to do or to feel something or to have something happen to me. I can be bound, but not obliged, to succeed or fail, to cry or to feel tired. I can be obliged to surrender, but only bound to be caught; obliged to jump, but only bound to fall. Since inanimate objects do not perform actions, they can only be bound to do what they do. The shopkeeper may be obliged to raise his prices, but his prices can only be bound to go up. If I am obliged to do so and so, I have no alternative to doing it other than acting incompatibly with my moral, legal, logical or desired position. If something is bound to happen, there is no alternative to its happening unless some other part of the situation is altered. Thus, the inhabitants are bound to be massacred unless the relief column arrives before nightfall; it is bound to rain unless the wind changes. Whereas 'obliged' carries an 'otherwise' rider, 'bound' has an 'unless' rider.

Many philosophers (e.g. Nowell-Smith, *Ethics*, pp. 206 ff.; Hart, *The Concept of Law*, pp. 80, 85; Gauthier, *Practical Reasoning*, pp. 177–9; K. Baier, 'Moral Obligation', *Am. Phil. Quart.* (1966), p. 212a) have suggested that the alternative which I am obliged to take must be less desirable, less desired, or less advantageous than the other alternatives; that 'the logic of obligation requires a conflict between the obligation to do something and the inclination not to do it' (Nowell-Smith, *Ethics*, pp. 210–11; cf. Kant). This is a mistake. Being in the position of being able to choose among alternatives, of being able to do whatever I want, is more desirable and perhaps more desired than being restricted in my choice by having to do something whether I want to or not. But it does not follow from this that the alternative to which I am restricted is less desirable or desired than the alternatives once open to me; nor that I cannot be said to be obliged to do what is advantageous to me. A candidate who wishes to offer paper *D* may be obliged to choose his further option from papers *X* and *Y*, but this need not be a less desirable course to him than choosing between papers *P* and *Q*. To be free to live either within or without the city boundary is more desirable than to be obliged to live within it; but there need be no suggestion that it is less desirable to live where one is obliged to live than to live elsewhere. The fact that exchanging a pawn for a queen or other piece is an advantage in chess does not preclude this change's being obligatory in certain circumstances (*pace* Gauthier, *Practical Reasoning*, p. 177). It is simply false to suppose that 'to say to someone that he has an obligation to refrain from torturing children plainly implies that he would want to torture them if he had a chance' (Baier, 'Moral Obligation', *Am. Phil. Quart.* (1966), p. 212a). Often, of course, the obligatory action is less pleasing than the alternatives and is one which I would not have taken if I could have avoided it; but not necessarily so. Furthermore, even where the obligatory course is undesirable, it is not this quality which makes it obligatory, but the fact that it is the only course open to me. It is not the fact that I consider a visit to the dentist undesirable *per se* that allows me to say I am obliged to go (e.g. Gauthier, *Practical Reasoning*, p. 178), but the fact that it is the only course open to a person who wants to stop his toothache. The obligatory course is the course I have to take whether I want to or not; not the course I would not take unless I had to. It is not a question of whether I want the course or not; since the course is obligatory, that question does not arise. The fact that we often excuse ourselves by pleading that what we did was not what we wanted to do but only what we were obliged to do does not show (*pace* Nowell-Smith, *Ethics*, p. 206) that being obliged to do something implies not wanting to do it. Nor is it relevant (e.g. Gauthier, *Practical Reasoning*, p. 178) whether the end to which the obliged alternative may be a means is pleasant or unpleasant. If I have only five minutes to get through my dinner before an appointment, I will be obliged to rush through the meal irrespective of whether the appointment is for an evening at the theatre or for a boring committee meeting.

Nor should we confuse, as some philosophers have done (e.g. Gauthier, *Practical Reasoning*, pp. 179 ff.; cf. J. Austin, *Lectures on Jurisprudence*, xxii–xxiii), the circumstances which may oblige me to do something and a general objective whose preservation may depend on my doing the obliged action. In virtue of my general objective I may have several alternatives open; I am not obliged to take any particular one of them. What obliges me to take one of them is that factor which closes the others. It is the wind, and not his desire to avoid being swept out to sea, which obliges the yachtsman to alter course. Certainly, I would not do the obligatory deed unless I wished to attain my objective, and sometimes it is necessary to mention what this objective is. Thus, I may be obliged to support a colleague on one measure on Senate because I want his support on another. But to say that I am obliged to do X if, or because, I want Y, or in order to get Y, is not to say that it is the desire for Y which obliges me to do X, or that I am obliged to do X by my desire for Y. My desire for Y is not the obliging factor. What does oblige me to do X is that factor which rules out any alternative ways of getting the desired Y. What obliges me to support my colleague on Senate is not the desire to have his support in return, but the fact or the knowledge that his support of me is dependent on my support of him. This fact or knowledge limits my choice of means of getting his support. I know that only by supporting him can I get him to support me. What obliges me to do X partly explains why I do X, but it is a mistake to suppose (e.g. Gauthier, *Practical Reasoning*, p. 183; Nowell-Smith, *Ethics*, p. 204; Hart, *The Concept of Law*, p. 80) that it is my reason or motive for doing X; or that being obliged to do X means doing X in order to get or preserve Y.

I already have my general reason or motive for doing X, namely a desire for Y, which is a reason for doing whatever is a means to Y. What the obliging factor does is to restrict my choice of means. Motives or reasons do not oblige me to do anything. Hence, there is no need to try to distinguish between obliging and non-obliging motives (e.g. Nowell-Smith) or between the kinds of reasons that motives provide for action and the kinds of reasons that obligations provide (Gauthier).

Because the law usually attaches sanctions and penalties to failure to do what one is legally obliged to do, jurisprudents and moral philosophers (e.g. J. Austin, *Lectures on Jurisprudence*, xxii–xxiii; Nowell-Smith, *Ethics*, pp. 200, 204, 209, 242) have sometimes identified the obliging factors in law with the sanctions, and supposed that to say that one is legally obliged to do so and so means that it has to be done in order to avoid unpleasant consequences. But this is a mistake. Sanctions are not legal bonds; they are measures employed to strengthen these bonds. To be physically obliged, e.g. by a fall of snow, to take one rail route rather than any other is to have the alternatives physically closed, thus making it a physical impossibility to take any alternative other than the obligatory one, though not, of course, physically impossible to abstain from action altogether. To be legally obliged, on the other hand, e.g. by railway regulations, to take one route rather than any other is to have the alternatives only legally closed. There need be no physical difficulty in taking an alternative other than the legally obligatory one. Hence, the law usually introduces sanctions and penalties to prevent people from doing, or to punish them for doing, what it is legally, though not physically, obligatory not to do. But reference to such a sanction is no part of the meaning of 'legally obligatory'. Similarly, any reference to the part played by social pressures or qualms of conscience in getting people to do what is morally obligatory is quite irrelevant to the meaning of 'morally obligatory'.

4. 'OBLIGED TO DO' AND 'OUGHT TO DO'

Among moral philosophers the notion of *being obliged* is often assimilated or confused with the notion of *ought*.[1] But an examination of these notions shows that both in morals and elsewhere they are quite distinct.

Whether X is said to be what one ought to do or what one is obliged to do, there is in either case a reference to some basic conditions in relation to which the judgment is made. Given that p is q or that A wants Y he ought to do X or he is obliged to do X. The main difference between saying that X is what A 'ought' to do and saying that X is what A is 'obliged' to do is that 'ought' is used where there are, in the given conditions, several alternative courses of action open to A of which X is judged to be a good course, a better course or the best course, while 'obliged' is used to indicate that X is the only course open to A.

'Ought' implies choice and therefore voluntary action; whereas what we are obliged to do we have no option but to do. No question of what ought to be done arises for the yachtsman obliged by the wind, or for the manufacturer obliged by his contract, to do what he does. Each has to do it; he has no alternative compatible with his general position. Not to know what I ought to do is to be ignorant of what is reasonable or best to do in this situation. Not to know what I am obliged to do is to be unaware of what is the only thing to do in this situation. To tell someone what he ought to do is to advise him

---

[1] Hare, *Freedom and Reason* (1963), p. 170, calls a feeling of obligation 'a desire to do what one ought'. Von Wright, in *The Varieties of Goodness* (1963), ch. 8, assimilates 'ought' and 'must'; in *Norm & Action* (1963), ch. v, sect. 12, he says 'it is obvious' that 'ought to be done' means 'must not be left undone' and 'ought to be left undone' means 'must not be done'. But this does not fit the ordinary use of the term, e.g. 'With all that grass you ought to get another mower' does not mean 'You must not omit to get another mower'. 'You ought to leave the rest of your work till tomorrow' does not mean 'You must not do the rest of your work now'; 'There ought to be a law against it' does not mean 'There must not not be a law against it'. K. Baier, *The Moral Point of View* (1958), p. 283, holds that there is one use of 'must' in which it is equivalent to 'ought'. H. A. Prichard, *Moral Obligation* (1949), pp. 89–90, thinks that 'is morally bound' is a useful synonym for 'ought' because ' "ought" does not admit of difference of tense'. He also (90–1) seems to think that the 'ought' in 'If you want X, and Y is necessary to do X, then you ought to do Y' means 'ought', whereas the 'ought' in 'you ought to tell the truth' means '(morally) obliged'. The reverse of this is nearer the truth.

about the goodness of the courses, to guide or influence his choice of what course to take; to tell him what he is obliged to do is to point out the only course open to him. The police may advise me that if I am going on holiday I ought to cancel my order for a morning paper, but they will inform me that if I am going abroad I am obliged to have a G.B. registration plate on my car.[1] If I know that there is only one alternative, I do not tell someone that he ought to take it, but that he must take it. If he knows that there is only one alternative, he cannot properly ask whether he ought to take it. Where there is no choice, there can be no guidance or advice and, hence, no 'ought'. This is why it is logically odd to attempt to derive an 'ought' from an 'is' by arguing (e.g. M. Black, 'The Gap between "Is" and "Should" ')[2] that if A wants X, and Y is the only way to get X, therefore A should do Y. In such circumstances A is obliged to do Y. We must distinguish between a statement like 'If you want X, and Y is the only means to X, you are obliged to do Y' and a statement like 'If you want X, and Y is a means to X, you ought to do Y'.

'If you want X, you ought to do Y' points out that X is one way of getting X. 'If you want X, you are obliged to do Y' points out that Y is the only way of getting X. The reasons for asserting that one is obliged to do Y point out what makes Y necessary; the reasons for advising that one ought to do Y point out what makes Y reasonable. A man might know that he is not obliged to do Y and yet rightly think that he ought to do it. Similarly, to say that something 'ought' to have happened by now implies that there are good reasons for its having happened, whereas to say that it 'must' (or is bound to) have happened by now is to say there are conclusive reasons for its having happened.

To ask whether one ought to do Y, given that one is obliged to do it if one wants X, is to raise the possibility of giving up

---

[1] Von Wright, *The Varieties of Goodness*, p. 160, assimilates informing that a necessity exists and giving advice.

[2] Black, *Phil. Rev.* (1964), pp. 165–81. Black's position depends on his holding (p. 170) 'the differences between the meanings of the two words "must" and "should" are unimportant here'. He also talks of 'evaluating' an action as 'preferable or obligatory'.

the pursuit of X. It is, indeed, often the realisation that to get Y one will be obliged to do X that makes one abandon the idea of trying to get Y. One may not feel that the end justifies the means, even though one does not dispute that the end requires these means. The existence of a moral obligation is a reason, though not necessarily a conclusive reason, for holding that I ought to do so and so. If I have conflicting obligations, then I have to decide between the tenets of the general position in virtue of which these obligations arise. In morals, as in nature, one factor may oblige me to do one thing and another factor oblige me to do the opposite. The steepness of a hill may oblige me to change gear, while the risk of damaging a faulty gear box may oblige me to stay in the same gear. My promise to my wife may oblige me to be home for dinner, while my duty as a doctor may oblige me to stay late at the hospital. In cases of conflicting obligations, I have to decide what to do. Do I stay in the same gear to save the gearbox and thus fail to get up the hill; or change gear to get up the hill and so damage the gear box? Do I leave the hospital early to keep my promise and so fail in my duty as a doctor, or stay at the hospital to do my duty as a doctor and so break my promise to my wife? In deciding between these conflicting obligations, we are not deciding which is our 'real' obligation (e.g. Ross); we are deciding what we ought to do.

If two courses are equally right, then whichever course we take we will be doing what we ought to do, but not doing what we are obliged to do. Moore (*Ethics*, pp. 34–6) admitted this, but denied that if X and Y are equally right, then it follows that I ought to do X or that it follows that I ought to do Y. But his argument depends on his (correct) assertion that if X and Y are equally right, then it does not follow that I am obliged to do X nor does it follow that I am obliged to do Y, together with his (incorrect) identification of 'obliged' and 'ought'.

Several reasons may be suggested why moralists have assimilated what I am obliged to do and what I ought to do. First, the two things may often in fact coincide. If, in a given case, I can do what I ought to do only by doing X – e.g. because there is an explicit rule to that effect or because it can be proved that there can be only one best course and that this is it – then I am obliged to do X. But since X is what I ought to do, then what I am obliged to do and what I ought to do are, in this case, the same thing, namely X. Secondly, a moralist may hold[1] that there necessarily can be, in any moral situation, only one thing one ought to do, since what one ought to do is what is best and there can be only one best course. Indeed, the considerations which show that X is morally the best course may also show that X is morally the only course. Thus, what one ought to do and what one is obliged to do necessarily coincide. But it does not follow from this that the concepts of *obliged* (or even *morally obliged*) and *ought* are the same. For, although the morally best course may be the only course one can morally take – that is, one is morally obliged to take the best course – the idea of the morally best course and the idea of the only moral course are distinct ideas.

A recent attempt to deny 'Hume's thesis' that one cannot derive an 'ought' from an 'is' is based on a misunderstanding of the notion of obligation. (J. R. Searle, 'How to derive "ought" from "is" ', *Phil. Rev.* (1964), pp. 43–58.)

The writer argues that from the fact that someone has promised to do X it follows logically that he is under an obligation to do X and from this it follows that he ought to do X. The writer holds that the statement 'All promises are obligations' and the statement 'One ought to fulfil one's obligations' are tautologically true. Now obviously it is only plausible to say that a man who has promised to do X is necessarily under an obligation to do X if this means that he is under a moral obligation to do X. He is not physically, legally or regulatively obliged to do X. But to say that someone is morally obliged to do so and so is to grant certain moral rules. And this is to make a judgment of value.

This becomes clearer if we contrast being morally obliged with being obliged in other ways. The yachtsman who is

---

[1] Thus, Moore, *Principia Ethica*, sec. 89, held that 'the assertion "I am morally bound to perform this action" is identical with the assertion "This action will produce the greatest possible amount of good in the Universe".' K. Baier, *The Moral Point of View*, ch. 3, holds that 'What ought I to do?' or 'What shall I do?' means 'What is the best thing to do?'

physically obliged by the wind to alter course is obliged because
of a physical closure of his alternatives; the manufacturer who
is legally obliged by his contract to deliver the goods within a
fortnight is obliged because of a legal closure of his alternatives; the player whose draughtsman lies next to an opponent's piece is obliged by his present position to jump his
opponent because the rules of the game forbid any alternative
move. In an exactly similar way the man who is morally
obliged by his promise to do so and so is obliged because the
moral rules to which he and we subscribe forbid any alternative in this situation. In all these different types of case one
is obliged by some factor to do so and so only because of one's
physical, legal, regulative or moral position. One is obliged to
do X, otherwise one will be acting inconsistently with one's
physical, legal, regulative, or moral position. Failure to see that
the existence of an obligation implies the existence of an
'otherwise' clause, which in moral obligation is the subscription
to an evaluation, is the cause of the false belief that there is no
evaluation in the statement 'All promises are obligations'.

If, on the other hand, one holds that the statement 'to
promise to do X morally obliges one to do X' is a tautology,
then one must hold that one of the conditions necessary to make
the uttering of the words 'I promise' into the making of a
promise is that the utterer is morally obliged by the utterance
to do X. And to hold this is to make an evaluation. Such a
condition cannot properly be called a 'straightforwardly
empirical condition'.[1]

[1] Searle really admits this in his remark that 'The whole proof rests on
an appeal to the constitutive rule that to make a promise is to undertake an
obligation' (p. 56), for such a constitutive rule involves recognition of a
moral system.

5

DESIRES AS CAUSES OF ACTIONS

David Pears

I T is not easy to explain how people know what they are going to do. The phenomenon occurs: obviously we often do know what we are going to do; but its explanation is less obvious. When I say this, I do not mean that we have some mysterious method by which we discover what we are going to do, like forecasting tomorrow's weather. Usually we know without any investigation, and without the use of any method of discovery. You know some of the things that you are going to do tomorrow immediately – i.e. you know them without the mediation of any evidence. This is a rather mysterious phenomenon, and it is not at all easy to classify it. How is it possible for there to be any immediate knowledge of something which lies in the future? Is it like the kind of immediate knowledge of the past which is supplied by memory? If so, does this analogy help us to understand our knowledge of our own future actions? Or is memory equally mysterious?

These are large questions. But the first point that I want to make towards answering them is a small and obvious one. It is that, however mysterious foreknowledge of one's own future actions may be, at least it is not as mysterious as premonition. You do not just find yourself knowing what you are going to do. Your view into the future is based in some way on what you at present want. This obvious fact might tempt us to revise the thesis that such knowledge is immediate. For it suggests that, although at first sight your knowledge of your own future action does not seem to be based on any evidence, in fact it is based on the evidence of your present desire. However, that would swing us too far in the opposite direction. For your desire is not something which you use as a piece of evidence. You look straight through it into the future, and your present state of mind is, as it were, entirely transparent. The whole thing is very unlike a weather forecast. Of course, you might say that you could see tomorrow's sunshine in today's high pressure. But this connection is learned by experience, and, before you learned it, you could not have claimed to see the sequel in today's high pressure. This gives us a very sharp contrast with the desire to perform a certain action tomorrow. You do not first learn how to identify the desire in the present, and then learn by experience what action it will produce in the future. You already know that it will be the desired action, because you can see the action in the desire.

Here there really is some analogy with certain forms of memory. When you recall a telephone number which you were told yesterday, you do not have an experience in the present from which you infer what you heard in the past. If such recollections involve experience at all, the experiences are effects in which their causes can be seen immediately. In a roughly similar way, desires may be causes in which their effects can be seen immediately.

But this is much too vague. How can it be made more precise? One very striking fact about desires to perform actions is that such desires are distinguished from one another by descriptions which mention the actions which they are desires to perform. So perhaps the point which I have been making by using the metaphor of transparency could be put more explicitly in the following way: we could say that you see your future action in your present desire because it is the desire to perform that action. Desires do not conceal their objects. You do not first realise that you have a desire, and then try to discover what it is a desire to do. Something similar is true of memory-impressions.

However, this is not the whole of the point that I was trying to make in metaphorical language. For my point was not only that you see your action in your desire. It was also something more than this: it was that you see your actual future action in your present desire – i.e. you see that your desire will produce it. This is a further point. The first point could have been illustrated equally well by regret instead of by desire. When you regret a past action, your regret is distinguished as regret that you performed that particular action. That is the first point. But your knowledge that you performed the action does not come through your regret: you already know independently that you performed it, and the regret supervenes. So regret cannot be used to illustrate the second point. If we want to illustrate the second point, we need something like a desire to perform an action. For here we really have got something through which it is possible to see the occurrence of a temporally distant event.

I want to emphasise the distinctness of these two points, because I shall rely on it at a later stage in my argument. So let us separate them again. Your knowledge of your own future actions is not like premonition, because you do not just find yourself with the conviction that you will perform them. But it is quite like crystal-gazing. For you have in your mind a specification of the projected action, and this specification is analogous to the image of a future event which might be hallucinated in a crystal. That is the first of the two points in the metaphor of transparency: your desire is distinguished by the specification of the action, in much the same way that the experience of the crystal-gazer is distinguished by the image which he sees. The second point, which is quite distinct, is that you see your actual future action in your present desire, just as the crystal-gazer would claim to see the actual future event in the present image.

Incidentally, there are two places at which this analogy with crystal-gazing breaks down. First, nobody thinks that the crystal-gazer's image would cause the future event: it would only be a sure sign that it would occur. Secondly, it is sufficient for the crystal-gazer that a certain image should appear; whereas, in the other case, it is not sufficient that the idea of the project should occur to you; you must also have a favourable attitude towards it. However, in spite of these differences, the analogy does bring out the distinctness of the two points which I wanted to emphasise.

But there is still a third point in the metaphor of transparency. The third point, which is perhaps the most important one, is that you do not have to learn by experience that your desire to perform a particular action will produce that action. For this fact about the desire is already wrapped up in the way that you identify it. You do not first learn to identify this type of desire, and then learn by observation what type of action it produces. Here there is a very sharp contrast with crystal-gazing. For it would be possible to discover by experiment that images seen under certain conditions were veridical. Experiment might also establish what each image meant. We tend to forget this second kind of experiment, because we assume that the crystal-gazer's images are not in a code. But if they are not in a code, that is a fact which could be established empirically.

So far I have merely been setting out a few basic facts about foreknowledge of one's own future actions. I shall now put up a theory which is supposed to fit the facts. The theory is that a desire to perform a particular action causes that action. Now there are many well-known arguments both for and against this theory. But I am going to examine only one argument against it – the argument that it does not fit the facts which I have just set out.

The argument is that A cannot be regarded as the cause of B unless A can be specified in some way that does not mention B. Here, of course, the specification of A has to be the specification under which it operates as a cause. It would be no good specifying your desire as the one that you felt when you woke up this morning. It has to be given a general specification, and, what is more, the general specification under which it operates as a cause. But, as we have just seen, such desires cannot be specified without mentioning the actions which they are supposed to cause. Therefore, according to this argument, they cannot really cause them.

This argument is invalid, as can be seen from countless examples. Fear of a particular accident may cause that accident, and it is only a contingent fact that magic wishes do not bring about the events which are their objects. This, in spite of the fact that the relevant fear and the relevant wish cannot be specified except in ways that mention the very things that are suggested as their effects. So this objection to the causal account of desire tries to exclude too much, and fails.

However, the objection becomes more powerful if its scope is restricted. Suppose that we say that A cannot cause B unless A can be specified in some way that does not mention the fact that it causes B. This version of the objection does not try to exclude so much. It does not try to exclude all causes whose specification involves any mention of their supposed effects, but only causes whose specification stipulates that their supposed effects should actually occur. That is to say, it refuses to allow that such cases really are examples of causes. This modification of the objection depends on the distinction between the two points which I emphasised just now. It is one thing to specify a cause by saying that its supposed effect is its object – e.g. by saying that the cause of an accident was fear of precisely that accident: and it is quite another thing to specify a cause by saying that it is actually followed by its supposed effect – e.g. by saying that the cause of an accident was whatever caused it.

This version of the objection is stronger. It relies on the more plausible suggestion that the thesis that desires cause actions is empty. The thesis is supposed to be empty, because it is thought that an essential part of the specification of a desire to perform an action is the stipulation that the desire should actually produce the action. There are really two stages in this argument. First, there is the idea that a person who does not do what he says that he really wanted to do cannot really have wanted to do it. Secondly, there is the suggestion that the existence of a particular desire can be established only through this criterion. It is this second suggestion that the objector is making when he says that the criterion is an essential part of the specification of a practical desire. He does not just mean that the criterion is a valid one. He means that it is the only thing which enables us to establish the existence of a particular practical desire. Of course, when you report your own practical desire, you do not use this criterion directly. But, according to the objector, you do rely on it indirectly. For you identify your desire as the kind of desire that causes that type of action. This is the nerve of the objection. Everyone would admit that a cause can be specified in a way that stipulates that it produces its effect – e.g. there is nothing wrong with saying that a person's death was caused by a fatal dose of barbiturate: there is nothing wrong with saying this, because we can remove this specification of the cause, and, when we have removed it, we still have another underlying specification which gives us a line onto that particular dose – say, forty grains. But, according to the objector, when we remove the specification which stipulates that a particular desire should cause the relevant action, we have no other line into it.

I said that this version of the objection is stronger. But it still has various weaknesses. One obvious weakness is that it is far too simple to suggest that someone who does not do what he says he really wants to do cannot really have wanted to do it. For there are many well-known possibilities, any of which, if it occurred, would explain non-performance by an agent who really did want to perform the action. So the most that could be said is that someone who does not do what he says that he really wants to do cannot really have wanted to do it, unless there is no occasion to do it, or it turns out to be impossible, or he lacks the necessary pertinacity, etc. This criterion can be expressed as a disjunction. Now there is a well-known difficulty about this disjunctive criterion, which is that the phrase 'etc.' is not just an abbreviation for a list of disjuncts which we can finally complete. It marks the fact that the list is genuinely open to new discoveries. However, this difficulty does not affect the question whether the thesis that desires cause actions is vulnerable to the objection which I am considering. For if the criterion of a practical desire is an open-ended disjunction, its effect will be reported in the same open-ended disjunction, because the criterion and the supposed effect are one and the same thing. The point of the objection is that the so-called effect is, but ought not to be, the only criterion which distinguishes one practical desire from another. This point is not affected by the openness of the disjunction which is supposed to report both the criterion and the effect.

There is a second criticism of the objection which can be disposed of quickly. The objection might be criticised on the ground that it relies on the dubious doctrine of analyticity. It might be argued that there is only a well-confirmed contingent connection between a practical desire and the set of alternatives which, from now on, I shall call 'the sequel'. The idea would be that a word like 'desire' can be introduced into a language by way of a contingent connection between its denotation and some public phenomenon like the sequel. This idea may well be correct, but it does not affect the objection to the causal thesis. For the point of the objection is that we only have one line attaching practical desires to public phenomenon, and, whatever view we take about the strength of this line, we cannot treat it in two different ways at the same time. If we now treat it as criterial, as we have to, we cannot simultaneously treat it as an ordinary causal statement. For how could it conceivably be falsified. Of course, if at some later date this criterion were replaced by another one, we could begin to treat it as an ordinary causal statement. But that would only be because we had two lines onto practical desires. At the moment, we only have one.

However, there is a third criticism of the objection which is less easy to dispose of. Suppose that someone claimed that we already have two different lines onto practical desires, so that the objection never really gets started. He could say that the objector has simply overlooked the fact that to have a desire is to have an anticipatory feeling which is very like the feeling of satisfaction when the goal is achieved. People could use this similarity in order to establish the existence of practical desires instead of using the sequel. Indeed, something like this must happen with idle wishes, which have no connection with action. Admittedly, the anticipatory feeling must be about the goal, which, in the case of practical desire, will be the project. But, as I have already explained, there is nothing wrong with the suggestion that the object of a feeling might be brought into existence by the feeling. So here we have a radical criticism of the objection: the assumption on which it is based, that we have only one line onto practical desires, is simply rejected as false.

There is something in this criticism, but not as much as is claimed. It is true that we have this second line onto practical desires, but it is not true that it alone would enable us to establish their existence. It would perhaps determine the kind of feeling about a project which we call 'a practical desire', but it would not determine the degree of that feeling. In order to establish its degree, we must rely on the sequel. To say that someone really wants to do something is to say that he wants to do it enough to produce the sequel. All other ways of assessing practical desires are derivative from this basic norm. We do not have an independent scale for measuring them, and then discover that a particular point on this scale is, as a matter of contingent fact, the point at which the sequel will be produced. The production of the sequel is a primary criterion for the concept of practical desire, and not a secondary adjunct.

This answer to the third criticism sounds as if it made the criterion unrealistically strong. It suggests that, if the sequel did not occur, it would simply follow that the person had not really wanted to perform the action, even if he had felt sure that he did want to perform it. However, the criterion need not be made so strong as this. The connection between practical desire and sequel could be interpreted probabilistically, in order to allow for hitherto undiscovered factors which would explain non-performance by an agent who really did have the practical desire. Then, in an isolated case in which someone felt sure that he really did want to perform an action, but the sequel did not occur, we would say that very probably he had not really wanted to perform it, allowing that it was just possible that some new factor was at work. A long run of such cases would require different treatment. It would suggest that conditions had changed in a way that made it impossible to apply the concept of practical desire without first changing its criterion. Of course we could not actually make the required change in the criterion until we had discovered what the new factor was.

This weakening of the criterion is obviously needed if we are going to give a realistic account of our concept of practical desire. But it does not upset the answer which I have given to the third criticism. For it still remains true that we only have one criterial line onto the degree of a practical desire. The only difference is that, instead of saying that a practical desire is primarily identified as a feeling of the degree which is necessarily followed by the sequel, we say that it is primarily identified as a feeling of the degree which is very probably followed by the sequel.

So far, I have been defending the objection against criticisms designed to show that there is no case to be answered. I think that I have shown that there is a case to be answered, because it is difficult to see how a practical desire can be said to cause the sequel, if the fact that it causes the sequel is an essential part of the criterion for its existence. When the objector says that this is an essential part of the criterion, what he means is that we should not be able to establish the existence of a practical desire, if we did not use this part of the criterion either directly or indirectly. For, according to him, we have nothing else which we could use in its place.

One very simple answer to this objection is that the causal theory does not require that there should be some replacement for the criterion available at the moment. It is sufficient that some independent identification of practical desires may become available later, perhaps through neurology. Meanwhile, we do not have to regard the concept as one which is completely and finally exhausted by its existing criteria. Practical desires are things of a kind, and they may soon be discovered to have further connections, some of which, after their discovery, may become criterial. This possibility allows us to treat them now as the causes of the phenomena through which alone we are able to identify them at present.

I think that this answer to the objection makes a valid and important point. But it does not close the case against the objection, because it seems to concede another point which ought not to be conceded. It seems to concede, or, at least, it does not deny that practical desires are at the moment in the position of occult causes, waiting to be given some empirical content. But this point ought not to be conceded because it is invalid.

The point is invalid for the simple reason that the person who has the practical desire can identify it without waiting for the sequel. Admittedly, he identifies it under a description which connects it with the sequel: i.e. he identifies it as the sort of desire that very probably produces that sequel. But he does not have to wait for the sequel before he applies this description to his present state. So the implied comparison with occult causes is invalid.

This immediately suggests a very bold answer to the objection. Maybe there is absolutely nothing wrong with this kind of criterial connection between cause and effect. Perhaps there is no need to appeal to the possibility that some new way of identifying practical desires may be discovered. Even if we now knew that our knowledge of them could never advance beyond its present state because there is nothing more to be discovered, we might still be able to regard them as the causes of the usual sequel. For, unlike occult causes, they can be identified in advance.

I shall spend the remainder of this lecture trying to determine whether this bold answer is correct, or whether perhaps it goes too far.

First, it might be resisted on the ground that the identification of an action must mention the desire from which it issued, so that the connection between the two cannot be causal. This argument is interesting, because it is precisely the reverse of the argument used in the objection which I am examining. The idea is that a practical desire may cause a bodily movement, but not an action, because the identification of the action as the action that it is would make the causal statement analytic. According to this argument, the occurrence of the cause is an essential part of the criterion for the occurrence of the effect, just as, according to the other argument, the occurrence of the effect is an essential part of the criterion for the occurrence of the cause.

However, this reversed argument is invalid in a very simple way. The causal theorist only has to point out that he is using the word 'action' proleptically. That is to say, when he says that practical desires cause actions, he means that they cause bodily movements, which, because they are so caused, are the actions that they are. The word 'action' is applied to the effect in a way that anticipates the result of the operation of the cause. This is no more reprehensible than saying that a man married his wife in 1947. The reason why it is not reprehensible is that there is another description which applies to the effect whether or not it was caused by that practical desire, viz. the description 'bodily movement which may or may not be an action'. So this argument is invalid in a way in which the other argument was not invalid. For, as we have seen, there is no available underlying description of the practical desire which does not involve its tendency to produce the sequel, one of whose alternative elements is the action itself.

Nevertheless, the other argument may be invalid, and the bold answer to it may be correct. Is it correct? There is not much room left for manœuvre in this discussion. For the facts are plain. It is a fact that people do identify their practical desires in advance, and it is a fact that they identify them under descriptions which connect them with their sequels. It is, however, worth observing that the description of the desire often does not match the description of the action: e.g. I might say that I went to the travel agent because I wanted to buy a ticket. This non-matching of the two descriptions is important, because it allows one and the same action to be caused by a variety of desires, and so provides a further way in which the analogy between desires and occult causes breaks down: whereas, when the two descriptions match, as they do when an action is performed for its own sake, there is only one way in which the analogy breaks down, and that is that there is an empirical difference between the case where the action is caused by the desire to perform it, and the case where there is no desire at work, and so no action, but only a mere bodily movement. But, although the frequency of non-matching descriptions is important, it does not affect the present discussion. For in the case mentioned it must also be true that I bought a ticket from the travel agent because I wanted to buy a ticket from the travel agent, and that I went there because I wanted to go there. So this manœuvre still leaves us facing the blank wall of the question whether the bold answer to the objection is correct or not.

Before I try to solve this problem, I want to restate it as clearly as possible. The difficulty is that, though we have two lines onto practical desires, they are not completely independent lines. First, the sequel gives us a line onto them, and I am trying to interpret this as a causal line. But then I need a second line which I can treat as criterial, and this second line has to be independent of the first one, because that is the pattern required for causal statements. Now the second line is, in a way, independent of the first. For a person can identify his practical desire without waiting for the sequel. But the independence is not complete, because he identifies it under a description which connects it with the sequel, viz. the description 'practical desire of the kind which is nearly always followed by this sequel'. Is this degree of independence enough to justify the causal theory, even on the assumption that there are no further specific descriptions of practical desires waiting to be discovered? That is the question.

The first point that I want to make towards answering it is that it is a contingent fact that people have these psychological states called 'practical desires', which have a high correlation with the sequel, and which can be identified in advance. This suggests that there ought to be a description of a practical desire under which its connection with the sequel would be clearly contingent. But what would the description be? Can it be the description 'identified by the person himself as a specific practical desire?' Certainly psychological states under this description are contingently connected with the sequel. For the person concerned might have had no such states, or, though he had them, he might have been bad at identifying them. I used to think that this line of thought might lead to a complete solution of the problem. But, unfortunately, the causal theorist cannot use the description 'identified by the person himself as a specific practical desire'. For, if he did use this description in his theory, he would only be saying that the sequel is caused by a state which is rightly or wrongly supposed by the agent to be a specific practical desire. No doubt this is both true and contingent. But it is not what his theory ought to be saying. It ought to say that the sequel is caused by a state which is rightly supposed by the agent to be a specific practical desire, or, in other words, that it is caused by a specific practical desire, recognised as such by him. Yet, if the state is actually described as a specific practical desire, the connection with the sequel is already involved in its description, and there is no further causal connection left to be asserted by the theory. So this solution, although it contains a valid point, will not quite work.

Perhaps, then, we might appeal to the fact that the description of a practical desire only involves a probable connection with the sequel, and not a universal connection. This certainly seems to be a fact, because we do not treat the absence of the sequel in a particular case as decisive against the person's claim to have really wanted to perform the action. I used to think that we might be able to exploit this fact in the following way: we might say that, when a given practical desire is followed by the sequel in a particular case, this only happens contingently, because it might have belonged to the small percentage of cases which are not followed by the sequel.

However, this solution to the problem will not work at all. No doubt, it is true that it is a contingent matter whether a given practical desire belongs to the high percentage of successes or to the low percentage of failures. But suppose that it does belong to the successful group. Then the singular statement, that it very probably caused the sequel, entails the general statement that desires of that kind are nearly always followed by the sequel. Now this general connection with the sequel is involved in the description under which the desire was identified. So it cannot be regarded as contingent. Yet, if we take away the entailed general statement, the original singular statement will only mean that that particular desire was in fact followed by the sequel. It will have been robbed of the very feature which made it a causal statement. So this solution must be rejected. It would be rejected even more swiftly by anyone who believed that all singular causal statements entail general statements which must be universal.

If there is a defence of the causal theory, given the assumption that there are no further specific descriptions of practical desires waiting to be discovered, it must lie elsewhere. But it cannot be far away. Let us start again with the most hopeful feature of the causal theory; which is that we really have got two lines onto practical desires, even if they do not yield completely independent descriptions of them. I shall incorporate this feature into a slightly different formulation of the causal theory. What this formulation says is that there is a degree of feeling about a project which is causally connected with the sequel, and which is identified in advance. This is a causal hypothesis which certainly is not empty. It would be falsified if there were no such degree of feeling because people's reactions were chaotic and it would be falsified if there were such a degree of feeling, but it could not be identified in advance. Of course, the second way of falsifying it is only a speculative possibility, since we could hardly establish that there were practical desires which could not be identified. That would amount to proving that there were such occult causes. Still, we might establish something less extreme in that direction – viz., that some people are not so good as others at identifying this degree of feeling in advance.

Anyway, the important point is that the causal theory, when it is formulated in this way, is theoretically open to these two kinds of falsification. This is simply because it is now formulated existentially: it says that there is a degree of feeling which has two properties – it is causally connected with the sequel, and it is identified in advance. Because this formulation is existential, it makes it very clear that the theory is not open to the ordinary kind of falsification, which would consist in the discovery of a case of the alleged cause without the alleged effect. If a degree of feeling was identified in advance without being followed by the sequel even in a long run of cases, that would leave the theory unscathed. For the theory only claims that there is a degree of feeling with these two properties, and obviously the degree of feeling identified in this case would not be the right one. If we try to get round this deficiency in the ordinary method of falsification by insisting that the degree of feeling must be correctly identifiable as a specific practical desire, in spite of the absence of the sequel in a long run of cases, we know that that will not work, because it is conceptually impossible. For we know that we could not discover a long run of cases in which we would be persuaded by the person's conviction that he really did want to perform the action in spite of the absence of the sequel. We know that in such an eventuality we would say either that he had not really wanted to perform it, or that the conditions for the application of the concept had broken down.

So the causal theory is an existential theory which cannot be falsified in the ordinary way. But it can be falsified in its own appropriate ways. It is a mistake to expect it to be falsified in the ordinary way, and a further mistake to suppose that, because it cannot be falsified in the ordinary way, the connection between practical desire and sequel cannot be interrupted causally. So the bold answer to the objection is, after all, correct.

This solution to the problem may seem too contrived. It may sound like an elaborate restatement of the problem rather than a solution to it. In order to remove this impression, I shall end by outlining an analogous case, in which the pattern of falsification would be the same. Near the beginning of this lecture I pointed out that your knowledge of your own future actions is not like the kind of premonition which consists merely in the inexplicable verified conviction that a certain event will happen. But it is quite like the kind of premonition which consists in thinking about the event with inexplicable intensity, and then finding that it happens. Suppose that you claimed to have the latter gift, because in your case you had noticed that thoughts of a certain intensity were always followed by the event so thought about. Suppose, too, in order to make the parallel more exact that you could not specify the degree of intensity except by saying that it was the degree which experience had shown you to be a sufficient indication of the future event. Would you not say that you had premonitory thoughts which were sure signs of the future? Naturally, you would not regard them as the causes of the future events. If there were a causal pattern here, it would be a different one: e.g. the horse's physique in some mysterious way would give you the intense thought, and in an obvious way give it the victory. But this difference in causal pattern does not affect my use of the analogy. The challenging question is this: Would you regard the hypothesis that you have premonitory thought as unfalsifiable, on the trivial ground that you could not conceivably have a premonitory thought which was not followed by the event? Or would you regard it as falsifiable, either because you might have had no thoughts with this connection with the future, or because though you had them, you might not have been good at identifying them?

6

MENTAL CAUSES

C. H. Whiteley

THE question I shall consider is whether there are any mental causes, that is, whether there is anything which is both a state of mind and a cause of other mental or physical happenings. The obvious common-sense answer to this question is Yes. In ordinary discourse (that is, outside philosophy and psychology) we constantly refer to human actions and experiences in what appears to be causal language; we seem to be saying that some states of mind are causes of other states of mind, and of some bodily activities. Sometimes we do this by using the word 'cause' itself – 'His driving into the ditch was caused by his seeing a child run into the road', 'The cause of his silence was his wish to protect his friend'. More often we use expressions which in physical contexts are admittedly causal – 'A glimpse of the look on her face made him hesitate', 'Ambition was the driving force of his career'. Most philosophers have taken for granted the genuineness of these causal attributions. But recently it has been frequently denied that any state of mind can be properly described as the cause either of other states of mind or of physical occurrences, at any rate if by a state of mind one means a state of consciousness. Some philosophers who deny this are materialists, advocates of the Unity of Science. They believe that everything that happens in the universe can be causally accounted for by reference to a single set of fundamental laws, the laws of physics, and since a state of consciousness is not, as such, a physical state of any kind, it cannot have a place in the causal explanation of any event, and must be an epiphenomenon. Others are believers in an indeterminist interpretation of human freedom, and hold that to introduce the category of cause and effect into the explanation of human actions is to deny that there is any genuine free will. I shall not be concerned with either of these general metaphysical objections, neither of which convinces me; but I shall consider some more specific objections to the admission of particular sorts of mental causes.

Is there anything which is both mental and a cause? In this lecture I shall be using 'mental' in a restricted sense, and shall count as mental states or events only those events which are states of consciousness – that is, which consist in somebody being conscious of something. One would expect it to be perfectly easy to determine which states or events answered to this description. Instead, one is surprised to find that there is a great deal of dispute among philosophers as to what sorts of mental events, in this restricted sense, do occur – or in other words, as to which of the expressions occurring in our accounts of mental history denote occasions of being conscious of something, and which of them denote something else. Since there are these disputes, I shall employ the following criterion to help settle them. I shall assume that if a person is in some state of awareness, then he is able to take note what state of awareness he is in, without having to infer this from evidence or clues of any kind; whereas other people can find out what state of awareness he is in only by inferring, judging or guessing on the basis of some evidence other than the state of awareness itself. Moreover, whereas other people can be misled by the evidence into thinking that he is in some state which he is not, he cannot be so misled. Consequently, when a predicative expression is so used that in applying this predicate to himself a person does not have to infer from clues, in the way that other people must, and when in deciding whether the predicate truly applies to him we grant his unique authority in the matter, and do not consider the possibility that he is mistaken (though we may have to consider the possibility that he is lying) – when, in a word, he can deceive other people about his state but they cannot possibly deceive him, than I shall say that this predicative expression stands for a mental state or event. If these

conditions do not hold, I shall say that it does not stand entirely
for a mental state – though it may do so partly. (For instance,
when a man says that he hears the cuckoo, in so far as he says
what sort of sound he hears, he describes a mental event, and
cannot be corrected, but in so far as he says that it is a cuckoo
that is making the sound, he may be mistaken, and may be
shown to be mistaken by further evidence available to other
people.)

So much for 'mental'; now for 'cause'. This will take longer,
because more than one version of the concept of cause is current
at present, and I must make clear which one I am using (not
everybody who engages in this controversy does this). Hume,
whose treatment of the matter dominates contemporary dis-
cussions, argued as follows. The fact that one event *A* is the
cause of another event *B* cannot be learned merely by observing
A and *B*; the only relevant fact about *A* and *B* that we can
observe is that *A* precedes *B*. But we can also have observed
that events of the same sort as *A* have been regularly followed
by events of the same sort as *B*, and it is this which leads us to
call *A* the cause of *B*. This being so, what we mean when we
call *A* the cause of *B* is that *A*-followed-by-*B* is an instance of
the general law that events of type *A* are invariably followed
by events of type *B*. The assertion of a causal relationship is,
or at least implies, the assertion of a regular sequence; the
concept of Cause cannot be separated from the concept of Law.
Now this last thesis is false. It is of course true that when we are
looking for the cause of thunderstorms or of cancer we are
looking for a law, for some *X* of which it is true that whenever
X occurs a thunderstorm, or a case of cancer, ensues; so Hume's
analysis works all right when it is applied to scientific investigations, which are by definition general. But it is not true that
whenever we say that some particular *X* was the cause of some
particular *Y* we are making, explicitly or implicitly, any
generalisation about the regular sequence of events of type *Y*
on events of type *X*. If a doctor says that the cause of John
Smith's death was cancer of the rectum, he does not commit
himself to asserting that all cases of cancer of the rectum are
fatal – a proposition which he knows to be false. Nor does he
commit himself to the assertion of any other generalisation

linking some characteristics of the alleged cause with some characteristics of the alleged effect. He may believe that there is some such generalisation of which this sequence of events is an instance; but he does not know what it is, and his ignorance does not prevent him from saying, and saying correctly, that Smith's death was caused by cancer of the rectum. The causal relation is asserted to hold just between these two events. The doctor is not saying that cancer of the rectum is either a necessary or a sufficient condition of death in all cases and under all circumstances. He is saying that this particular cancer, in all its detail, occurring in all the circumstances in which it actually did occur, was sufficient to ensure Smith's death, and in those circumstances it was necessary to Smith's dying, not of course in the sense that otherwise he would not have died at all, but that but for the cancer he would not have died as and when he did die. Thus Hume was wrong in linking the concept of cause to that of invariable sequence. We say, for instance, that anxiety often causes indigestion, and that indigestion is often caused by anxiety (otherwise put, that indigestion is a common effect of anxiety, and anxiety a common cause of indigestion) – expressions which on Hume's view would be self-contradictory, being equivalent on that view to 'anxiety often is always followed by indigestion', and so on. So Hume was wrong in supposing that our belief that A is the cause of B is based on observation of an invariable sequence of events of type B on events of type A. Even if there are any *observed* sequences which are invariable (are there?), it is certain that the vast majority of our causal judgments are based on observed sequences which are not invariable. Nevertheless, Hume was right in holding that causal relations are not matters of direct observation, and that the only reason we can have for believing that A is the cause of B is that we either have observed, or have reason to believe, that events of a type to which A belongs have been followed by events of a type to which B belongs in some cases at any rate. Notice that on my interpretation of causation, it is possible for more than one event to be referred to as the cause, or as a cause, of a given effect. For it may be true of X that, in all the circumstances (including Y), if X had not happened Z would not have happened, and also true of Y that, in all the circumstances (including X), if Y had not happened, Z would not have happened, as and when it did.

A mental cause, then, is an occasion of being aware which is such that in all the circumstances it is sufficient and necessary for the occurrence of some other event, whether mental or not. Are there any such things as mental causes? I shall put the likely candidates under three headings.

Firstly, there are the occasions when a person notices, perceives, thinks of, remembers, concludes, bears in mind that something is the case. (I do not put 'believe' in this list, since 'believe' is normally a dispositional word; but the actualisations of the belief-disposition are often cases of thinking, remembering, realising or bearing in mind.) At first sight it is plausible to interpret the role of such occurrences in causal fashion. In the given circumstances (including, of course, the circumstance of his being the sort of person he was) the sight of the child running into the road was enough to make him swerve, and if he had not seen her he would not have swerved. In the circumstances, his coming to the conclusion that his shares were likely to depreciate was enough to make him decide to sell them, and if he had not come to this conclusion he would not have sold. We support this interpretation in the same way that we support similar judgments about inanimate causes: namely, by noting that the agent behaves in similar ways in similar circumstances, and that other people relevantly similar to him also behave in similar ways in similar circumstances. He, and other people, when they notice a human being in the path of cars they are driving, try to avoid running them down. He, and other people, when they come to believe that their investments will become less valuable, try to realise them. Of course, such correlations are not simple stimulus-response affairs: the effects involved (avoiding a collision, selling investments) are no more physically determinate than the causes. Nevertheless, avoiding collisions and selling investments are determinate kinds of behaviour; and the fact that their specification may involve psychological or social concepts, while it is a reason for putting them outside the sphere of merely physical causality, is no reason for putting them outside the sphere of causality altogether.

Objections to regarding the relation between an awareness and a subsequent action as causal are often based on a distinction between causes and reasons. It is argued that a person who acts for a purpose in the light of certain observations or beliefs acts because of reasons: that the child ran into the road is a reason for swerving (given the other circumstances, and given that the driver does not care for running children down); that the shares are likely to depreciate is a reason for selling them (given that one does not want to lose money). And reasons can't be causes; an explanation of an action by reference to reasons is not a causal explanation – and, some say, is incompatible with any causal explanation. The grounds for insisting on this radical difference between reasons and causes are not often made explicit. (Ordinary language, despite some statements to the contrary, makes no such systematic distinction: 'What made you do that?' and 'What was your reason for doing that?' can be equivalent, and I can be said to have caused a student to enter for a scholarship by giving him some good reasons why he should.) Perhaps the argument may run like this. A cause makes, compels or forces its effect to ensue, whereas a reason does not compel, but is the ground of a free action; what we do for a good reason is done freely and unconstrainedly. A man caused to act in a given way has no option, can do no other; but a man acting from reasons is free to accept or reject the course of action he contemplates. Again, it may be said that when a man acts or decides rationally, on account of reasons, it is because he sees some logical connection between premises and conclusion in a theoretical or practical inference, and it is this logical connection, the 'force of the argument' as we call it, which determines what he does. But the force of an argument is a logical or rational force, not a causal force; premises do not causally necessitate their conclusions, and to be determined to do an action by reasons is not to be determined by a natural force or a causal law.

If these are the arguments, they are not good enough. Of course it is true that the relation between premises and conclusion, whether in a theoretical or a practical syllogism, is not a causal relation: premises neither bring about their conclusions, nor compel anybody to draw them. Logical connec-

tions serve to make inferences valid or invalid, to justify them
or fault them; and the question of validity is not a causal
question. But for that very reason the logical explanation or
validation of an inference in terms of implication- or proba-
bility-relations does not exclude or conflict with a causal
explanation of the fact that some person has passed from an
acceptance of the premises to an acceptance of the conclusion.
People sometimes speak as though one could adequately
explain a human action by showing that the action was a
reasonable thing to do in the circumstances, that it conduced
to the fulfilment of some normal or worthwhile aim. But while
such an explanation may serve to justify the agent, it does not
of itself account for his having done the act. The fact that
selling the shares was a financially sensible thing to do will
account for the shareholder's having sold them only on two
further assumptions: first, that when making up his mind to sell
he bethought him of the likelihood of suffering loss if he did not
sell; and second, that if he had not bethought him of this he
would not have sold. If, being short of ready money, he would
have sold the shares anyhow, then the likelihood of their
depreciating was not his reason for selling and does not explain
why he sold. But to say that he thought of the likelihood of
depreciation and so decided to sell, and that if he had not so
thought he would not have so decided, is on the face of it a
causal assertion. As with other causal assertions, its truth cannot
be known by mere inspection of the present data. While there
are many cases in which there can be no serious doubt what
an agent's reasons were for doing a given act (the same is of
course the case with many examples of physical causation),
there are plenty of other cases in which not only outsiders but
the agent himself may doubt which of a number of considerations before his mind was his reason – his real reason, we
sometimes say. And this doubt is a doubt about what he would
have done if this consideration had not been before his mind;
it is a doubt about the hypothetical proposition 'If he had not
thought of X, he would not have done Y', which is essential to
the application of the category of causality. Thus there seem
to be good grounds for saying that the apprehension of some
proposition can cause a person to conclude that some other

proposition is true, or that some action should be done. To say this is compatible with, but different from, saying that the premise is a good reason for the conclusion; for, of course, a person sometimes comes to believe that q as a result of believing that p when p is not a good reason for q.

As for freedom, there are some contexts in which the connection between freedom and rationality is important; but in this context it is out of place. Leaving aside the point that causation and compulsion are not the same thing, it seems to me sometimes correct, not merely to say that a man thinking rationally has been caused to come to a conclusion, but also to say that he has been compelled to do so; when the reasons are clear and the conclusion is unpalatable, this is just the sort of language we use. In any case, while it is a condition of freedom in some important senses of the word that one should be capable of considering reasons and acting considerately rather than impulsively, yet in the matter of drawing conclusions from premises the notion of freedom is totally out of place. In the appreciation of the validity of an argument there is no option. It is only irrational men who believe what they choose; rational men want to have their beliefs imposed upon them in accordance with the evidence and the principles of logic.

Moreover, the distinction between being determined by reasons and being determined by causes is impossible to draw in any sharp fashion. A man who parts with his wallet to another who threatens his life is surely being made, forced or caused to act as he does. But at the same time he has excellent reasons for his action – what better reason could there be than that the action is necessary to save his life? A man who is drugged or drunk or feverish does things which he would not do in a normal condition; and we reckon the changes in the composition of his blood as causes of his odd behaviour. But his behaviour need not be without reasons, and they may be very good reasons if we allow for the changes in his inclinations or values which the chemical causes have brought about. And if we are to reckon the abnormal state of his blood as a cause of his present abnormal behaviour, by what right do we ignore the normal condition of his blood in accounting for his normal behaviour?

H   H.A.

The second group of alleged mental causes I shall discuss comprises desires, wants, motives, emotions, passions – those mental forces which are supposed to move men to action and cause them to have the aims they do have. It is clearly only in conjunction with some aim that a thought or perception can determine action; and we must consider the sorts of mental causes which are said to determine these aims. Obviously we do sometimes attribute human actions to desire for this and that, and sometimes characterise actions as due to such components of the mind as fear, avarice, gratitude, compassion, indignation, remorse – the things that earlier generations of philosophers labelled as the 'passions' of the soul.

Now there is a serious objection to classifying any of these entities as mental causes. For, despite what many past philosophers and psychologists have assumed, it can be argued that none of these expressions, neither 'desire', 'want', 'motive' nor the names for the various passions or emotions, stands for any mental event; they are not states of awareness, discernible by introspection, occurring on specific occasions and being followed by actions of which they may be taken to be the causes. Not being in my restricted sense mental, they cannot be causes either. For a cause has got to be a distinguishable event occurring at a definite time, and followed by some other event with which it can be connected by some law.

As to wants and desires, to say of a person that he has or had a want or desire is not to describe or refer to any specific state of consciousness, it is not to say how he felt at the time when he acted. There are indeed various kinds of feelings which are characteristic of desiring or wanting situations. There is the feeling of longing for something unattainable or unattained; there is the feeling of grief or discomfort at the absence of something whose presence we think would give us joy; there are the glows of agreeable anticipation of what we expect to attain and enjoy; there are the 'urges', the incipient movements towards something desired, the beginnings of action in the direction of getting what we are said to want. These are marks and signs of desire. But they are not desire itself, nor is it any other state of awareness. For a person can be correctly described as wanting or desiring something on occasions on which none of these feelings is present. I can be properly said to want a cup of tea, or to want to finish this lecture on time, without there being any suggestion that any such longings, urges or pleasant expectations pass through my mind. I can be properly said to want something without realising it, when nothing relevant passes through my mind at all. And whatever be my feelings, if I declare that I want a cup of tea, and when the tea is offered me leave it untasted, or if I assure you how much I long for leisure to write my philosophical masterpiece, and yet am found assiduously filling in whatever free time I have with committees, evening classes or social engagements, I shall have to admit that I did not really want what I said and believed that I wanted – what I took to be a desire for tea, or for writing my masterpiece, was not really that at all. But that concerning which I can be mistaken, and other people can correct me, cannot be a state of my consciousness. Normally, indeed, a man knows what he wants. But he knows this because he knows how in a given set of circumstances he will behave. A want is not essentially the occurrence of any event in consciousness. It is essentially a readiness or disposition to pursue the object of the want. To say that a person wants X is to say that if he has the opportunity to acquire or achieve X he will, other things being equal, do so. It is then a necessary truth that men do what they want to do. If a man under no external pressure to drink tea does drink tea, then he wanted to drink tea, regardless of his state of consciousness. Thus a want is not a separate happening explanatory of the action. Its connection with action is not causal but logical, in that to say that a man wants X but never takes any of the steps which would enable him to get it would be at least logically odd. The want is just the likelihood that a certain sort of action will take place, and so it accounts for action only verbally.

Similarly with such mental states as fear, anger, avarice, ambition, love. To attribute a man's actions to one or other of these passions is not to describe the contents of his consciousness at the time immediately preceding the action. There are indeed feelings characteristic of each of them; but to say that a man acted out of fear, anger, avarice, ambition or affection is not to say that he felt any of these characteristic feelings at the time when he acted, still less is it to say that his having these feelings caused him to act as he did. For one can act from anger without feeling angry, and from avarice without feeling avaricious – if indeed 'feeling avaricious' is a proper description of any sort of feelings. These words are primarily descriptive, not of states of awareness, but of patterns of behaviour which commonly occur in certain characteristic sets of circumstances. To say that a man is afraid is to characterise, in a general way, his likely behaviour over a short period – the duration of the emergency. To say that he is ambitious is to describe in a general way his likely behaviour over a longer period. If these expressions essentially refer to patterns of behaviour, then the relation between a man's fear or ambition and his fearful or ambitious actions is not the relation of cause to effect, but something more like the relation of general to particular. The actions are not consequences of the mental state, but examples of it; together with other actions and inclinations to act, they constitute it. Thus the function of this group of concepts is not to assign causes to human actions, but to classify those actions; just as the function of the meteorological term 'depression' is not to assign a cause to the low pressure, cloudiness, humidity and inclination to rain which occur so frequently together, but to give a name to this dismally familiar weather-syndrome. The approach of a depression is the onset of these conditions. Their causes are to be sought at a different level of abstraction. Similarly, any causes of human behaviour there may be are to be sought at a different level of abstraction from that at which the concepts of the passions are in place.

These arguments are sound as far as they go. But there is something more to be said. When we classify Smith's action as due to, or as an example of, his avarice, kind-heartedness or jealousy we do more than judge it to be behaviour of a certain type. We also judge that there is something persistently operative in the character of Smith which affects or is concerned in his behaviour on the various occasions on which these concepts are applicable to it. Likewise, when we bring Smith's and Jones's actions under the same concept, we suppose there to be something in the character of Jones significantly similar to that in the character of Smith which makes him behave

in similar ways. We suppose that fear and anger, avarice and
patriotism, love and hate, are analogous conditions on the
different occasions and in the different people by whom they
are displayed. If we were to discover that similar-looking
actions by Smith and by Jones were due to altogether dissimilar
causes, we should be reluctant to apply the same word to them.
That is to say, the concept of a passion does contain a causal
element in that where the same verbal characterisation is used,
similar causes or 'motives' in the literal sense are supposed to
be operative. The same of course is true of more academic
concepts such as 'instinct' and 'drive'. Only the words 'fear',
'avarice', 'patriotism', 'jealousy', 'self-display', etc. do not
specify the nature of these causes; they are specified solely in
terms of their effects. To account for Smith's action by saying
that it was caused by his ambition explains his action only as
far as one explains the breaking of a piece of china by reference
to its fragility. From one point of view the fragility is no
explanation of the break, but merely a restatement of the fact
that the thing was liable to break. But from another point of
view it does give some explanation, in that it says that there was
something about it rendering it liable to break in circumstances
in which other things would not break, without saying what
this something is. Compare what a physician does when he
diagnoses a case of measles. To give this name to a particular
set of bodily conditions is to classify symptoms rather than
causes. But to use the name implies, in the first place, that a
number of different symptoms – spots, fever, weakness – have
a common cause, and in the second place that similar sets of
symptoms in different patients have similar causes. If this turns
out not to be the case, different names are devised for those sets
of symptoms which differ in their causes. The diagnosis can be
made without knowing what the causes are, but not without
the belief that there are such common causes. If the comparison
with the passions is just, then the attribution of a person's
action to fear, love, or ambition is not an assignment of it to
some mental cause to the exclusion of physical causes, but is
quite consistent with an attribution to some physical cause.
Just as the attribution of shivering to influenza is quite compatible with attributing it to the presence of a virus in the body,

so attributing an action to fear is quite compatible with attributing it to some chemical change in the body. As in the former case we could say that the presence of the virus *is* influenza, so in the latter case we could properly say that the chemical change in question *is* fear.

Similarly, when we say that a person wants or desires something, we assert that there exists in him a disposition to pursue it; and this disposition we regard as a condition in which he may be for a considerable length of time – we talk of desires waxing and waning, and ultimately dying. But what this disposition consists in, how it is brought about and what would stop it are matters for further investigation. '*S* wants *x*' makes a dispositional statement about *S*. It says something about *S*'s condition, but specifies that condition only in terms of the behaviour which tends to issue from it. Thus in so far as action is causally attributed to desire, it is attributed to a cause not specified apart from its effects.

There is a third class of expressions that may appear to refer to mental causes, a particularly important group in that if they are causes at all they would seem to cause not only other states of consciousness but bodily movements. Among the movements executed by a person's body, we distinguish those which he did intentionally, on purpose, wilfully, deliberately, meaning to do them, from those which occurred (we hesitate to say that he did them) unintentionally, involuntarily, automatically, against his will. And amongst the consequences of such movements we distinguish those which he intended, meant or was trying to do from those which happened inadvertently, unintentionally, by accident. Now if intending, meaning, purposing or trying to do something is an occurrence of any kind, it is a mental occurrence in my restricted sense. For whether a person is intending, meaning, purposing or trying to do something, and what it is that in the course of a series of bodily movements he is intending or trying to do, are matters about which the person cannot be ignorant, and cannot be deceived. He cannot intelligibly be said to be intending or trying to do something without knowing that this is what he is intending or trying to do; and to know this he does not need to judge on the basis of evidence, whereas other people do have to judge on the basis of evidence, and may be deceived. We do indeed sometimes rely on publicly available evidence of a person's intentions in preference to his own avowals. But this is not because we doubt his means of information, but because we doubt his sincerity; if we could get a truth drug which was 100 per cent. reliable we should not need the circumstantial evidence. If these words 'intend', 'mean', 'wilful', 'on purpose', 'try' stand for occurrences, the occurrences are those known to philosophers as acts of will or volitions, and often supposed to be the causes of those bodily movements which count as genuine actions.

Are there such occurrences? It is often argued nowadays that there are not, and that since there are no such events as volitions or acts of will, neither such acts, nor the 'will' itself, can be regarded as causes of bodily movements, and the nasty question of how the mind (consciousness) can affect the body cannot arise at any rate in this form. The argument goes something like this. If volitions really occurred and were noticed by the people who gave them or execute them, then they could be described by various epithets. We could say in what respect one volition differed from another, and give a list of those we had performed over a given period of time. We should be able to describe them without reference to the bodily movements which are their alleged consequences. For if we could not do this, then we should not know how to pick out the right volition to perform in order to produce a given movement. Nor could we formulate any causal generalisation, for to do this we must be able to specify the cause independently of its effect. But we cannot supply the requisite descriptions. When we look within ourselves for these acts of will, to inspect and describe them, we are met with a blank. If I am asked to say what volition preceded and caused the movement of my arm, I can only say that it was the will or intention to move my arm; that is, I can identify it only by reference to its supposed effect. And then the proposition that the raising of my arm was caused by the will to raise my arm appears clearly, not as a causal explanation, but as a limp tautology. The volition supposed to be the cause of the movement is conceivable only by reference to its supposed effect; the connection between the two is not causal but logical. Reference to the act of will can be no more than a misleading way of saying that I did raise my arm in the ordinary way.

This argument has force. But acceptance of it leaves us in a very uncomfortable position. In the first place, how we manage to distinguish so confidently between what is and what is not done on purpose, between the intended and the unintended consequences of our actions, is left mysterious. It is no good referring to awareness of what the body is doing or about to do, for I can be very well aware of what movements are going on or are about to go on in my body, and at the same time very far from making these movements willingly or on purpose – for instance, in being sick. Nor is it any good referring to the general context of the performance; for this is as well known to the bystanders as to myself, and yet they are not aware as I am aware of what I am intending or trying to do. In the second place, if the conclusion of the argument is to be that the relation between volition and bodily movement or other characteristics of action must be logical rather than causal this conclusion is plainly false. For the connection between willing, intending or trying to do something and doing it is not necessary but contingent. It is quite common for people to intend and try to do something and not to do it, but something else instead. Most people, indeed, when they mean to raise their arms, do raise their arms – though even here there are exceptions; I have been one for the past dozen years. But most people, when they will, intend or try to hold their arms quite still for a minute, draw a circle, recite a tongue-twister twenty times, or play the Appassionata Sonata as Beethoven wrote it, do something other than what they intended. In such cases, there is no logical connection between the will and the deed, and the volition *is* describable without reference to what the agent actually does.

There is a view of the character of volition which is vulnerable to the kind of criticism I have been considering. It is based on taking the rather rare deliberate, pondered, momentous choices as the only, or the typical kind of human willing. From this point of view willing consists of a series of distinct choices or decisions, separated by intervals of non-willing, each of these being a Humean impression, an item in the content of the mind, distinguishable from other such volitional items, so that one might enumerate the acts of will one had performed over a period, note down their times by the clock, and give each its separate description as a phenomenon. If we are to believe in the influence of consciousness on bodily movement we need a different sort of interpretation of what willing is. In the first place, it is not an occasional and optional feature of consciousness, but a constant and necessary one; all the time we are awake we are doing something, and meaning to do something (usually, but not necessarily, the same thing). We cannot count our volitions, any more than we can count our auditions (acts of hearing) or our thoughts, because the volitional process is continuous, and any breaking up of it into separate items is more or less arbitrary. (There is no answer to Professor Ryle's question 'At what moment did the boy will to take the high dive?' because he was willing this throughout the whole operation.) In the second place, willing is a mode of consciousness. Just as we can distinguish one act of hearing from another only by reference to what is heard, and one act of thinking from another only by reference to what is thought, so we can distinguish one act of willing from another only by reference to what is willed. My volitional intention, like my auditory attention, shifts from one object to another. But it is not a mere noticing of what the body is about; it is not the inert spectatorship which Hume took it to be. Awareness is always in the mode of action and passion, of acceptance and rejection, of saying Yes or No. Whatever takes place in my experience comes as welcome or unwelcome, with my concurrence or despite my repudiation. It is this sort of conscious activity which the words 'will', 'mean', 'intend', 'try' essentially refer to. That volition in this sense, the assent or dissent of the conscious person to what is going on in his experience, makes a difference, that the raising of my arm takes place if and only if I assent to its going up, is not an immediately given fact of experience, but a hypothesis to be confirmed. We do not know straight off what we can do, which of the movements within and without our bodies we can control; we have to learn. But the hypothesis is reasonable; and in the case of a great number of movements which my body makes, it can be confirmed in the same way as other causal hypotheses – namely, that when I do will, intend or try to make these movements they usually take place, and when I don't they usually do not. In view of this regular correlation it seems to me that more formidable arguments than I have yet met are needed to show that the connection between the will and the deed is not a causal connection.

7

'TIME'S ARROW'

AN INFORMATIONAL THEORY TREATMENT

The Earl of Halsbury

TIME's arrow is not a property of time but of events: the way in which they succeed one another in our experience and, as many believe, in a reality independent of our experience. I hope to throw a little light on one aspect of this difficult matter by treating it from the standpoint of logic, topology and information theory. If I succeed in my hope I shall still be leaving many other matters unresolved. Let me state briefly what these other matters are in order not to exaggerate the scope of any contribution I hope to make.

Physics is a subject with a consolidated centre of knowledge surrounded by an incomplete boundary of speculation. Our sense of wonder at the achievements of those who have consolidated the centre must not be allowed to lead us into supposing that the task is finished or that physics is a completed subject. The two parts of the speculative boundary which are causing most trouble at present are the ultra-macroscopic or Cosmical studied by mathematicians and astronomers, and the infra-microscopic studied by so-called 'particle physicists'.

On the Cosmical scale the General Theory of Relativity turns out to be too general to be applied unambiguously to the Universe as a whole. To do so we have to introduce some extraneous assumption without any basis for preferring one to another. The most we can do is to compare the results of incorporating alternative extraneous assumptions with observations and determine whether one model or another corresponds more or less closely with reality. Unfortunately the type of decisive observational test which would discriminate between them usually turns out to be beyond our present powers to make. We are, therefore, left with models associated with their proponents and very little means of discriminating between them: Einstein, de Sitter, Einstein/de Sitter, Friedmann-Lemaitre, Weyl, Eddington, Milne, Dirac, Godel, Hoyle, and so on. Many of these models, but not all, possess an absolute time scale. That is to say, the dissection of space–time allowed by Special Relativity Theory into a space and a time proper to each observer, the relativity of this choice by different observers being determined by their relative motion, is from the Cosmic point of view a local matter according to most models. There is, however, no philosophic reason for supposing Truth to be necessarily associated with majority views and we have therefore no final basis for believing the choice of time axis to be relative or absolute. Our ignorance is really profound. To this basic problem I have nothing to contribute.

At the other extreme the analysis of matter right down to the fundamental particle is attended by one commonplace, common-sense feature being a straightforward extrapolation from the macroscopic to the microscopic: 'parts' always turn out to be 'smaller' in the common-sense interpretation than the 'wholes' which they compose. This apparently stops at the level of the fundamental particles, of which over one hundred are known and all of which appear to have a diameter of about 10^{-13} cm. irrespective of whether they are taken singly or in union with one another. The time required by light to cross such a spatial interval, i.e. a time of the order of 10^{-24} second, appears to mark a limit beyond which temporal succession may not be a continuous process. This is one difficulty. A second difficulty is that the temporal order of complex particle-events appears to become ambiguous so that the description of events in terms where causes precede their effects appears to enter on level terms with counterpart descriptions in which effects precede their cause. Thirdly, the invariance or otherwise of various processes under time reversal is an unresolved issue. To these basic problems I have, again, nothing to contribute.

Let me, therefore, turn to the consolidated part of physics and begin with the semantics of temporal succession in our

experience. We may properly say that the body of water in a
river flows in its bed, but we must not say that the bed flows.
The language we use must, therefore, make it clear whether
we are talking of the body of water in a river or the bed of the
river. The word 'river' by itself is ambiguous and can refer to
either the water or the bed in which it flows. We have to learn
to avoid the use of ambiguities of this kind. Regarding the
passage of any drop of water past a point in the river bed as an
event, we may say that the succession of such events flows in
time. We may say that the river flows in time if we are careful
to note the ambiguities involved and clarify what we say as we
go along. We ought not to say that the bed flows in time (save
in so far as meanders are a dynamic phenomenon) though it
preserves a continuity therein. And under no circumstances
must we say that Time flows or Time flows in time. 'Time itself
is not a process in time.'[1]

These ambiguities are particularly likely to infect the concept
of a block-universe or William James stack, of which I will give
a description (Fig. 1). Consider a strip of 35-mm. film, consisting
of a lengthwise display of picture-frames. The projective potentialities of the camera have produced in each frame a two-
dimensional representation of a three-dimensional field of view.
The exposures were made in temporal succession but, owing to
the motion of the film between exposures, this temporal succession of exposures is represented by a spatial succession of
frames. Neglecting its thickness, the whole film is a two-
dimensional object in which the length has an ambiguous
character. It is used to represent temporal succession from

---

[1] 'Time itself is not a process in time.' G. J. Whitrow, *The Natural
Philosophy of Time* (London, 1961), p. 292. A long and distinguished list of
views to the contrary indicates how widespread the mistake is: (i) 'Time is
a moving image of Eternity', Plato, *The Timeaus of Plato* (trans. R. D.
Archer-Hind) (London, 1888), p. 119; (ii) 'Time travels in divers paces
with divers persons', Shakespeare, *As You Like It*, III. ii. 326; (iii) 'We
evidently must regard Time as passing with a steady flow', I. Barrow,
Lectiones Geometricae (trans. E. Stone) (London, 1735), lect. I, p. 35; (iv)
'Absolute, true and mathematical time of itself, and from its own nature,
flows equably without relation to anything external', I. Newton, *Mathematical Principles* (trans. A. Motte, ed. F. Cajori) (Berkeley, 1934), p. 6;
(v) 'Time like an ever-rolling stream bears all its sons away', *Hymnist*.

frame to frame, and also to represent one dimension of the
projected field of view. The ambiguity can be removed by
using a pair of scissors to cut the frames off, one by one, and
later stacking them vertically above one another in a vertical
order corresponding to the horizontal order of their original
succession. This is what is called a William James stack. It is
a three-dimensional object corresponding to and representing
a four-dimensional process. A four-dimensional structure which
cannot be visualised is thus reduced to a three-dimensional
object which can, by exploiting and inserting it into the three

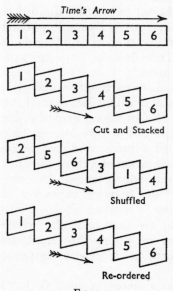

Fig. 1

dimensions of physical space utilising the projective power of
the camera to economise by one dimension in representing the
field of view. This gives a dimension to spare and it can be used
to represent time. In doing so events have been geometrised.

At this point a word of warning should be uttered against
taking geometrisation too seriously. One can probably geometrise anything. Cows eat grass and secrete milk which we
can convert into butter. There is a strong correlation between

the carotene content of the grass and the Vitamin A content of the butter. We can display this correlation by plotting a graph of one against the other. In doing so we geometrise a metabolic relationship. We must not suppose, however, because we can display a metabolic relationship geometrically that it is itself of geometrical character. For exactly the same reason it must not be supposed, because a four-dimensional succession can be displayed as a three-dimensional stack in which temporal succession is represented by spatial succession, that there is any sort of identification between them. Representation is not identity.

This problem arises immediately we consider the William James stack in relation to our experience of succession. A block-universe consisting of a generalised all-inclusive William James stack represents events, past, present and future, as omnipresent in a non-temporal sense. We merely encounter them in succession. But in succession in what? In succession in time, of course. If we wish to encounter the temporal succession of the frames in this stack we must consider them in succession in time, or illuminate them in succession in time, or generally mark them by one device or another in succession in time. We have emphatically not exorcised time by our process of geometrising a temporal succession.

J. W. Dunne endeavoured to exorcise this difficulty by geometrising the going on of time in time (an impermissible expression) by utilising a fifth dimension and so extending the geometrisation. But this merely pushed the difficulty into a sixth dimension and then a seventh, and so *ad infinitum*. He therefore boldly accepted the infinite regress involved and postulated a 'serial universe' with an infinity of dimensions. Dunne was, I believe, an engineer and not a pure mathematician. Had he been one he would have noted that what he was postulating was quite a well-known structure known to pure mathematicians as Hilbert space and would have treated it with more discrimination and respect than he did. Hilbert space is subject to various metrical restrictions which Dunne did not know about, all of which would have been highly objectionable as features of a model universe. A Hilbert 'cube' with finite sides, for example, will have an infinite diagonal unless after some finite number of sides has been enumerated their lengths begin to diminish so that the sum of their squares converges and only makes a finite contribution to the diagonal. Hilbert objects of this kind have to be pancaked flatter and flatter in their higher dimensions until they become of arbitrary thinness so that the price paid for a convergent diagonal is a zero volume. Dunne does not seem to have been aware of the difficulty he was running into.

My reason for referring to Dunne's serial universe is not to voice disagreement but because it has the point of regress in common with what I shall propose. My regress, however, is an informational not a geometrical one, though some of its features can be given a convenient geometrical representation for expository purposes. I shall in fact be concerned with the regress: 'Information'.[1] 'Information about Information',

---

[1] 'Information' in communications engineering retains approximately its everyday meaning subject to being measured in the following way. Suppose a situation as known to us before and after some kind of disclosure, signal, observation or whatever it be relevant to the situation. Before receipt of the signal, etc., our *a priori* knowledge was, let us suppose, measured by p_B. After receipt, our *a posteriori* knowledge is measured p_A. p_B and p_A are probabilities ranging from 0 to 1, 0 standing for impossibility and 1 for certainty. The information in the signal is related to the ratio p_A/p_B. For convenience the logarithm of this ratio is taken and in particular its logarithm to the base 2, though this is not essential. Thus if $p_A = p_B$, then $p_A/p_B = 1$, and since $\log_2 1 = 0$, no information is received. The information measure accordingly relates to the rise in our knowledge of something following an observation. Thus if a coin is covered our *a priori* knowledge of its being a head or tail is $\frac{1}{2}$ in either case. On uncovering the coin and observing that it is, say, a head, our *a posteriori* knowledge regarded as certain has risen to the value 1.0. The information content of the observation is therefore $\log_2 1/\frac{1}{2} = \log_2 2 = 1$. The unit of information or BIT is therefore taken as measuring the rise in our knowledge of a situation from an even money chance of it being so to certainty that it is so. Information may be linked to a general physical event, or to a linguistic symbol whose meaning is purely conventional. The former class is called 'intrinsic', 'implicit' or 'bound' by different writers; the latter 'semantic', 'explicit' or 'free'. These definitions imply nothing as to the importance of what is conveyed by a signal of the second kind. The telegraphic answers WELL and DEAD in reply to an enquiry after someone's health contain the same information as measured above. Their significance to the recipient could, however, be greatly different. 'Noise' is the component of reception that contains no information. Thus our *a posteriori* knowledge of events at a transmitter following reception in a noisy receiver is less than certain, i.e. is measured

'Information about information about information', and so on, but not *ad infinitum*. I have a natural escape route from an infinite regress via the second law of thermodynamics, one of whose formulations states that information is progressively eroded by noise. A more familiar and earlier formulation is that entropy always increases. Information and entropy, however, are calculated in the same way and one is the negative of the other. To say that information decreases is logically identical with saying that entropy increases.

To give a rough idea of what I am going to propose before coming to the detail, the temporal sequence in a William James event stack is identical with the logical order of the informational regress in a cognate informational stack. And by logical order I mean the way in which order is defined in logic. This eliminates our 'encountering' the elements of the stack in temporal sequence. We can encounter them simultaneously or in random order if we insist on invoking a physical time for the encounter.

Provided only that we regard each element of the stack as a 'state of consciousness', we shall construct the logical order of information automatically out of the logical process which defines what order is and shall assert in consequence that this is the temporal order of events. In a pictorial sense Saturday is the day which contains information about itself and Friday, which was the day which contained information about itself and Thursday, and so on backwards in a regress. This entails the order Thursday-Friday-Saturday as a matter of logic. The state of consciousness labelled 'Saturday' therefore contains information about Friday and Thursday as being past by definition and construction, and no information about Sunday as being future by the same test. From this point of view 'Time's arrow' and 'becoming' are matters of logic rather than physics.

My states of consciousness depend, I am prepared to suppose, on my brain, which is a physical system. If I am to suggest (as I shall) that the theory I have propounded above is more than a

---

by a figure less than 1·0. Noise thus ranks as negative information. Entropy in thermodynamics is also defined as the logarithm of a probability. It is therefore very similar to information as defined by communication engineers.

subjective one, I must demonstrate that it can be illustrated by physical systems as well as mental ones and this I shall do later by constructing a hypothetical machine devoid of a mental counterpart which acts in conformity with my theory.

In the meantime I want to say something about the logical foundations of order and measure in order to prepare the ground for what comes later.

If one tackles the problems in which Plato was interested, using only the tools that Plato had available, one may add to the innumerable commentaries on Plato that have been written since his day but one will not, I think, make a contribution to knowledge. For surely everything that can be said about Plato's problems using Plato's tools has by this time been said already by Plato or his successors. It is very difficult to find anything new to say unless we reformulate the problem in modern terms and use modern tools. In the last hundred years many new and wonderful tools have been sharpened by Weierstrass, Dedekind, Cantor, Frege, Peano, Russell, Whitehead, Hausdorff and others, and they cut through many of the ambiguities involved in traditional formulations.

The first of these advances was made by noticing a dualism between pairs of propositions, one of which contained (say) a reference to 'the number 2' and the other a reference to 'the set of all numbers less than 2'. Within a framework of quite definite rules one member of a dual pair of propositions can always be translated into the other. This made a world of difference to the treatment of irrational numbers such as $\sqrt{2}$, which is a slippery sort of object, a number and yet not a number. 'The set of all numbers whose squares are less than 2' is, however, a very much more definite sort of object provided that one is prepared to accept our intuitive interpretation of 'the set of all X such that Y' as having validity. Subject to this, dualism enables one to deal with incommensurables such as $\sqrt{2}$ on level terms with rational numbers such as 2 by a simple process of translation, and so finally to dominate the concept of the continuum which has caused so much difficulty in relation to both Time and Space.

The Euclidean point and the temporal instant were other slippery entities which Whitehead was able to tame by treating them on set-theoretic lines as the limits of nested sequences of intervals, each contained in its predecessor so that it became possible to say what one wanted to say about them without actually referring to them as entities which both were (in one sense) and were not (in another), as in Euclid where a point is defined as having position (implying that it exists) but no magnitude (implying that it does not exist).

Another classical teaser was concerned with the relation between position and extension or, in modern terms, between topological and metrical properties. A line can be regarded, quite legitimately, as an ordered set of points. It is also seen and felt intuitively to be in some sense the possessor of a property known as 'length' which does not appear to be a logical consequence of its construction as a sequence of points none of which has any property which can be referred to as length. Generations of men have tried to understand how the one can arise from the other without making much progress. The modern solution is that the problem is in a sense spurious as pertaining to logic and mathematics, and purely physical/ factual in relation to real objects. Topology and metric are essentially distinct logical concepts. We attach one to the other by assignment. They are not involved with one another automatically as a matter of logic, though they may be concomitants of one another as a matter of physics. The postulates run as follows. First the concept of a point a, say. Next the concept of distinguishable points, a, b, c . . ., etc. Then point pairs (unordered) (a, b). Then intervals defined by point pairs (ab). Lastly the measure of an interval $\mu(ab)$ which we assign according to certain rules if we choose to do so. $\mu(ab)$ is a number, not a point or length and, subject to the rules, we can assign it as we please. The rules are simple and chosen to coincide with and generalise our intuitive ideas based in the first instance on Euclidean geometry. The first rule is that $\mu(aa) = 0$. This expresses the intuitive idea that the distance from a point to itself is zero. The second states that $\mu(ab) = \mu(ba)$, i.e. the length of an interval is independent of the direction in which we measure it. The third rule is called the triangular inequality and states that $\mu(ab) + \mu(bc)$ is equal to or greater than $\mu(ac)$, e.g. that any two sides of a triangle are greater than the third. (Equality covers the case where the triangle just fails to form or to enclose a space.)[1] This treatment of 'measure' has considerable importance in relation to some relativistic models of the Cosmos. For 'length' in geometry we must substitute 'duration' in time. Either is a measure of interval and both are subject to an arbitrary element of choice in assignment. Having chosen a μ we have adopted a convention. Any other μ, $\mu' = \log \mu$ say, would be equally legitimate provided the ground rules were obeyed.

Thus given a Cosmos that exploded in a finite time in the past, the question of what happened before then can be neatly side-stepped[2] by adopting an alternative 'measure' for temporal intervals. According to the 'Big Bang' theory the Universe exploded at time $t = 0$. This is according to one convention for measuring time-intervals. If we chose a logarithmic convention, then since $\log 0 = - \infty$, we push the explosion back into the infinite past. We have of course to be consistent and adopt the same convention in all contexts so that the laws of physics in logarithmic time-measure appear different from those required by an alternative convention, but there is no logical reason to prefer one to the other, though our intuitive ideas may cause us to feel a preference without being able to explain why.

The last matter bearing on this subject but the most important for my purpose is that of 'order'. It is a large subject seen from its different aspects such as partial ordering, total ordering, well ordering, and so on. I shall, therefore, confine myself to the simple logical definition of a discrete ordered n-tuple in order to see how the logician avoids circularity by referring, say, to an ordered triple $\langle ABC \rangle$ as 'First A. Second B. Third C', the words 'first', 'second' and 'third' themselves being expressions of a concept of order which has still to be defined.

[1] The ground rules are given above in the form in which they are generally set out in works on topology and are assigned by analogy with Euclidean spaces and other spaces with a positive definite metric. One can formulate alternatives however, e.g. Minkowski space–time.

[2] Side-stepping means what it says. One does not answer a question by agreeing not to discuss it! One way of restricting a discussion is to restrict one's vocabulary in such a way that a particular question cannot be asked. It may still need answering however.

Nor can this definition be escaped by an intuitive approach through contemplating A, B and C in temporal order, for it is the nature of temporal order that we seek to define.

Consider accordingly the undefined terms 'set' and 'element (or point)' and the undefined relationship 'member of'. This enables us to write, for example: 'x is a member of the set X'. Where distinguishable elements $x, y, z \ldots$ are all to be regarded as members of the same set X we write $X = \{x, y, z \ldots\}$.

Consider accordingly the set whose members are A and B, namely $\{A, B\}$ or $\{B, A\}$ as being an unordered pair, there being no difference between the two expressions. To order it we proceed as follows. We first form the set whose only member is A, namely $\{A\}$, noting that A and $\{A\}$ are not to be confused or identified. Next we form the set $\{AB\}$ or $\{BA\}$. Lastly we form the set of sets $\{\{A\}, \{AB\}\}$ which can equally well be written $\{\{BA\}, \{A\}\}$ the two alternative expressions defining the same set of sets. This set of sets is taken as the definition of the ordered pair $\langle AB \rangle$. A is the singleton in this definition, and we may define what we mean by 'first' in this way. 'The second' may be defined as the member of the pair which is not the first.

An ordered triple $\langle ABC \rangle$ may similarly be defined as the set of sets $\{\{A\} \{AB\} \{ABC\}\}$ and 'the third' can be defined as the member of the triple which is not the first or the second. And so on to ordered n-tuples $\langle a_1 a_2 \ldots a \rangle$.

The next definition is that of precedence. A is said to precede[1] B, $A \prec B$, in the ordered pair $\langle AB \rangle$ if A is the singleton in the set $\{\{A\}, \{AB\}\}$. From this the transitive character of precedence can be deduced, namely that if A precedes B and B precedes C, then A precedes C.

Lastly a set-inclusive character involved in order must be noted, namely that in the ordered triple $\langle ABC \rangle$ the set $\{A\}$ is included in $\{AB\}$ and $\{AB\}$ is included in $\{ABC\}$, the three sets $\{A\}$ $\{AB\}$ and $\{ABC\}$ forming a nesting sequence. (A set X is

[1] The word 'precede' must not be interpreted in a spatial or temporal sense. Cf. Hausdorff, *Set Theory* (Chelsea Publishing Co., New York, 1957), p. 49: 'Of course the space-like or time-like characteristics which seem to attach to this explanation because of the use of the prepositions "before" and "after" are of no consequence, and we will convince ourselves by the use of other definitions that what we have here is nothing but an application of the concept of function.'

said to be included in a set Y if all the members of X are members of Y.)

The three ideas of ordered n-tuple, precedence and nested inclusion are closely associated with one another. Any one can be made the starting-point for a treatment of the subject. The method chosen here has perhaps the merit of simplicity in presentation.

It will now be clear that any regress of the type 'Information', 'Information about Information', 'Information about information about information', etc., is a nesting sequence which provides a natural link to the concept of what order means as defined above. The natural order of the regress is the logical order of the nesting sequence.

With this much logical preamble let me turn to a William James stack and see how far we can reconstruct its historical order after shuffling it so that the historical order is destroyed and how far the reconstruction depends on the nature of the phenomenon recorded.

Consider a stack of three frames only: three negatives of a white ping-pong ball photographed against a black curtain in motion across, say, a black table. What appear on the negatives are three black discs against a transparent background. On superimposing them it can be seen instinctively that they form an ordered sequence of positions. The problem of restoring their historical order from their shuffled order is simply that of ordering them front to back in the same order as that in which they appear from left to right.

There remains, however, one ambiguity I must leave unresolved, namely that of which way up the stack should be viewed. Was the ping-pong ball travelling from right to left or left to right? Nothing recorded on the photographs gives a clue to this. I might seek further information, not on the photographs. Question: 'What was the nature of this object?' Answer: 'It was a ping-pong ball.' Question: 'Is there a law of nature requiring ping-pong balls to travel preferentially leftwards rather than rightwards?' Answer: 'No.' Comment: 'I cannot resolve the ambiguity.'

This example illustrates Newtonian physics with invariance under time reversal.

Next consider a stack consisting of a sequence of photographs of a hot body in contact with a cold one, each carrying a thermometer. The temperature differential between the thermometers provides a criterion of order which enables one to restore the historical order from the shuffled one. Again, however, there is an ambiguity to be resolved. Which is the first and which the last element of the ordered set? I cannot determine this from the information on the photographs so I ask for more. Question: 'What am I looking at?' Answer: 'A hot body in contact with a cold one, and the mercury levels of two associated thermometers.' Question: 'Is there a law of nature which states how heat flows under these conditions?' Answer: 'Yes. The second law of thermodynamics requires heat to flow from the hotter to the colder body.' Comment: 'In terms of this extra information I can resolve the ambiguity. The frame with the largest temperature difference recorded on it is the first not the last element in the ordered set.'

This example illustrates a macroscopic thermodynamic process asymmetrical as between past and future. (Microscopic processes, however, are subject to fluctuations which would invalidate the foregoing argument.)

In my first example the ambiguity was unresolvable in terms of auxiliary unrecorded information.

In my second, auxiliary unrecorded information was sufficient to resolve the ambiguity on the macroscopic scale.

My third example will require no auxiliary information and the ambiguity will be resolved entirely in terms of recorded information. Moreover, the order that emerges is both logical, natural and absolute, and does not depend on any intuitive approach.

Consider an object rather like a picture frame, whose relative dimensions are as $1 : \sqrt{2}$. This enables me to bisect it into sub-frames whose relative dimensions are also as $1 : \sqrt{2}$ though turned through a right-angle relative to the main frame. I will call the left-hand sub-frame the clock frame because it will contain a clock, and the right-hand sub-frame the display frame because it will contain a photographic display of the whole frame. In front of the frame let there be a camera capable of photographing the whole frame on a scale reduced linearly by

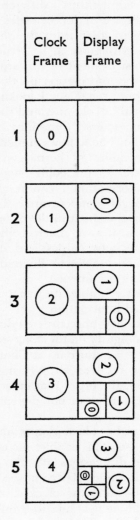

FIG. 2

$\sqrt{2}$ or superficially by 2 so that a photograph of the whole frame reduced in scale by $\sqrt{2}$ can be turned through a right-angle and inserted into the display frame.

With the clock frame displaying the symbol O, and the display frame empty, I photograph the whole and insert the photograph in the display frame. I wait till the clock reads 1 and re-photograph the assembly inserting the photograph in the display frame after removing its predecessor. I wait again till the clock reads 2, re-photograph the assembly and insert the photograph in the display frame, after removing its predecessor. And so on, repeating the procedure at each successive clock interval thereafter and until the resolution of my apparatus fails. It is this limit on resolution which prevents my landing in an infinite regress. To pass beyond the limit of resolution I should need two of these assemblies, one set to start off approximately half-way through the cycle limiting the other. My record would alternate cyclically between the information on each of them by means of their overlap.

The build-up of information would appear as in Fig. 2.

Note the nesting property of the above sequence numbered Nos. 1–5. The whole of the information in No. 1 is part of that in No. 2. The whole of the information in No. 2 is part of that in No. 3, and in general the whole information in the nth frame is part of the information on the $(n+1)$th up to the limit of resolution.

Note also that these nested regresses coincide in structure with the logical definition of what order means and that there is no ambiguity as between the first and the last.

Now let me modify the apparatus slightly in imagination so as to make it completely independent of my intervention.

For the optical camera I will substitute a television camera. In the display frame I will insert a closed-loop television display tube connected to the camera by a single-frame delay element. The clock will be synchronised to the time base of the television equipment in such a way that one clock interval equals one frame interval. The result is a pure machine which generates information about the physical world, stores it, arranges it in a sequence of regresses which provide it with a natural and logical order coincidental with historical order and disposes of it at the limit of resolution through erosion by noise, noise being the ultimate factor controlling that limit, so that each regress is finite. Two such arrays with cyclic overlap and an infinite sequence of such regresses would of course be needed to record an infinite time, but each regress would be finite and the historical order would be unambiguously reconstructable from the logical order subsequent to no matter how many shufflings and permutations of a dissected record. Even if the clock numbers were written in Linear Minoan A or some other undeciphered script; even if one did not know the physical nature of the instrument whose records one was analysing after shuffling, this would remain true.

Why not then pass to a firm identification of the historical with the logical order and assert that the historical order is the logical order of information storage in a Cosmos (locally at any rate) capable of storing it?

The foregoing entails a resemblance with and also a distinction from the views of McTaggart on this subject. He first distinguished two series:

B Series $\rightarrow T_1\ T_2\ T_3\ T_4\ T_5$ — characterised by the relations 'before' and 'after'

A Series
$\downarrow$

$\begin{array}{l} T_1\ t_2\ t_3\ t_4\ t_5 \\ T_1\ T_2\ t_3\ t_4\ t_5 \\ T_1\ T_2\ T_3\ t_4\ t_5 \end{array}$ — characterised by the terms 'past' and 'future', indicated here by majuscule (past) and minuscule (future) type

He then argued against the reality of either of these, being an idealist philosopher for whom space and time were unreal. Postulating that they were misconceptions of a true and a real C series, he defined the latter in terms of an inclusion relation of spiritual and non-temporal character:

$$C_1 \subset C_2 \subset C_3 \subset, \text{ etc.}$$

He then attempted to explain why the C Series was mis-conceived as an A or B Series.

The regresses I have demonstrated, however, include the counterparts of McTaggart's A, B and C Series. The equivalent of an A, B and C Series were all incorporated in a single display;

all three were co-present. No question of mistaking one for another arises, however. *A* and *B* are concomitants of, not mistakes for, the inclusion relation *C* granted the informational regresses.

What of circularity? Have I unconsciously and surreptitiously presupposed time's arrow and inserted it into my regressive storage machine? Could the machine be made to run backwards so that the temporal order of the regress was in fact reversed? In one sense the machine certainly could not run backwards for a physically real delay element cannot be converted into a physically real anticipatory element or crystal ball. The hands of a clock can be run counter-clockwise by gearing, but the clock is still going forward in time. A delay element is not of this character. What can be done to run the display backwards in the logical sense? In the forward mode the machine generates information and stores the whole upon the part. In the backward mode it must store the part upon the whole and erase information. If the lower half of the display frame is blown up by $\sqrt{2}$, turned through a right-angle and projected on to the whole display frame through the delay line the regress will progressively disappear in time in the backward mode just as it was progressively formed in time in the forward mode. If the clock is geared to run backwards, then the backward and forward modes appear completely symmetrical. There is, however, an underlying asymmetry which requires analysis.

The informational regress in the forward mode is of indefinite length. I will suppose that when the clock reads 100 the original reading of 0 has spiralled down to the centre of the display frame and is just about to disappear at the limit of resolution, so that when the clock reads 101, the number 0 has disappeared and the number 1 is at the limit of resolution. A hundred units of time later the situation repeats itself in relation to the figure 201 on the clock, and 101 is at the limit of resolution on the display frame. At some intermediate period the same was true of the state when 151 was on the clock and 51 was at the limit of resolution on the display frame. The finite regresses overlap in such a way that it always remains possible to order Nos. 0–100 in relation to Nos. 101–201.

In the backward mode the situation is completely different.

Starting with the display running from 201 to 101 and working in the backward mode, the display would run from 200 to 101, then from 199 to 101, and so on backwards to 103 to 101, 102 to 101, 101 itself and then nothing.

A progressive blank would be growing at the centre of the display; the numbers 100, 99, 98 and so on would never appear at the centre because they never were (or could have been) stored there. The logic of this is not difficult to see. Information can be eroded by but cannot be generated from noise. Having permitted the second law of thermodynamics to enter into the forward mode in order to secure finite regresses, it becomes an automatic barrier to reversibility in the backward mode. Thus the backward mode has a finite lifetime as opposed to the forward mode whose lifetime is indefinite.

The second asymmetry concerns the status of the clock. In the forward mode it stands as the first link in a causal chain and drives the whole regress forward in such a way that causal order has the signature of logical order written on it. In the backward mode it is a synchronised epiphenomenon which plays no part in the disappearance of the regress. In the forward mode blanking out the clock for one time interval would cause a blank to be stored in the regresses. In the backward mode, blanking out one of the regresses for one time interval would never blank out the clock. The clock is thus an essential component of the forward mode. In the backward mode it can be disconnected and removed without in any way affecting the *modus operandi*.

This concludes my exposition of what I have tried to analyse. I have not attempted to propound a new theory of time either physical or philosophical. I have tried instead to remove an apparent inadequacy in a very common representation of time, namely the block-universe geometrised representation in which time's arrow is commonly thought to be missing. I have tried to show that it is present in logical form, regarding time's arrow as proceeding in the direction in which free information is generated[1] and bound information eroded by noise, the

---

[1] Cf. Whitrow, op. cit.: 'The direction of time in our personal experience is that of increasing knowledge of events', p. 270, and also 'The order of our awareness [is] of the growth in our information of what occurs', p. 271.

regressive potentialities of storage marking the direction logically and unambiguously.

Time, however, is not space and the 'block-universe' is not the real one. Nevertheless the relative structure of the real universe must be or be held to be to some extent isomorphic with any representation of it that works or appears to work. To that extent this paper is relevant to theories of time though it does not itself contain such a theory.

Deeply bound up with the block-universe representation are the historical problems of Natural law, determinism, causality and free will. Information theory has, of course, no intrinsic connection with one physical law rather than another, but appears capable of exercising a unifying influence on our classification of different types of physical law, particularly in relation to the way in which time enters into them.

We have first the low noise-level non-turbulent type of physics embodied in Newtonian orbital theory. By low noise level I mean that the Brownian movement of a planet in orbit is negligible by very many orders of magnitude compared to its orbital motion. Here there is conservation of information in the sense that the information arising from an observation remains relevant independently of the time at which it was established. This enables us to make tautological predictions of the form, 'If the system has been doing for an indefinite time past what it is doing now, then at any particular point in time past it was doing so and so.' Alternatively, 'If it will be doing for an indefinite time to come what it is doing now, then at some particular point in time future it will be doing such and such.' In this case Laplace's omniscient mathematician is in a position to predict the future as Laplace postulated on the basis of knowledge he can have. However the relevance of his information only runs between singularities. No amount of information with respect to the seven elements of a planetary orbit suffices to say how it got into orbit or when, if ever, it will have a collision with another body. While these encounters have in the past been rare, orbiting rockets can in the future be expected to collide in due course with the 'disjecta membra' of their predecessors now constituting an embarrassing, because unrecorded, clutter in space.

If the relevance between singularities of observational information occupies a time interval comparable to the time required to obtain it, then Laplace's omniscient being begins to run into difficulties. If he can no longer fabricate tautologies on the lines of, 'If this particle of a viscous fluid continues to do what it has been doing, then etc. . . .' because such is not the case, his power to predict becomes evanescent. This takes us into the domain of turbulent motion where in the immediate past and the immediate future there has been and will be interference with the trajectory of a particle by other elements of the motion with respect to which no observation on the particle itself provides any information. In terms of mathematical physics these difficulties are expressed by unresolvable mathematical difficulties of a theoretical character. Turbulent motion cannot be predicted in detail. The conservation laws of Energy, Momentum, Angular Momentum and so on only enable us to write down equations which become insoluble at the point where inertial and viscous forces become comparable. Most philosophical discussion of Determinism ignores this deplorable situation.

Laplace's omniscient being has thus to consider just how much information he can obtain with respect to a whole system viewed from inside as opposed to a part of it seen from outside. This takes him into the domain of thermodynamics where we may conceptually divide any system into two parts, the environments of an observer and an observed respectively. It transpires that the observer can only obtain information with respect to the observed at the cost of destroying more information in his own environment than corresponds to the information he has obtained from the other. This, alas, is what the second law of thermodynamics prescribes. It is effectively impossible to obtain from inside a closed system sufficient information to categorise it completely. Laplace's omniscient being cannot therefore make a beginning. He is spurious. This is not to say that God is not omniscient but only that his knowledge is not obtained by physical observation. No serious theologian ever supposed that it was. There remain the Quantum Laws embodied in the uncertainty principle and in which Planck's constant h replaces the Boltzmann constant k of thermodynamics. Here, too, we have to trade information for information, though not as in thermodynamics at a loss, though not at a profit either. My final conclusion is that the type of prediction which treats the future as already established is either tautological or impossible. In so far as this is not generally accepted it may be that philosophers and scientists have fallen into the trap of believing one another's propaganda! Scientists take the philosopher's concept of causality at its face value and confuse it with law. Philosophers accept the scientist's laws and suppose that they are experimental verifications of their concept of causality. I believe that each party is in its own way mistaken with respect to the identifications in which these procedures involve them.

I have already dealt with the psychology of the block-universe having a geometrised time representation and explained that we do not encounter its cross-sections in historical order so much as arrange them as states of awareness in their natural logical order as part of the process of awareness. There is, however, another aspect of the matter of psychological interest, that of the specious present. Any goal-seeking device set to home on a moving target needs two related pieces of apparatus, a recorder and a predictor. The combined recorder/predictor has to be optimised from the design point of view so as to optimise the behaviour of the control system. The recorder must not seek to stretch too far into the past or its stored information will tend to be irrelevant; and its predictions must not stretch too far into the future or they will be inaccurate. I would suggest, therefore, that the psychologist's specious present merely represents the temporal limits of the recorder/predictor in our brains and that, on a guess that it is a self-optimising device, the specious present would be itself a variable.

Deep problems would undoubtedly remain respecting moral responsibility and choice in a block-universe representation of reality. Whether we encounter its cross-sections in a historical order or arrange them in logical order as part of the process of overall awareness as outlined in this paper, they are on either view of the matter 'there' and the model provides small opportunity for choice.

In this context I would like to draw attention to a well-known topological model which suggests that the issue may be a good deal more subtle and complicated than would appear on presenting it as a choice between free-will and determinism.

Topologists are concerned with sets of elements which they usually call points. These sets are themselves usually treated as sub-sets of other sets, and so on. Thus a line is thought of as a sub-set of points forming a plane having certain properties of connectivity, etc. The terms 'points', 'lines' and 'planes' are not necessarily to be identified with geometrical elements in the physical sense. In classifying points on a line topologists commonly distinguish between end points, ordinary points and branch points as follows. An end point is one in which every sufficiently small circle centred on it cuts the line in one point only. An ordinary point is one in which every sufficiently small circle cuts the line in precisely two points. A branch point is one in which every sufficiently small circle cuts the line in three or more points (Fig. 3).

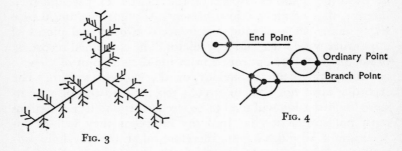

FIG. 3

FIG. 4

An elegant definition then arises of a simple closed curve as a line all of whose points are ordinary points. It occurred to Brouwer to investigate whether it was possible to construct a curve in the form of a line all of whose points are branch points and what sort of an object it would be.

One can see intuitively what it might be like. It would be the limiting case of a feathery sort of structure in which each spicule had lesser spicules on it and they in turn had . . . etc. (Fig. 4).

Could we, however, actually construct such a limiting object? Brouwer proved that he could. Starting with an equi-

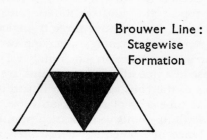

Brouwer Line:
Stagewise
Formation

Fig. 5

lateral triangle we bisect the sides, join the points of bisection to form a triangle having a quarter of the area of the original and remove it, either notionally by colouring it black or physically by cutting it out. (Colouring it black is more convenient.) We repeat the construction in the three triangles remaining. At stage 2 we remove three triangles, leaving nine. At stage 3 we remove nine triangles, leaving twenty-seven, and so on. If we carry this process on indefinitely we do in fact reach the limiting case of a line all of whose points are branch points. The first stages of the construction are illustrated in Fig. 5.

The potential time axis of a block-universe, constructed in such a way that all its points were branch points, and in which a particular choice of branchings constituted an actual time axis, would seem to have a block structure richer in potentiality than actuality and to be capable of accommodating moral responsibility as well. It would appear to be consistent with the view expressed in the form that an act of awareness is coterminous with the arrangement of the information content of its subject matter in natural logical order. For arrangement we must substitute 'choice and arrangement'. Some such Aristotelian conversion of δυνάμις into ἐνεργέια seems inevitable if free-will is to be reconcilable with a block-universe.

Whether the model discussed here will appeal to anyone not a student of topology is perhaps doubtful. But topology is an increasingly important branch of pure mathematics and lay interest in its findings may be on the increase.

ACKNOWLEDGMENTS

In working out the foregoing I have so constantly studied and had recourse to *The Natural Philosophy of Time*, by Professor G. J. Whitrow, that detailed references to its pages would be impracticable. I am also greatly obliged to Professor Whitrow for reading this paper in manuscript and for a number of suggestions and corrections which have greatly improved it.

8

AGENT AND SPECTATOR
THE DOUBLE-ASPECT THEORY

G. N. A. Vesey

ONE of the theories defined in Baldwin's *Dictionary of Philosophy and Psychology*, published in 1901, is 'The Double Aspect Theory'. It is 'the theory of the relation of mind and body, which teaches that mental and bodily facts are parallel manifestations of a single underlying reality'. It 'professes to overcome the onesidedness of materialism and idealism by regarding both series as only different aspects of the same reality, like the convex and the concave views of a curve; or, according to another favourite metaphor, the bodily and the mental facts are really the same facts expressed in different language'.

What was a favourite metaphor in 1901 is still in use. In a talk significantly entitled 'Brain and Will' on the B.B.C. Third Programme ten years ago,[1] and more recently in a contribution to an anthology called *Brain and Mind*,[2] Professor D. M. Mackay has advanced what might be called a 'double language' theory of action. On the one hand there is 'subject-language', to which belong words defined from the standpoint of the actor in the situation, that is, words describing mental activity; on the other, there is 'object-language', comprising words defined from the standpoint of an observer of the situation, words like

---

[1] Reprinted in *Body and Mind*, ed. G. N. A. Vesey (London, Allen & Unwin, 1964), pp. 392–402. Further references to this sourcebook of readings on the body–mind problem will give only its title and the page number.

[2] Ed. J. R. Smythies (London, Routledge & Kegan Paul, 1965), pp. 163–200.

'brain' and 'nerve-cell'. How are these languages related?
Suppose my hand jerks. Either it is because of an involuntary
spasmodic contraction of the muscles, or I jerk it deliberately
(perhaps I am trying to shake off a fly that has settled on it).
In the former case, if I am asked 'Was this of your will?' I
know directly what is meant and can answer 'No'. In the latter
case, the answer to the same question is 'Yes'; and expressions
like 'I willed my hand to jerk' and 'I chose, or decided, to jerk
my hand' are expressions in subject-language, the language of
the actor in the situation. They report my mental activity.
That a subject-language account of the action can be given
does not exclude the possibility of an object-language account
being given, an account of the physical causes of my action,
something happening in my brain. In such a case the mental
activity is not the cause of the brain activity; and the brain
activity is not the cause of the mental activity. This is because
the mental activity and the brain activity that is its immediate
physical concomitant are not two activities, but two aspects of
one and the same activity, and we can only say '*A* causes *B*'
when *A* and *B* are two activities (or events or sets of events).

That, in brief, is Mackay's theory.[1]

Mackay is a scientist, but he is not putting forward this
theory as a scientific one. For instance, he does not say with
what kind of experiments one could test it. In a reply to a
comment, he describes himself as holding 'a view of man as a
(mysterious) unity with multiple aspects'.[2] He is philosophising.

The question I propose to consider is: Is it good philosophy?

First, let us have a look at its origins.

Many early holders of the Double Aspect theory acknowledge a debt to Spinoza. In the Note to Proposition II of Book III
of his *Ethics*[3] Spinoza says that 'the decision of the mind, and
determination of the body, are simultaneous in nature, or
rather one and the same thing, which when considered under
the attribute of thought and explained through the same we

----

[1] He has read this paper and has asked me to add that by two 'languages'
he 'did not mean two translations of the same facts, but two linguistic
projections of the same multi-dimensional situation, which in its full
nature cannot be expressed in either language alone'.

[2] Ibid., p. 200.   [3] *Body and Mind*, p. 58.

call a decision, and when considered under the attribute of extension, and deduced from the laws of motion and rest, we call a determination'.

This theory about decisions and determinations of the body being one and the same thing only considered under different attributes follows from the account Spinoza gives, in Book II of the *Ethics*, of the relation of body and mind. It is not an easy account to follow, owing to some expressions, like 'the object of the idea', being used in unfamiliar ways. One might, at first, suppose that when Spinoza says 'the object of the idea constituting the human mind is the body, and that actually existing', or 'the object of our mind is the existing body and nothing else' he means that we never think of anything but our bodies. But it soon becomes obvious that he is using the expression 'the object of an idea' in a technical sense, connected with his theory of there being one substance with an infinity of attributes, and there being a correspondence between modifications of the spatial attribute of this one substance and modifications of what might be called the 'ideational' attribute. The human mind consists of those ideational modifications which correspond to those spatial modifications that are a human brain. It is to this correspondence that Spinoza is referring when he says that 'the object of the idea constituting the human mind is the body, or a certain mode of extension actually existing, and nothing else'.

Now, it is obvious that people do not go around saying 'There is one substance with an infinity of attributes' without there being some good reason. What was Spinoza trying to explain? What was the problem he was trying to solve?

There is a clue in the note to the Proposition (Prop. XIII of Book II) from which I have been quoting. Spinoza says that his account of the mind as the idea whose object, in his technical sense, is the body, enables us to 'understand not only that the human mind is united to the body, but also what must be understood by the union of the mind and the body'. This suggests that others had been talking about 'the union of the mind and the body' and that there was not agreement as to either its being the case that body and mind are united, or what it means for them to be united.

This is not a misleading suggestion. Leibniz had written on the topic. So had Malebranche. And so had Descartes. In fact, it was Descartes who set the stage for the discussion with his insistence on the distinctness of mind and body.

Descartes's starting-point was the question 'What am I?'. His answer was on the following lines:

> If I think, I cannot be nothing; therefore, I must be something. I can be deceived in thinking that I have bodily attributes, but not in thinking that I am thinking; therefore, the thing I am is essentially a thinking thing. A thing can be made to exist in separation from its non-essential attributes; and a substance is, by definition, a thing which so exists that it needs no other thing in order to exist. Therefore, I am a substance whose essence is thought, distinct from the substance of my body, whose essence is extension.

Descartes's departure from common sense in giving the answer 'a thinking substance' to the question 'What am I?' involved him in departing from common sense in other respects. If I am a person, as 'person' is ordinarily understood, then a sentence such as 'I raised my arm' is perfectly intelligible as it stands; but if I am really a thinking substance then 'I raised my arm' must be regarded as an elliptical way of saying something like 'Something (a 'volition') in the thinking substance which is me somehow caused the arm of the body I call mine to rise'. And, similarly, 'I saw a table' must be regarded as an elliptical way of saying something like 'Something (a 'sensation') in the thinking substance which is me was somehow caused by a table'.

Notice the word 'somehow' in these two analyses: 'A volition somehow caused my arm to rise', 'A sensation was somehow caused by a table'. It seemed easy enough to understand how a movement in one extended substance could cause a movement in another, or how, say, deliberation could lead to decision, and decision to volition; but when it came to an event in a material substance bringing about an event in a spiritual substance, and vice versa, it was another matter.

In the Sixth Discourse of the *Dioptric*[1] Descartes explains how the movements by which an image is formed in our brains cause a sensation in the soul. He writes:

> We must hold that the movements by which the image is formed act directly on our soul *qua* united to the body, and are ordained by Nature to give it such sensations.

And in Part I of *The Passions of the Soul*, Articles 41 and 44,[2] Descartes explains how a volition causes a bodily movement. The last sentence of Article 41 is as follows:

> The action of the soul consists entirely in this, that, simply by willing, it makes the small gland to which it is closely united move in the way requisite for producing the effect aimed at in the volition.

And part of the heading of Article 44 is:

> That each volition is naturally connected with some movement of the gland.

Descartes's explanations of mind–body interaction, accordingly, are in terms of two notions:

(1) the soul's being united to the body, and
(2) its being 'ordained by Nature', or its happening 'naturally' that certain mental events should accompany certain bodily events, and vice versa.

This gave rise to two questions: (*a*) What can it mean to talk of two distinct substances being united? and (*b*) What are we to understand by this reference to 'Nature'?

I do not know of any passage in Descartes's works in which he explains what he means by 'Nature'. But about body and mind being united he wrote, in a letter to Princess Elizabeth dated 21 May 1643:[3]

> As regards the soul and body together, we have merely the

---

[1] *Descartes: Philosophical Writings*, trans. and ed. E. Anscombe and P. T. Geach (London, Nelson, 1954), p. 246.
[2] *Descartes's Philosophical Writings*, trans. Norman Kemp Smith (London, Macmillan, 1952), pp. 298–300.
[3] *Body and Mind*, p. 49.

notion of their union; and on this there depends our notions of the soul's power to move the body, and of the body's power to act on the soul and cause sensations and emotions.

But he was not entirely at ease with this notion. In a letter dated 28 June 1643[1] he wrote:

> What belongs to the union of soul and body can be understood only in an obscure way either by pure intellect or even when the intellect is aided by imagination.

And later in the same letter[2] he wrote:

> It seems to me that the human mind is incapable of distinctly conceiving both the distinction between body and soul and their union, at one and the same time; for that requires our conceiving them as a single thing and simultaneously conceiving them as two things, which is self-contradictory.

Descartes's explanation of mind–body interaction, I said, was in terms of (1) the soul's being united to the body (or there being a union of body and mind), and (2) the concomitance of mental and bodily events being 'ordained by Nature'. Malebranche was not satisfied with either of these notions. In his *Dialogues on Metaphysics and Religion* he put into the mouth of Aristes views very like those of Descartes:[3]

> I believe that God has united my mind to my body so that in consequence of this union my mind and my body can act reciprocally upon one another, in virtue of the natural laws which God always follows very closely.

Then, as Theodore, he commented:[4]

> This word 'union' explains nothing. It is itself in need of explanation. Thus, Aristes, you may like to take vague and general words for reasons. But do not think you can pay us in this coin, for though many people accept it and are satisfied with it, we are not so easily dealt with.

---

[1] *Body and Mind*, p. 51.   [2] Ibid., p. 52.
[3] Ibid., p. 81.   [4] Ibid., p. 82.

Malebranche himself supplied the explanation which he thought the word 'union' needed. He did so by reference to God. He said:[1] 'It is clear that, in the union of soul and body, there is no other bond than the efficacy of divine and immutable decrees', and[2] 'There is no other nature, I mean no other natural laws, than the efficient volitions of the Omnipotent'. He held, in other words, that on the occasion of a bodily event (something happening in the brain as a result of stimulation of the sense-organs) God wills a mental event (a sensation); and on the occasion of a mental event (a volition), God wills a bodily event (whatever happens in the brain which causes a bodily movement). This was known as the theory of 'Occasionalism'.

Leibniz, also, thought that Descartes had left his followers with a problem. Section 33 of his *Discourse on Metaphysics* was entitled 'Explanation of the commerce of the soul and the body, which has passed for inexplicable, or for miraculous'.[3] The 'inexplicable' was a reference to Descartes; the 'miraculous' to Malebranche.[4]

Leibniz, in his generosity, supplied two explanations of what he referred to as 'that great mystery "the union of the soul and the body" '. One was rather like Malebranche's. But instead of God having to produce the concomitance, the 'harmony', of bodily and mental events, by incessant willing, he was allowed to do so in one go, so to speak. The harmony was pre-established. God pre-ordained the history of each soul and of each body (or, rather, of the substances which comprise the reality of each body) in accordance with plans which complemented one another within his overall plan, the blueprint for the best of all possible worlds.

That explanation was intended for his religious readers. For his fellow-philosophers Leibniz had another explanation, in terms of what a substance is. He defined a substance as that which satisfies a description so complete as to distinguish it

---

[1] *Body and Mind*, p. 76.   [2] Ibid., p. 76.   [3] Ibid., p. 66.

[4] For Leibniz's account of the difference between the theory of pre-established harmony and that of occasionalism, see his letter to Arnauld, dated 30 April 1687, in Leibniz, *Discourse on Metaphysics, Correspondence with Arnauld, and Monadology* (Illinois, Open Court, 1902), pp. 184–9.

not only from all other substances in this actual world, but also from substances in all logically possible worlds. Such a description will have to involve a reference to every single thing that makes this actual world the world it is. Otherwise a particular substance in this actual world would not be distinguished from substances like it in the infinite possible worlds which differ from this one in respect of each of the countless things that make this world the world it is. Leibniz describes the consequence of this by saying that each substance 'mirrors' or 'expresses' all the other substances in the world of which it is a part. He then talks of there being 'degrees' of this 'expression'. My soul expresses and is expressed by the substances of my body 'more clearly' than it expresses and is expressed by other substances. This clear expression gives rise to those appearances of mind–body interaction that other philosophers had tried to explain in terms of mind and body being 'united'.

Spinoza's account of 'what must be understood by the union of the mind and body' was like Leibniz's first explanation of their harmonious working in being a God-referring one. But it was also like Leibniz's second explanation in being in terms of the definition of substance. For from Spinoza's definitions of substance, and of God, together with a number of other definitions and axioms, it followed that there could be only one substance, God, with an infinity of attributes. And, as I said earlier, for Spinoza mind and body are modifications of two of the attributes of this one substance, related through the human mind being the 'idea' whose 'object', in a technical sense, is the body.

The double-aspect theory is Spinozism popularised. God, the one substance, is dropped. Attributes, with their substance–philosophy connotation, are replaced by 'aspects'. Double-aspect theorists feel that they are not being more than marginally metaphysical.

There have been a variety of double-aspect theories. It may help in classifying them if I first of all say something rather obvious about our everyday concept of an 'aspect'. It is, I suggest, part of this everyday concept that there should be three 'elements': (*a*) that which presents the aspects, (*b*) the aspects themselves, and (*c*) the person to whom the aspects are presented. All double-aspect theories depart from this threefold pattern to some extent. Let us take (*a*), that which presents the aspects, first. For Spinoza, as I said, thought and extension were the two known attributes of a substance with an infinity of attributes. Corresponding to this, in double-aspect theories, would be the idea of an underlying reality of which states of consciousness and brain processes would be two aspects.

In his contribution to a book called *Human Senses and Perception*[1] Professor R. J. Hirst writes:

> We can now provisionally state a double aspect theory of 'mental' activities. It is that such activities are 'whole' activities of the person *qua* living organism, and that they present two aspects: an outer one which consists of a complex of brain activity and is on principle, at least, externally observable; and an inner one, the various experiences which the person has, and can introspect, in the actual performance of these activities. This latter aspect is available only to the person concerned; it is the actor's view as it were, not the spectator's, of the whole activity.

Hirst talks about 'whole activities', but I do not think he wishes to suggest that there is really some third thing besides the two aspects. He writes:[2]

> Further theoretical development is required, even though it is an advance to regard conscious (or introspective) experiences and brain activity as co-ordinate aspects of whole activities of the person rather than as cause and effect. For it might still be supposed that they were aspects of some third thing, of some process of a different character forever unknown to us except for its misleading appearance in these aspects. And then one would have a theory as uneconomical as Interactionism in postulating a special order of being.

A question that very naturally arises, and has in fact been asked, is: What is achieved by calling states of consciousness and brain processes 'aspects' if the word 'aspect' is deprived of its ordinary meaning by the removal of one of its elements,

[1] By G. M. Wyburn, R. W. Pickford and R. J. Hirst (Edinburgh and London, Oliver & Boyd, 1964), p. 321.
[2] Ibid.

that which presents the aspects. This is a question which was recently asked by Professor C. J. Ducasse in his book, *The Belief in a Life after Death*,[1] but it was asked in almost the same terms about seventy-five years ago by Karl Pearson in his *Grammar of Science*.[2] Pearson wrote:

> What the actual relations between the psychical and physical aspects of thought are, we do not know, and, as in all such cases, it is best to directly confess our ignorance. It is no use, indeed it is only dangerous, in the present state of our knowledge with regard to psychology and the physics of the brain, to fill the void of ignorance by hypotheses which can neither by proved nor refuted. Thus if we say that thought and motion are the same thing seen from different sides, we make no real progress in our analysis for we can form no conception whatever as to what the nature in itself of this thing may be.

I shall return to this question of what it is which presents the aspects in a moment. First I must say something about the third element in our everyday concept of an aspect – the person to whom the aspects are presented. The situation here is somewhat complicated. Double-aspect theorists tend to start out with the idea of there being a person, or 'subject', to whom the aspects are presented, but then they seem to have second thoughts when they realise that this has left them with an entity distinct from both states of consciousness and brain processes. At this point they tend to equate the person, or subject, with the successive states of consciousness. C. A. Strong, for instance, in his book, *Why the Mind has a Body*,[3] writes:

> The antithesis between consciousness and its immediate objects is fallacious. The things we are immediately conscious of are always modifications of consciousness itself, and the existence of consciousness is their existence.

It would seem, from what I have said, that double-aspect theorists are left with only one of the three elements that go to make up our everyday concept of anaspect – the aspects them-

---

[1] Illinois, Thomas, 1961, p. 72.   [2] *Body and Mind*, p. 215.
[3] New York, The Macmillan Co., 1903, p. 289.

selves. This departure from our everyday concept of an aspect, particularly the omission from the scene of that which presents the aspects, leaves the theory considerably weakened. It is remarked, in Baldwin's *Dictionary*, that 'the theory, while professing to harmonise materialism and spiritualism, occupies a position of somewhat unstable equilibrium between the two, and shows a tendency in different expositors to relapse into the one or the other'. This relapse takes the form of allowing the aspects themselves to play double roles. Either the states of consciousness are given the role of the things that present the aspects, or the brain processes are given this role. The former theory may be called 'psychical monism' or 'spiritualism', the latter, 'physical monism' or 'materialism'.

The view of the psychical monist is that we do not know the nature of things as they are in themselves, so, for all we know, the brain, and all the other things we apprehend as material, may, in themselves, be mental. On this supposition our apprehending them as material is to be explained by reference to the manner in which we apprehend them. Since we apprehend them by sense-perception they appear to us as material.

The view of the physical monist is that mental states may in fact be brain processes. On this supposition our apprehending them as mental is to be explained by reference to the manner in which we apprehend them. Since I apprehend my brain states by introspection it is only to be expected that I should apprehend them as introspectible, that is, as mental.

Historically, psychical monism has priority, so I shall start by saying something about it. Psychical monists of the latter half of the nineteenth century usually claim Kant as their inspiration. Kant had said that we can know nothing about things in themselves, and that he could, therefore, very well admit the possibility[1]

that the substance which in relation to our outer sense possesses extension is in itself the possessor of thoughts, and that these thoughts can by means of its own inner sense be consciously represented. In this way, what in one relation is

[1] *Critique of Pure Reason*, trans. Norman Kemp Smith (London, Macmillan, 1934), A359.

entitled corporeal would in another relation be at the same
time a thinking being, whose thoughts we cannot intuit,
though we can indeed intuit their signs in the field of appearance. Accordingly, the thesis that only souls, as particular
kinds of substances, think, would have to be given up; and
we should have to fall back on the common expression that
men think, that is, that the very same being which, as outer
appearance, is extended, is, in itself, internally a subject, and
is not composite, but is simple and thinks.

For Kant this was a mere speculation, something we could
never know to be true or false. But his followers took it very
seriously. Perhaps the best known of the English psychical
monists was W. K. Clifford. In a paper in *Mind* in 1878,[1] he
advanced the famous 'mind–stuff' theory.[2] The article was
entitled 'On the Nature of Things-in-Themselves'. I have
already mentioned one of the American psychical monists,
C. A. Strong. Chapter xii of his book has the title 'Things-in-
Themselves: their nature'. Another was Morton Prince, who
later became famous for his work with the split-personality girl,
Sally Beauchamp. In his book, *The Nature of Mind and Human
Automatism* (1885),[3] he advanced a restricted version of the
theory. Clifford, like Spinoza (*Ethics*, ii. xiii), held there to be
a mental side to everything. Even inorganic matter had its
portion of 'mind–stuff'. Morton Prince, on the other hand, was
content with only brains being in themselves mental. He
accounted for these mental realities appearing as material ones
on the following lines: Suppose that brain processes were, in
themselves, states of consciousness, such as thoughts and feelings.
And suppose we were to look at another person's thoughts and
feelings. We would expect them to appear to us as visible
things, since it is through our organ of vision that we are
affected by them. The only way we could apprehend them is
objectively as visible neural vibrations, whereas the only way
the person whose thoughts or feelings they were, could apprehend them, is as they are in themselves, namely thoughts and
feelings.

[1] *Body and Mind*, pp. 165–71.
[2] Not to be confused with the 'mind–dust' theory.
[3] *Body and Mind*, pp. 187–96.

William McDougall, in his book *Body and Mind*,[1] distinguishes between Spinoza's doctrine and that of Clifford and Strong, calling the former 'identity-hypothesis *A*', the latter, 'identity-hypothesis *B*'. Among other holders of 'identity-hypothesis *B*' he mentions is G. T. Fechner, who is best known to first-year psychology students for his work on the measurement of mental states. Fechner, like Clifford, held an unrestricted version of identity-hypothesis *B*. McDougall comments:

> Fechner's view necessarily involves the assumption that all the objects and events composing the physical world are, like the processes of the cortex of our brains, the outward appearances of what is really consciousness or consciousnesses. For to set certain of the processes of the brain apart from all other physical processes, attributing to them alone this peculiar relation to consciousness, would be but to deepen the mystery of the psycho-physical relation. Fechner, far from shrinking from this necessary implication, revelled in it; and his two chief lines of endeavour were, on the one hand to provide some empirical evidence of the psychical nature of all that we call physical processes, and on the other to show how pleasing and inspiring the world becomes when thus regarded.[2]

Whereas psychical monism had its roots in transcendental idealism, physical monism had its roots in behaviouristic psychology – or perhaps I should say in the attempts by behaviouristic psychologists to say something about sensations. Psychologists like E. C. Tolman and E. G. Boring, in the United States, and C. S. Myers in Britain, writing in the early 1930s, toyed with various versions of the identity hypothesis. The philosopher Roy Wood Sellars, in his book *The Philosophy of Physical Realism*,[3] came close to being a physical monist. He wrote:

[1] London, Methuen & Co. (1911), ch. xi.

[2] William James discusses this last aspect of Fechner's psychical monism in the chapter on Fechner in his *Pluralistic Universe*. For James's reactions to the theory, see W. T. Bush, 'William James and Pan-Psychism', *Columbia Studies in the History of Ideas*, vol. ii, 1925.

[3] New York, Macmillan, 1932, p. 414.

Consciousness is the qualitative dimension of a brain-event. It is the patterned brain-event as sentient. It is because of its status that we, as conscious, participate in the being of brain-events. Here, and here alone, are we, as conscious beings, on the inside of reality.

But the theory has come to fruition only in the last ten years or so with the articles 'Is consciousness a brain process?' by the psychologist U. T. Place, 1956, and 'Sensations and Brain Processes' by the philosopher, Professor J. J. C. Smart, 1959.[1]

Judging from Smart's paper the part played by Kant's doctrine of unknowable things-in-themselves in psychical monism is played, in physical monism, by a doctrine about the 'reference' of the expressions a person uses. If a flash of lightning is in fact an electrical discharge then, whether I know this or not, in talking about a flash of lightning I am talking about an electrical discharge. Similarly, if sensations are in fact brain processes then in talking about sensations I am talking about brain processes, and it cannot be objected to the identity hypothesis that, since a man may know about his sensations without knowing about his brain processes, the things he is talking about cannot be his brain processes.

And the part played, in psychical monism, by Morton Prince's argument about states of consciousness necessarily being apprehended by others as sensible things, is played, in physical monism, by a corresponding argument about brain states necessarily being apprehended, by the person whose brain it is, as states of consciousness. Thus R. J. Hirst[2] writes that the difference between conscious experience and brain activity

> lies in and is due to the radical difference in modes of access. . . . There is an immense difference between inner private awareness of one's own 'mental' activities by performing, experiencing, and introspecting them, and the outer public awareness which some other person or even oneself

---

[1] Both these articles are reprinted in *The Philosophy of Mind*, ed. V. C. Chappell (New Jersey, Prentice-Hall, 1962). The second article is reprinted in *Body and Mind*, pp. 424–36.

[2] *Human Senses and Perception*, p. 322.

may obtain by use of sense-organs and scientific instruments. And it is because of this difference that the one event or activity presents different appearances.

In reading the works of psychical monists and physical monists I have looked for an argument that would support one theory without there being a corresponding argument to support the other. I have failed to find one. My impression is that for any argument for, or against, one theory, a parallel argument can be found for, or against, the other.

Consider, for instance, the desire for a monistic scheme of the universe. McDougall mentions this in connexion with psychical monism. He writes:[1]

Many philosophers seem to experience this desire to conceive the universe as at bottom consisting of only one kind of real being; and not a few claim that this desire is a demand that our intellectual nature inevitably makes, and one that carries with it a guarantee of the validity of the monistic interpretation. Closely connected with this in many minds is the conviction that a universe monistically conceived, that is, conceived as a unitary whole of which all the parts are of one nature, is infinitely nobler than one consisting of ultimate real beings of diverse natures.

It does not seem to me far-fetched to regard what Smart says at the beginning of his paper 'Sensations and Brain Processes' as an expression of this same desire for a monistic scheme of the universe:

Sensations, states of consciousness, do seem to be the one sort of thing left outside the physicalist picture, and for various reasons I just cannot believe that this can be so. That everything should be explicable in terms of physics . . . except the occurrence of sensations seems to me to be frankly unbelievable.

At its crudest, we are asked to believe, by holders of one theory, that material events are really mental; by holders of the other, that mental events are really material; without there

---

[1] McDougall, *Body and Mind*, pp. 145–6.

being any argument for one theory for which there is not a corresponding argument for the other. What is more, we are asked to believe these theories without even being told what it would be to find out that they were true or false. According to Kant, his speculation could never be known to be true or false, for things-in-themselves are, by definition, the things to which the categories of the understanding, whose application to 'appearances' yields knowledge, do not apply. And physical monists never say what are the criteria of the alleged 'strict identity' of sensations and brain processes.[1] It is as if we were asked to believe something without being told what.

The situation is no better if we revert to a form of double-aspect theory in which neither of the aspects is given the role of that which presents the aspects. If the objection to psychophysical parallelism is that it involves a colossal coincidence, it is hard to see how a double-aspect theory in which there is nothing of which the aspects are aspects escapes a similar objection. All we are left with is an empty metaphor.

There is only one thing to do. We must go back to the person who started us on our journey, Descartes, and see whether the directions he gave us were reliable. I do not propose to comment directly on his manner of answering the question 'What am I?'. It will be sufficient for my purposes to consider the paradoxical views to which his dualism led him.

I shall begin with perception. A consequence of Descartes's view that I am really a mental substance is that 'I saw a table' must be regarded as an elliptical way of saying something like 'Something (a 'sensation') in the mental substance which is me was somehow caused by a table'. It is this 'sensation' which physical monists assert to be identical with, or an aspect of, a brain process. They do not always use the word 'sensation'. At the Los Angeles Conference on 18 to 22 March 1966,

---

[1] This is not quite true. Anthony Quinton, in *Brain and Mind*, ed. J. R. Smythies (London, Routledge & Kegan Paul, 1965), says that the criterion is that of rough spatio-temporal coincidence, supported by concomitant variation of properties (p. 214). His reason for saying that mental states and events have 'a real position' in space is that if they had not they could not be individuated (p. 211). It seems not to have occurred to him that experiences are individuated by reference to the people whose experiences they are.

Professor Herbert Feigl used the expressions 'the qualities of immediate experience', 'the "raw-feels" of experience', and 'raw-feel qualities'. He said: 'The qualities of immediate experience are the subjective or private aspect of neurophysiological processes'. The term 'raw-feels' he had got from the psychologist, E. C. Tolman, to whom I referred earlier. Tolman had said:[1] 'Raw feels may be the way physical realities are intrinsically.'

The idea behind the use of the expressions 'the qualities of immediate experience', 'raw-feel qualities', etc., seems to be that redness, hotness, sweetness, and so on, are not qualities of the things we see, feel, and taste, but are qualities of our apprehension of them. This idea is well expressed in the following quotation from the Cambridge psychologist, D. E. Broadbent's book, *Behaviour*:[2]

> When a man sees blue, his experience is intensely real to him, but the essence of it cannot be communicated. All he can do is to say a word which labels that experience, so that he can tell other people whether or not some fresh situation gives him this same quality of awareness. No man can tell whether another is really feeling the same as he does himself when he looks at a colour.

Popular though this idea – the idea that colour words are words we use to label experiences – may be, it is open to an objection. What is meant by the word 'experience'? Is to say that two people are having different experiences to say, for instance, that to one of them something looks blue, but to the other it looks green? If this answer is given, it cannot then be said that the words 'blue' and 'green' which occur in the explanation of how experiences are differentiated are words that we use to label experiences. That would be circular. 'Blue' cannot be the name of the experience of something looking blue.

To this it might be replied that the words 'blue' and 'green' are like the words 'weary' and 'giddy' in being words which primarily apply to our feelings but which we often use to

[1] *Purposive Behaviour in Animals and Men* (London, C.U.P., 1932), pp. 426–7.

[2] London, Methuen, 1961.

describe things. A weary road, a giddy height; similarly, a blue sky, a green leaf. We 'project' the colour, which is really a quality of our experience, onto the object that arouses the experience. To say that a painting is blue is like saying that it is melancholy. It is not objectively blue any more than it is objectively melancholy.[1]

The trouble about this reply is that it overlooks an important difference between words like 'weary', 'giddy', and 'melancholy' on the one hand, and 'blue' and 'green' on the other. It is not the case that the only uses we have for the words 'weary', 'giddy', and 'melancholy' are to describe people's feelings and, by 'projection', the things they feel about (roads, heights, pictures). We use them to describe people. People can *be* weary, giddy, and melancholy; and what is more, they can be seen to be so. This is important, for if we had no use of these words to describe people it is hard to see how we could come to have a use to describe people's feelings. I do not mean that feeling weary is feeling one's weariness, feeling dizzy, feeling one's dizziness, etc.[2] I mean that people would not come to say 'I feel weary' if there were no possibility of noticing that this is what other people say when they are weary. One could not notice this if people could not be seen to be weary. In this linguistic way the possibility of feeling weary depends on the possibility of being weary.

But if 'blue' and 'green' are the names of experiences, what is to correspond to the experience of which 'blue' is the name as being weary corresponds to feeling weary? I do not know. And so, if 'blue' and 'green' are primarily the names of experiences, I do not know how they get into our language in the first place.

---

[1] R. M. Chisholm, *Perceiving – A Philosophical Study* (New York, Cornell U.P., 1957), p. 138.

[2] A. R. White, in *Attention* (Oxford, Blackwell, 1964), p. 90, says that in feeling inclined to do something and in being inclined to do something, it is not the same inclination which is felt on one occasion and unfelt on another. I do not know whether he would contend, also, that feeling depressed is not feeling the depression one is in (cf. P. F. Strawson, *Individuals* (London, Methuen, 1959), pp. 108–9) and that feeling hot is not feeling the heat of one's body (cf. D. Armstrong, *Bodily Sensations*, London, Routledge & Kegan Paul, p. 39). On the last of these, see my 'Berkeley and Sensations of Heat', *Phil. Review*, vol. lxix (1960), pp. 201–10.

Are they even derivatively the names of experiences? Broadbent writes of blue, not as a quality of what we are aware of, but as a 'quality of awareness'. I do not know what to make of this. I know what is meant by describing awareness as visual or auditory, but what is meant by describing it as blue I do not know. Like G. E. Moore, in his neglected paper on 'The Subject-matter of Psychology', it seems to me that there is no difference, so far as the awareness is concerned, between being aware of blue and being aware of green.[1] The awareness is the same although what one is aware of, and presumably what is going on in the optic region of the brain, is not the same. If by the term 'sensation' is meant the awareness, rather than what one is aware of, then any theory that sensations and brain processes are identical, related as aspects, etc., is a non-starter. Awareness is characterless.

Perhaps all this will become clearer if we turn from a consideration of the consequences of Descartes's dualism for the philosophy of perception to its consequences for the philosophy of action.

Imagine the following case. We see people running. First Smith. Then Jones. Then the police. Smith is shooting at the police, obviously trying to shake them off. But is Jones a good citizen, trying to catch Smith to hand him over to the police? Or is he, also, running away from them? If we could see what he did when he caught up with Smith, that would settle the matter. But it does not become true (or false) that he was chasing Smith only when his behaviour makes this indubitable. It was true that he was chasing Smith, and not running away from the police, while he was still chasing him. Reflection on this may lead one to ask: 'His chasing Smith does not consist in his bodily motions, since they are equally in accord with his running away from the police. In what, then, does it consist?'

The answer to this question that would be given by Descartes refers to a mental occurrence – a decision or act of will. It is this mental occurrence that is alleged by the double-aspect

[1] *Body and Mind*, pp. 236–45. See esp. p. 238. Cf. C. J. Ducasse in *The Philosophy of G. E. Moore*, ed. P. A. Schilpp (Chicago, Northwestern University, 1942), pp. 223–51.

theorist to be the subjective aspect of the brain process that causes the running. But what decision, or act of will? Presumably the decision to chase. Chasing, then, consists in running, having decided to chase. And if Jones had been running away from the police, the volition that, along with the bodily motions of running, would constitute his running away, would be the volition to run away.

I began this lecture by saying something about D. M. Mackay's 'double-language' theory of action. Mackay talks of a 'subject-language' comprising words defined from the standpoint of myself as the actor in the situation, that is, words describing mental activity. Taken literally, the implication of this is that the meaning of the word 'chasing' is taught to a child by pointing at someone running and saying 'Chasing consists in this, plus having a volition to chase'. But it could not be taught in this way, any more than 'blue' could be taught as the name of an experience. Volitions are as characterless as experiences; they are accessible only through what they are volitions to do. To explain 'chasing' we would point at the police; to explain 'running away', at Smith. The child would soon pick up our way of talking.

But surely, it will be said, there must be a mental difference between Jones chasing and Jones running away, for how else could Jones tell which he was doing when his behaviour is equally in accord with one as with the other? And, it will be said, this mental thing is what is identical with, or an aspect of, his brain processes.

Well, how can Jones tell what he is doing? In one sense, of course, nothing is easier. He tells us what he is doing by saying 'I'm chasing Smith'. But that is not what is behind the question. How does Jones know what he is doing?

This seems to invite an answer on the following lines: He observes, by introspection, certain mental events which characteristically precede or accompany his chasing someone, and concludes that this is what he is doing. This is the sort of answer B. F. Skinner gives in his book, *Science and Human Behaviour*.[1] It is, on the other hand, just the sort of answer Wittgenstein was attacking in his 1946–7 Philosophy of

[1] New York, Macmillan, 1953, p. 262.

Psychology lectures when he talked about the asymmetry of psychological with non-psychological verbs. Applied to verbs of action, what Wittgenstein said would amount to this: Other people may know what I am doing, but what I am doing is not something I know. I do not conclude or infer that I am doing what I am doing. The utterance of first-person psychological verbs is not based on observation.

On what, then, is it based?

It might be said that we have a special faculty of knowing things without observation, and that it is through the use of this faculty that a person can say what he is doing. But this merely mystifies.

Should we say that the utterance of first-person psychological verbs is not based on anything? Should we say that in one sense of 'what I am doing', if (knowing what I am talking about, and not intending to deceive) I *say* 'I am chasing Smith', then I *am* chasing Smith? This would be the sense of 'what I am doing' in which even if, unbeknown to me, Smith had gone in the opposite direction, I could still be said to be chasing him. That is what I am doing. And it makes no sense to add 'or, at least, that is what I think I am doing'. What I am doing, in this sense, is not anything about which I can be said to be right or wrong. Only other people can be right or wrong about it.

If this is said, then the following question seems to arise: How is it that, having learnt what 'chasing' and 'running away' are by observing in what circumstances the words are used by others in first-person and third-person statements, a person starts using them himself, in first-person statements, but not on the basis of observation of his behaviour or introspection of his mental condition? Is not this remarkable?

Yes; if you look at it in a certain light, it is remarkable.

9

MIND AND BRAIN
THE IDENTITY HYPOTHESIS

R. J. Hirst

Life Science Library now claims to examine 'the most complex of all biological organs: the human mind', and scientists quite commonly make no distinction between mind and brain – they delight in talking about the brain classifying, decoding, perceiving, deciding or giving orders. And while resisting the conceptual muddle involved in talking of the brain doing what persons do, the identity hypothesis tries to provide a philosophically respectable basis for the equation of mind and brain, maintaining that 'mind' is just a term for a group of activities and dispositions, and that these in turn are in some sense to be identified with brain activities or traces. On the other hand, from the point of view of religion and traditional philosophy the suggestion is completely unplausible – creative or inventive thought, and aesthetic, moral or religious experiences seem so far removed from mechanical or physiological processes that a good deal of softening up is necessary if any kind of identity theory is to get a fair hearing. This softening up is best carried out by considering the difficulties in the main rival philosophical view, interactionism.

Interactionism has two main theses:

(i) The dualist hypothesis that the human mind is one entity or substance and the human body is another. This was put most strongly by Descartes, who claimed that the mind and body were substances of diametrically opposite qualities and were distinct in that they did not depend on each other in any way for pursuing their essential roles of consciousness in the one case and space-occupying in the other. In a milder form this thesis involves the claim that it makes sense to suppose that the mind can exist on its own independent of the body. On either version the true person or human being, the essential you, is the conscious being, the mind (or soul), and this is perhaps only temporarily lodged in the body – though claims about present and future existence are not necessary to philosophical mind/body dualism.

(ii) The interactionist thesis – that while the mind or essential person is lodged in the body, it interacts with it. The body acts on the mind in sense perception including pain and other sensations, in the effects of gland secretions, drugs, drinking, fever, etc.; conversely the mind acts on the body in voluntary deliberate action and decision, in the bodily effects of emotions or thoughts (e.g. fear making one's hair standing on end), or in psychosomatic diseases.

Now for the difficulties, first in the dualist thesis.

(i) There is no evidence for mind as a mental substance. It is certainly not open to overt public observation nor is it available to private observation by introspection. Introspection can reveal qualities of sensations or other experiences and, in conjunction with memory, an awareness of a continuing self; but it does not show that the experiences are mental in the sense of being activities of a mental substance or reveal that the continuing self or ego is a mental substance. So far as introspection is concerned, the self may be the biological organism, a unity at once conscious and corporeal.

(ii) It is unsatisfactory to divide a person up into two parts, a mental and a physical substance. It is contrary to Occam's Razor, i.e. to the principle of economy in explanations, to suppose two substances where one would do, i.e. when the concept of a person as a unity with both mental and physical characteristics would fill the bill. Mr P. F. Strawson goes further in defending this position and argues that if persons were just bare mental egos with private experiences and if we could not observe them as physical organisms, we should not be able to identify them or ascribe experiences to them.[1] Not infrequently in the history of mankind, however, invisible gods,

[1] P. F. Strawson, *Individuals* (Methuen, 1959), pp. 104 ff.

spirits, or demons have been thought to take over trees, stones, bushes, idols or bodies of mediums or madmen; similarly it seems possible to claim that persons as non-physical minds animate bodies in this life and can be identified by what they make these bodies say and do, also that from this bodily behaviour we are entitled to attribute to them experiences similar to our own. But although this is conceivable, it seems uneconomical and so theoretically unsatisfactory. Strawson also claims that according to our concepts of them a person's activities and states are likewise of this double nature, i.e. are both mental and physical, are both privately and publicly observed, and that to ignore this is to ignore the structure of our language and concepts. But does this matter? – it may be that our language and concepts are just scientifically or philosophically naïve. Hence the fundamental anti-dualist contention must be that of economy.

(iii) A rigid distinction of mind and matter generally is unsatisfactory. It exaggerates the difference between conscious mental activity and mechanical processes by taking a very simple-minded view of the latter. Dualists, even 20th-century ones, tend to argue as if the highest kinds of physical processes, i.e. machines, were just clockwork. But there are now electronic computers, translating machines, missiles which 'home' on the target, machines that can find their way through a maze or play chess, and others that imitate animal behaviour in their plasticity, i.e. their ability to reach a goal by different routes according to circumstances. Admittedly there is still a range of human experiences and behaviour – creative or inventive or artistic – which is not fully covered: machines have to be programmed and have no consciousness, emotions or self-awareness; their chess playing lacks insight and their translation is pretty feeble, e.g. the machine that translated 'out of sight, out of mind', as 'invisible imbécile'. All the same there are now important modifications in our concept of machine which greatly reduce the difference between mental and mechanical processes.

Furthermore the matter related to mind is not a machine at all but the living brain; this is immensely more complex than electronic computers and so may be adequate, when we fully understand it, for explaining mental activities.

(iv) There are special difficulties in the stricter dualism of Descartes and others. If the essence of mind is thought or consciousness what happens when the mind or person ceases to think or be conscious, as in a coma or dreamless sleep? Can a substance continue to exist when its essential characteristic is not being exercised? More difficult is the modern psychological notion of the unconscious mind as a governing factor in human behaviour, e.g. hysterical paralysis, Freudian forgetting, wishful thinking, rationalisation and unrecognised motives generally. On the Cartesian view unconscious mind must be a contradiction in terms; and if unconscious mental activities are really brain activities then they occur in material substance. Again the mind as a substance should be able to pursue its essential activity of thinking without having to rely on any physical activity, but all the evidence seems to show that a properly functioning brain is essential for thought and consciousness. Concussion, drugs, diseases and other kinds of brain damage can prevent thought.

Difficulties in the interactionism claimed are:

(i) So far as perceiving is concerned it involves the representative theory – the mind is aware of mental sense-data which are the effects of and represent the external physical world. The epistemological difficulties here are well known – how can we ever tell that there is an external world or what it is like if we can never observe it directly? A further special problem is: how can mental sensations or sense-data represent or resemble properties in the physical world if mind is so different from matter? Thus how can a non-spatial mind represent spatial properties? Even if, like Dr J. R. Smythies,[1] we talk of mental space, we have to make causal relations between mental and physical space plausible. Contiguity in space and in time are involved in the normal concept of cause, and physicists jib at action-at-a-distance within one space let alone action between spaces.

(ii) On any interaction theory the alleged causal relation between mind and body is mysterious and inexplicable. On

[1] J. R. Smythies, ed., *Brain and Mind* (Routledge & Kegan Paul, 1965), p. 252.

dualist principles mind and body are complete opposites so that one can conceive of no way in which they can work on each other. Matter can work on matter by impact or by electrical or other forms of physical energy; but if mind or consciousness are not in physical space they cannot act on physical energy or be acted on by it. Indeed mental force works by persuasion[1] either by rational argument or by emotional appeals, but one can no more persuade a brain cell than one can hit a dream image. Further, one is aware of mental events by introspection, a private mode of awareness, while physical events are open to public scientific observation. One has here two distinct series of events: the link between them, the supposed causal inter-action, is open to neither means of observation, so what is the evidence for it?

But you might say, surely perceiving and deliberate action occur; there is plenty of evidence of interaction, and its occur-rence is just a brute fact we have to accept. But the evidence is really of a correlation, the concomitant variation of conscious and physical events, and such a variation does not require a direct causal link between the variables. Often streaks may flash across the T.V. screen while a closely correlated crackling is heard in the loudspeakers: but though they are correlated they do not cause each other, the noise does not cause the streaks or vice versa. Likewise if mental and cerebral processes are identical or are two different aspects of one basic process, then there will equally be a close correlation and concomitant variation between them without a causal relation between them. Alcohol may act on the brain or excitation of the retina set up activity in the visual cortex, but one does not need another causal link between cerebral activity and conscious experiences. Perhaps then the reason the alleged mind–body interaction is so mysterious is that it never really occurs.

For reasons like these, all versions of the identity theory agree in rejecting dualism and maintain something like the Aristo-telian view that the soul or mind is a function or capacity of the organism as a whole. Thus in referring to a person's mind one is referring to certain types of activity, ability or disposition; when one says that so and so has an acute mind, or has some-

[1] Cf. J. Passmore, *Philosophical Reasoning* (Duckworth, 1961), p. 54.

thing in mind, or is in two minds, or is giving his mind to something, one refers to ability, to intention, to being undecided, and to concentrating his attention. As the term 'mind' is just a shorthand for referring to mental activities or to tendencies or abilities to perform them, it is on mental activities that philosophical investigation must concentrate. First one must differentiate mental activities from physical ones. This can be done roughly for our present purposes by saying that physical activities are essentially observable and differentiated from each other and from mental activities by their overt characteristics; whereas the typical distinguishing feature of mental activities is that they involve and are differentiated by conscious experiences and self-awareness. (Exceptionally they may be unconscious, i.e. be just brain activity, but even then they are best described as if they were conscious.) Mental activities also involve bodily processes, mainly brain activity, as well as conscious experiences, and hence I refer to them as whole activities, activities of the person as a whole.

The mind–body problem is now to be restated as: what is the relation between the conscious experiences and bodily processes in mental activities? If we suppose that there is a causal interaction between the conscious and the brain processes then it is difficult to avoid being pushed back into dualism. For if the conscious processes are effects of brain processes they must be different from them, and yet there seems no room for them in the physical organism – which tempts one to suppose that they are activities in a mental substance. To avoid this, the identity theory says with varying degrees of baldness that the conscious experiences just are brain processes.

I suppose even balder would be the behaviourist claim that mental activities themselves simply are cerebral or organic activity, but this is really reinterpreting the term 'mental activity' by saying that what distinguishes mental activity from physical is only that it is not overt or readily detectable: thus thinking is sub-vocal speech or silent soliloquy, perceiving is reacting to stimulation of the sense organs, dreaming or other imagery is reacting as if the sense organs were being stimulated and so on. But this is to ignore the main features I mentioned of mental activities, namely that they involve conscious experiences, feelings, sensations, images, and that these differentiate one such activity from another. Where the identity theory differs is that it tries to give due weight to these conscious experiences.

A well-known version of the theory is that of Professor Feigl.[1] He points out that there is no logical or definitional identity between mental and physical (or cerebral) concepts – i.e. no pair of terms from the two groups means the same – but maintains that there is, however, an empirical or contingent identity between the 'raw-feels' of direct experience and neural processes.

By 'raw-feels' he means pains and other bodily sensations, feelings of depression or elation, etc., visual, auditory and similar sensations; he claims that these are the objects of direct experience, i.e. of knowledge by acquaintance. The identity claimed with neural processes is really a two-stage one, i.e. the 'raw feels' are 'identifiable with the referents of certain . . . concepts of molar behaviour theory and these in turn . . . are identifiable with the referents of some neurophysiological concepts',[2] or in another version[3] 'what is . . . *knowable by acquaintance* is identical with the object of *knowledge by description* provided by molar behaviour theory and this is in turn identical with what the science of neuro-physiology *describes* (or . . . will describe . . .) as processes in the central nervous system'. I think that the jargon of 'molar behaviour theory' is unfortunate here, apart from suggesting that it is all something to do with one's teeth. What we know by description (mainly by inference from speech and other behaviour and from the physical situation) is that the person is having a pain, thinking of his lunch, feeling depressed, seeing a red after-image, etc. They are in fact familiar experiences and activities. To suggest that knowledge of these is part of behaviour theory on a par with talking about drives, instincts and repression is misleading. Also unfortunate is the talk of 'raw feels', partly

[1] H. Feigl, 'The "Mental" and the "Physical"' in *Minnesota Studies in the Philosophy of Science*, vol. ii (University of Minnesota Press, 1958), pp. 370–497.

[2] Ibid., p. 445.

[3] Ibid., p. 446.

because thoughts as well as feels are involved, and partly because 'raw' and 'knowledge by acquaintance' (i.e. direct awareness without any process of inference) suggest simple basic sense-data, a 'given' on which all other knowledge is inferentially based. But what are being identified with brain processes are really the various conscious experiences of a person; these may not be 'raw' at all. They may be the results of unconscious inferences and psychological adjustment, and their contents may not be just sensory qualia, i.e. not be like sense-data. In perceiving they will be the contents of perceptual consciousness, i.e. seeming awareness of objects, persons, etc.

The real points of differentiation of the two terms of the identity relation are these: the conscious experiences are private (available only to the person concerned); awareness of them is not obtained by mediation of sense-organs or instruments, and does not involve scientific theory and concepts. By contrast, the brain processes they are to be identified with are public (available to any suitably equipped person, even to the person concerned by use of mirrors and electroencephalograms – what Feigl happily sums up as an 'autocerebroscope'); they are to be observed by means of sense-organs and instruments, and their characterisation involves scientific theories and inferences, e.g. from electroencephalogram traces.

One must note that the identity should strictly be between events, i.e. having certain conscious experiences = having a pain = having certain nerve and brain processes. Feigl tends to talk as if the contents of the experiences are identical with the states described in mental activity or molar behaviour terms and hence with the brain processes, i.e. the sense-data, the qualia only, are identical with the processes. This seems a category mix-up and involves an extra theoretical jump in supposing that the contents and the consciousness are really separable. It also suggests that what we are aware of in conscious experiences are the brain processes, i.e. sense-data = brain processes. This equation is cruder and less plausible than the tripartite form: viz. experiences are identifiable with mental activity and that in turn with brain processes.

Next we may ask what this empirical identity between 'raw-feels' and neural processes amounts to. One view would be that it is a theoretical claim, a scientific hypothesis in fact, to explain the close correlation of conscious experiences and neural processes. The essential points of correlation are: (1) that so far as we know, conscious experiences do not occur without corresponding brain activity; (2) a given conscious experience and the associated brain activity are correlated in time and space, being at the same time in the same person; (3) there is a more detailed correlation, in that so far as we can judge from electroencephalograms and other devices, activity in certain parts of the brain starts and stops as a sensory experience or a mental activity like working out a problem starts and stops, and it varies with variations in the experience, at least as far as a number of sensations is concerned. This identity proposal simply claims then that the conscious experience and the correlated neural process must be regarded as one and the same thing, such a hypothesis being the most economical one. The apparent or qualitative difference in the two processes thus identified must be attributed to the different ways by which they are known – direct acquaintance in the case of experiences and scientific knowledge in the case of neural processes.

Some theorists are not satisfied with this; thus Professor Sellars[1] claims that an identity theory that only goes this far would be trite because 'most scientifically oriented philosophers think of raw feels and thoughts as brain states'. However even the rejection of dualism is far from uncontroversial, and the number of non-scientifically oriented philosophers – or even of so oriented ones who are dissatisfied with this degree of identity – is quite large. Be that as it may, U. T. Place, J. J. C. Smart and, tentatively, Feigl want to claim that the conscious experiences or 'raw-feels' will eventually be reduced to physical processes, i.e. be fully explained by some eventual comprehensive theory of neural processes. They will not be left 'dangling' as a different type of property identified with neural processes only by correlations or bridge laws, but their properties will be

---

[1] Wilfred Sellars, 'The Identity Approach to the Mind–Body Problem', *Review of Metaphysics*, xviii (1965), pp. 430 ff., esp. p. 442. Sellars also thinks that what is at issue is the identity of 'raw-feels' universals and brain-state universals. But how then can the identity be empirical and not logical?

included in and explained by super-neurophysiology. The analogy of the reduction of certain chemical or macro-physical properties to micro-physical ones is quoted – what would appear at one time to be quite different properties or concepts are now seen to be part of one system, e.g. valency explained by atomic structure, temperature by molecular motion, genes by RNA. This kind of reduction is certainly neat and economical: it may be argued that it is merely a development of a continuous trend towards the unification of the sciences. On the other hand a strong case can be made out against it.

1. It may be said the analogy breaks down at several key points. Thus the chemical, genetic or macro-physical properties concerned form part of a close-knit and ordered scientific system, whereas the conscious experiences do not; the latter are not homogeneous but cover a wide and varied range. Again, the chemical properties and atomic ones are both known by public observation or theoretical inferences based on it. But the whole point of this mind–body approach is that conscious processes are private and differently known. A scientific theory, however chimerical, could not include them because it is limited to what is publicly observable.

2. The reduction draws large blank cheques on the future – it has to rely on postulating enormous and novel advances in neurophysiology.

3. The reduction does not seem plausible if worked out. When one science, *A*, is reduced to another one, *B*, the laws of *A* are exhibited as dependent on or derivable from those of *B* (either logically or by empirical hypothesis). This would mean that the explanation of any logical or psychological passage from one conscious experience to another must be derivable from neurophysiological laws. Thus in an inference where a person passes from premise to conclusion by apprehension of logical necessity, the passing must be shown to have a more fundamental physiological explanation. But is this credible – could there by anything more fundamental than apprehension of logical necessity?

If one pursues this tough anti-reductionist line it may prove difficult to maintain the identity hypothesis, and I favour an intermediate view. First, the critics exaggerate the caprice of

M   H.A.

conscious processes – there are some laws of conscious experience or mental activity. The admitted logical apprehension provides one important example; psychological associationist laws are another; there are also laws of good Gestalt, or laws about the effects of cues, constancy, colour contrast, etc.: perhaps also deeper psychoanalytic ones. So there is sufficient order for the reductionist analogies to be valid. On the other hand the correlations and possible new reductionist laws will be between sequences of conscious experiences or mental activities on the one hand and mass action in the brain involving many neurones on the other. At present our neurophysiological laws are relatively small scale – about nerve conduction, synapses, etc. So neural mass action, integrated large-scale neural complexes, may require laws of a very different kind from those at present. And such laws may in fact be suggested by or mirror those of conscious processes – i.e. there would be no real reduction of mental to physical at all. This is in fact what the identity theory really involves. If conscious experiences are brain activity, or if, as I prefer, conscious experiences and brain activity are different aspects of mental activities, then thinking, dreaming, wishing, etc., are activities of the human organism. Any laws there are of them must be laws of the behaviour of the human organism. They must therefore be so different from present neurophysiological laws as to make emergence of new powers of the brain, rather than reduction, the concept required.

The most ardent reductionists are the upholders of the version of the identity theory that Mr Beloff dubs the Australian heresy. If we take Professor Smart[1] as an example, we see that not only does he claim that conscious experiences, are brain activities and will eventually be shown to come under physical laws, but also that there is nothing irreducibly psychical and non-physical in their characteristics, e.g. in the sensory qualia or the introspectible character of imagery.

Smart's attempt to meet the objection that the sensory qualia, the phenomenal qualities of sensations, are irreducibly

[1] J. J. C. Smart, 'Sensations and Brain Processes', *Philosophical Review*, 68 (1959), pp. 148–50. Cf. his *Philosophy and Scientific Realism* (Routledge & Kegan Paul, 1963), esp. pp. 94 ff.

psychical is not easy to follow. He claims that colours are not sensuous qualia but are powers in objects to cause discriminatory responses in human beings; but then he has to admit that they cause sensations (on which surely the discriminatory responses depend) and the apparently psychical character of sensations thus remains. To meet this, he appears to claim that all we report – or are entitled to report – when we have a sensation of, for example, orange is that 'there is something going on which is like what is going on when I have my eyes open . . . and there is an orange . . . in front of me'. The 'something' is 'topic neutral', i.e. it may well be a brain process even if the subject does not realise this. All we report when we report our sense experiences are differences or similarities between them; and we can say that *A* is like or unlike *B* without knowing what they really are.

Now one might claim that the introspectible contents of abstract thoughts are so vague that they can be topic neutral, i.e. be brain processes confusedly perceived as an elusive nonphysical 'something'. But it is difficult to understand how this can be claimed about ordinary sense experiences on which the question turns: they can be and normally are precise, definite and unmistakably sensuous in character – quite unlike neurological processes. What is there vague and elusive about the content of experience in seeing a yellow book or in burning one's finger?[1]

In fact it seems to me that Smart has simply lapsed into behaviourism; the sensory qualia or content of conscious experiences, he thinks, are just vague somethings, unnecessary appendages to the brain processes to which all mental life can be reduced. This is no longer an identity theory because the distinct, special character of conscious experiences is devalued and explained away.

From our discussion so far, it seems that the identity hypo-

---

[1] Smart, *Philosophical Review*, 70 (1961), p. 407, explains the elusiveness as 'our inability to describe sensations except by reference to stimulus conditions'. But we have no such inability, cf. 'loud', 'sour', 'pungent', 'dazzling', 'a dull ache', although as sensations are private (not elusive) we may find it easiest to convey information about them in unusual cases by referring to what presumably gives other persons the same experience.

thesis must fulfil the following requirements: (i) preserve the unity of the person as a living organism characterised by mental and physical attributes. (ii) Avoid behaviourism and any commitment to the reduction of conscious experiences to brain activities. (iii) Emphasise more than Feigl does the difference between one's awareness of one's own mental activities and public observation of brain processes. (iv) Recognise that the identity is concerned not with 'raw-feels' but with events – performing a mental activity, having a certain experience.

The only version that seems to me to meet these requirements is that which I put forward elsewhere;[1] we can perhaps distinguish this as the Aspect Version.

The main contentions are:

Mental activities like thinking, perceiving and deciding are activities of the person as a whole and are at once both conscious and physical (or rather cerebral): i.e. mental activities are whole activities which present two aspects, an outer one which consists of a complex of brain activity and is in principle, at least, externally observable; and an inner and private one, the various experiences which the person has, and can introspect, in the actual performance of these activities.

It is normally alleged that a double-aspect account is uneconomical as postulating a third order of being underlying the two aspects. But that is not so. The logic of the term 'aspect' is such that when we are said to see an aspect (or view) of anything we are seeing the thing in question; the point of the term is not that we see some screen behind which the real thing lurks, but that we do not see the whole of the thing or of its characteristics. When we see the southern aspect of a building, or get a bird's eye view of it, we are still seeing the building. So when the person concerned is having or introspecting the experiences such as imagery which constitute the inner aspect of thought, he is aware of himself thinking, of his 'whole activity' of thinking; and in so far as one can observe or record on an electroencephalogram the corresponding outer aspect, i.e. the brain activity, one is observing the person's thinking.

[1] R. J. Hirst, *Problems of Perception* (Allen & Unwin, 1959), ch. 7, and G. M. Wyburn, R. W. Pickford and R. J. Hirst, *Human Senses and Perception* (Oliver & Boyd, 1964), ch. 15.

The experiences are the 'mental' activity as observed from within, the brain activity is the 'mental' activity as observed from without. If thinking of Z or perceiving Z is one whole event in a person's life, his conscious experience at the time and the concomitant brain activity are both that one event as revealed on different modes of access or observation. Instead then of a mysterious causal relation one has a partial identity; conscious experiences and brain activity are not two distinct events between which one must postulate or discover a causal relation; they are co-ordinate aspects of one whole event or activity in a person's life, e.g. his thinking, perceiving, etc.; they are that one event or activity differently revealed.

Difficulty may be felt in accepting this because of the apparently very different nature of conscious experiences and brain activity. But this difference lies in and is due to the radical difference in modes of access. To this extent the ordinary analogies of aspect, e.g. north and south aspects of a building, are inadequate, for they presuppose the same mode of access, namely sight, and only a difference in viewpoint. A better analogy might be the use of two different senses to give quite different modes of access to one object, e.g. we may see the wine as a red transparent liquid, and taste it as cool, smooth and tangy. Disparate as are transparent red and cool tang, we have no compunction in saying that we see and taste the same wine, and we can accept the difference in perceived characteristics as due to the radical differences in the senses by which we perceive it. But there is an even greater difference between inner private awareness of one's 'mental' activities by experiencing, and introspecting them, and the outer public awareness which some other person or even oneself may obtain by the use of sense organs and scientific instruments. And it is because of this difference that the one event or activity presents different appearances. If the same or similar mode of access revealed appearances so disparate one would have to say that they were two distinct events; but that does not hold. Interactionism mistakenly talks as if we observe sense-data and physical objects in the same way – we are said to see a mental map or T.V. picture of the external world. But sensing sense-data is private, and even if it is ultimately due to the stimulation of the sense organs by light rays, sound waves, etc., the organs, rays and waves do not intervene between the sensing and the sense-data. It is therefore very different from public observation of someone else's (or even one's own) reacting brain by means of sense-organs and instruments. Because of this mistake interactionism takes the two aspects of a mental event to be quite different events and then identifies the mental event with only one of them (the conscious experiences) so that the other – the brain activity – becomes an embarrassment.

I propose now to consider some objections to my position.

First a comment on Mr Vesey's criticism in his lecture of a fortnight ago that the 'departure from our everyday concept of an aspect, particularly the omission . . . of that which presents the aspects, leaves the theory considerably weakened',[1] so that holders of the theory slide into psychical or physical monism. I would certainly wish to dissociate myself from either of these, and my criticism of Professor Smart and of reductionism show that I am not the physical monist Mr Vesey thinks I am. My position is that it is mental activities of the human being, whole activities not just brain processes, which present aspects and which are apprehended according to mode of access as conscious experiences or brain processes. This would allow the two aspects to be equally valid revelations of mental activities; the outer aspect is important as a link with physical processes generally, and the inner aspect at present provides our means of differentiating mental activities and most of our knowledge of them.

There is admittedly on my theory an extension of the ordinary concept of an aspect, in that normally we contrast an aspect, a partial limited view, with the thing itself as revealed by a superior viewpoint, by a conflation of views (all views being on the same mode of access – sight), or by some superior process, e.g. measurement. But that does not apply here: the modes of access differ widely and there is no other superior mode of access available to us (there might be to God). The mental activity has therefore to be regarded as the sum of the two aspects and each aspect is the set of its characteristics revealed on a mode of access. To suppose that something is missing, and that the activities must be more than brain activity and con-

[1] See above, p. 148.

scious experiences, is a revival of Locke's despised concept of substance, the notion that a thing or event must be more than what is observed in it, must possess a substratum in addition to its properties. Another conceptual block to understanding my view is the assumption that one can ignore mode of access or observation and treat what one observes as absolute properties. This kind of abstraction works well for practical affairs but is theoretically crippling, not only for the mind–body problem but also for perception (what is a colour or a sound?) and physics (the wave/particle duality of light and matter generally).

Now for some objections to any version of the identity hypothesis.

(i) The identity, even an empirical one, is roundly alleged to be impossible. If *A* and *B* are identical then whatever is true of *A* is true of *B*: e.g. if Harold Wilson and the Prime Minister are the same man, then smoking a pipe is true of both and smoking reefers is false of both. But brain activity is public and conscious experiences are private, and questions like 'over what area does it occur?' make sense of the former but not of latter.

The reply is that one is not simply asserting the identity of substances, like persons or stars, observed on the same mode of access though at different times. One is concerned with aspects, and even what is true of the north aspect of a building may be false of the south one. The aspects and what is true of them differ more radically here, however; experiences, mental activity and brain processes are identified in the sense that the experiences are the mental activity as known from within and the brain processes are that activity as observed from without. On the other hand the identification means that the whole mental activity (as opposed to just conscious experiences) may be said to occupy a certain area. I do not think that this is outrageous if it is realised that one is in this way describing public observable characteristics of an activity of the person as a whole. One must not beg the question by interpreting 'mental' on Cartesian lines.

(ii)[1] That it oddly makes consciousness a functionally

---

[1] Objections (ii)–(iv) are raised by J. Beloff in *Brain and Mind* (1965), ed. J. R. Smythies, pp. 47 ff.

redundant product of evolution; if the organism *qua* brain can do all that a person can, why did consciousness emerge? (The implication no doubt is that some behaviour cannot be explained solely in terms of neural processes.) But the identity hypothesis need not suppose that the organism *qua* brain alone, i.e. without consciousness, can do all a person can. Consciousness must have some biological advantage, perhaps in planning; to plan ahead the organism must be able to distinguish self from non-self and present perception from imagery of past or future. Representation in consciousness by image or symbol enables the results of various courses of action to be visualised and plans made accordingly; such a representation and its awareness will have neuro-physiological correlates, but must be presumed more efficient than a purely physical representation system. One may add that there is a parallel problem for dualism; where did mind as a separate non-material entity come from if the brain on which it depends evolved from lower forms of life?

(iii) The lack of congruence between the phenomenal and the neurological domains is said to preclude identity. Thus the sense-data of a circle do not coincide in shape with the correlated pattern of brain activity and so cannot be identical with it. It is difficult to see the force of this: the identity theory need not and must not claim that experiences and brain processes have identical characteristics, including spatial extent, still less that elements of each coincide. Anyhow it is equally odd that the very different pattern of brain activity should cause a circular sense-datum, as interactionism claims.

(iv) The most important objection, Beloff thinks, is that parapsychological phenomena such as telepathy have no known physical explanation. Either they must be explained by a dualist theory of mind or physical theory will have to change radically. Unfortunately he does not discuss the attacks[1] that have been made on this objection, which was originally J. B. Rhine's. A short reply is that physical theories have changed radically in the past (Newton to quantum mechanics) without becoming non-physical, and will no doubt do so again. Also dualism does not really explain parapsychological phenomena

[1] See R. J. Hirst, *Problems of Perception*, p. 203.

(why does the mind 'reach out' so capriciously or inefficiently in them?), and if 'mental' is made a blanket term for anything as yet not physically explained, it becomes meaningless.

(v) Professor H. H. Price writes: 'According to Brentano, intentionality is the distinguishing mark of the mental. Every mental event is 'of' something or 'directed upon' something. It has to have an object or accusative. For instance, there cannot be inspection unless there is something inspected, nor wishing unless there is something wished for, nor believing unless there is something believed. On the other hand, no physical event ever has intentionality.' [1]

The main difficulty here is to understand what 'intentional' means. Mr Kenny and Professor Chisholm, for example, produce several very artificial criteria none of which clearly distinguishes the intentional from the physical. If we take the simpler notion of 'directed upon' then a large range of purely physical or non-mental activities appear intentional, e.g. cutting, destroying. There cannot be cutting unless there is something cut, etc. If one amends this with Chisholm by saying that intentional activities are directed on something which may not really exist, [2] then, as Kenny says, [3] knowing (connaître) becomes non-intentional and so non-mental. By contrast the beetle in a box hunting for food, the sea anemone waiting for its prey, or the guns aimed at the invader, all display intentional and so mental powers.

Perhaps this is quibbling however. The real point is that even if intentional in the sense of 'directed on what may not exist' is accepted as differentiating mental activity, this does not impugn the identity theory. First, as has been emphasised already, the identity hypothesis asserts only a contingent and

[1] H. H. Price in *Brain and Mind*, ed. Smythies, p. 59. But, as Chisholm sees, the possible non-existence of the object is the important point, cf. Franz Brentano, *Psychologie vom empirischen Standpunkt* (1874), bk. ii, ch. 1, sec. 5, ed. Kraus (Leipzig, 1924), vol. i, p. 124, and vol. ii, pp. 133–4.

[2] Cf. R. Chisholm, *Perceiving* (Cornell, 1957), pp. 169–70.

[3] A. Kenny, *Action, Emotion and Will* (Routledge & Kegan Paul, 1963), p. 198. His own favoured scholastic criterion placing 'the intentionality of psychological actions precisely in the fact that they do not change their objects' rules out 'love', 'hate', 'fear' and other psychological attitudes which affect their human or animal objects if present.

not a logical identity, and does not demand identity of all characteristics. Secondly, the mere possible non-existence of the object is an external criterion and a slight one; it can hardly account for the great difference dualists claim between mental and physical, in fact it seems an effect of a more important characteristic of mental activities, viz. that they normally involve representation or symbolisation. But this characteristic will not help dualism for physical representation systems are possible.[1] Several different forms are found in computers, though, as I have suggested, representation by conscious experience must be supposed to be more efficient for living organisms.

(vi) Even if all these replies are accepted, dualists may still claim that the identity theory does not give due weight to conscious experiences – the difference between them and brain activity is so great that it cannot be explained as merely due to different modes of access. This dissatisfaction is likely to be greatest concerning the two main characteristics of mental activities which dualists think shows them to be non-material, namely their creativity and freedom. Human beings, they would say, can invent or create new concepts, theories, works of art, institutions and devices; they can decide freely on a course of conduct. A physical or mechanical process can do none of these, which must therefore belong to mental not material substance.

The point here is that an identity theory, though not reducing mental processes to physiological ones, must render them compatible. This is particularly clear about mental activities such as thinking and deciding. The theory does not need to assert that brains think or decide – it is persons who do this and to say brains do it implies that no conscious experiences are involved. All the same if the brain and neural processes are outer aspects of these mental activities, an eventual theory of brain processes must be non-deterministic, i.e. compatible with the freedom which we attribute to such whole activities as the result of the sense of deliberate choice which is their inner aspect. This is not absolutely necessary in the sense that determinism may be true, but for most people it is required to make the identity

[1] As D. M. Mackay points out in *Brain and Mind*, p. 174.

theory plausible. So also it must be possible on an eventual neuro-physiological theory for persons *qua* organisms to be artistically or intellectually creative. This I think can only be catered for on an emergence theory, i.e. by supposing that when new levels of physiological complexity and new levels of integrated action are reached, then new powers and properties of a radically different kind appear, such as creativeness or choice by the organism. But these will be new things the organism can do, not the arrival of a mental substance. So long as one is considering the outer aspect only, they are new powers of the brain, new behaviour. But when both aspects are considered they are not just behaviour, since they are activities of the organism which possess a conscious inner aspect, and moreover are best differentiated and explained in terms of the inner aspect.

True this supposition draws blank cheques on future theory, but not so badly as reductionists do. One must remember that dualism exaggerates the differences between mental and physical by taking the comparison to be between Einstein and clockwork. But the material side is not even computers let alone clockwork, it is the highly complex living brain, a brain moreover that has developed by an evolutionary process. It seems plausible to maintain that full consciousness, creative and inventive powers, and capacity for spontaneous decision, emerge when the brain is of sufficient complexity. Many people would hold that intelligence or mind in some sense is possessed by animals like dogs, cats, and chimpanzees. Even lower animals are capable of complex behaviour with mental traits of recognition and learning – rats can learn maze-running, bees dance to indicate where pollen is. One cannot draw a hard and fast line between mind and not-mind – the evidence suggests the gradual emergence of mental characteristics including rudimentary forms of consciousness, with a sudden jump in human beings, a jump parallel by their enormously greater brain development. Furthermore even if the atoms of the brain are subject to determinist laws, and this is doubtful, there is no need to suppose that enormously complex wholes made up of them are similarly bound. On the power of the brain required by emergence theories or the identity hypothesis we may let

Spinoza have the last word: 'no one has hitherto laid down the limits to the powers of the body, that is, no one has as yet been taught by experience what the body can accomplish solely by the laws of nature'.[1]

[1] Spinoza, *Ethics*, note to Proposition ii of Part iii.

10

IMPERATIVES AND MEANING

C. K. Grant

In recent years philosophers have given a good deal of attention to imperatives.[1] They have concerned themselves mainly with the logical grammar of sentences of this kind, that is to say their relations to each other and to interrogative and indicative sentences. Very often this topic has been raised in terms of the problem 'Is imperative inference possible, and if so, what kind of inference is it?'. Many philosophers have contended that there are logically valid inferences that involve imperative sentences.[2] Against this it has been argued that no such inferences are possible.[3] It has even been held that there are no such things as imperatives at all – regarded, that is, as types of expression logically *sui generis* and independent of indicative sentences.[4]

PART I

In this lecture I am not going to concern myself with these questions, but with the prior problem of the kind of meaning (and meaninglessness) that can properly be attributed to

[1] A valuable bibliography is to be found in *The Logic of Commands* (1966), by N. Rescher.

[2] For example A. Ross in 'Imperatives and Logic' in *Philosophy of Science* (1944), R. M. Hare in *The Language of Morals* (Oxford, Clarendon Press, 1952), and H. N. Castaneda in *Philosophy and Phenomenological Research* (1960) and in some of his other writings.

[3] B. A. O. Williams in the *Analysis Supplement* (1963).

[4] P. C. Gibbons, 'Imperatives and Logic', *Australasian Journal of Philosophy* (1960), and H. G. Bohnert, 'The Semiotic Status of Commands' in *Philosophy of Science* (1945), discussed by R. M. Hare in *The Language of Morals*, pp. 7 ff.

imperative expressions. As a necessary preliminary, I attempt to clarify the nature of imperatives, and in the course of this discussion I shall advance a thesis to the effect that the importance of the imperative mood is often overstressed, with the consequence that subsequent accounts of practical deliberation are distorted. Professor Hare's influential interpretation of imperatives (and also decisions) is, roughly, that they are appropriate answers to practical questions like 'What shall I do?'.[1] This view, as it was advanced in *The Language of Morals*, has been criticised on the ground that it is much too wide, and would classify as imperatives sentences that are not imperative at all, for instance a possible answer like 'If I were you, I'd get a divorce' to the practical question just mentioned. This objection by Mr B. Mitchell[2] is, I think, a sound one. Should we therefore narrow the definition by confining our attention to sentences in the imperative mood? This grammatical criterion is not altogether adequate if we bear in mind the fact that from the point of view of logic the imperative should be regarded as a linguistic device for influencing, in the strongest possible way, the actions of others. There are grammatically imperative constructions which do not have this action-guiding function; just as there are rhetorical questions which do not require an answer, so are there rhetorical imperatives which do not, and are not intended to, influence conduct – e.g. 'Go to the devil', 'Buy a book, ref!' and 'Tell it to the Marines'. *Per contra*, there are sentences in the indicative mood which by convention have imperative force; when the commanding officer says, 'You will advance to point X' he is not making a prediction, and similarly it would be preposterous, or a poor joke, to treat the utterance 'I wish you would stop doing that' as an introspective report about the speaker's state of mind. Nevertheless, it is true that most grammatically imperative constructions have action-guiding force, and we shall not go far wrong if we confine our attention to these, bearing in mind the fact that some indicative sentences can be used with imperative import.

[1] R. M. Hare, *Freedom and Reason* (Oxford, Clarendon Press, 1963), pp. 54–5.
[2] In his contribution to the symposium with B. Mayo, 'The Varieties of Imperative', *Proceedings of the Aristotelian Society*, supplementary vol. 31, 1957.

In these remarks I shall not be concerned with the 'illocutionary' aspect of the utterance, on particular occasions and in particular contexts, of imperative sentences. This needs to be made clear at the outset, because much recent discussion of imperatives has been condemned, I am inclined to think rightly, on the ground that it takes place in a logical Never-Never land, where it is unclear whether what is being discussed are imperative sentences, the acts of uttering them, or the orders thereby issued, etc.[1]

Now if we examine the ways in which we in fact use language to influence the conduct of others, it is clear that the employment of the imperative, whether or not the imperative mood is actually a feature of the expression, is by no means the only or indeed the most important means that is adopted. We request, suggest, propose, ask, warn, beg, entreat, persuade, etc., and we do these various things because for one reason or another we do not order, command or insist. Often the imperative is out of place on account of good manners; on occasion it may be excluded if the speaker lacks the necessary authority, though this is not to say that authority or title is essential in all cases – it is not present when, for example, the passenger, who knows the route, says to the driver, who does not, 'Turn right!' Cases like this are common enough, and therefore I cannot agree with N. Rescher's contention that some entitlement or authority must generally be present if a command is to be issued.[2]

I have suggested that the essential function of the imperative use of language is to influence action, but that this of itself does not mark off the imperative from the host of other linguistic methods of achieving the same end. At this point I should give some explanation of how the notion of 'influencing action' should be understood. I am not referring to the fact that there are ways of using language that can powerfully affect, in the sense of causally trigger-off, the actions of others. If *A* calls *B* a foul name, this language might well affect *B*'s behaviour, but this would not constitute an action-guiding use of language in my sense because the linguistic expression does not point out or

[1] Y. Bar-Hillel, 'Imperative Inference', *Analysis*, Jan. 1966.
[2] Op. cit., p. 16.

indicate the desired course of action on the part of the inter-
locutor.

To summarise so far. I have urged that we restrict the word
'imperative' to those utterances that are in the imperative
mood, or which like the military order which has the grammatical form of a prediction, are governed by linguistic con-
ventions giving them an imperative force. I have suggested
that it is misleading to employ the concept of the imperative
as widely as, for example, Professor Hare does when he interprets it as an appropriate answer to a practical question.[1]

I have said that the main reason why this is misleading is that
it distorts the nature of practical deliberation. Let us look at
this more closely. Language as it is employed in the issuing of
imperatives, orders, commands, etc., is primarily a matter of
inter-personal communication. To interpret practical deliberation as typically terminating in the issuing of an imperative[2] is
to assimilate an individual's relation to his own contemplated
action to the model of one way of influencing the behaviour of
others. This is wrong because, when I wonder what I am going
to do next, I am doing something very different from wondering
what someone else is going to do. There are, of course, cases
in which what the other is going to do is, as it were, up to me;
I may wonder whether the milkman is going to leave one or
two pints, but what this amounts to – unless I have an unusually
disobedient milkman – is that I am wondering what I am going
to do in respect of a request that I may or may not make to him.
Furthermore, as I have said, it is important to keep distinct,
even within the area of inter-personal communication, the
differences between giving orders or commands on the one level
and making requests, suggestions, proposals, etc., on the other,
though I have no wish to deny – in fact will later emphasise –

[1] *Freedom and Reason*, pp. 54–5.
[2] Hare does admit that the answer to the question 'What shall I do?' is
not normally expressed in words, but that the agent 'just acts'; however, he
goes on to say that in order to give a satisfactory account of moral reasoning,
we require an expression in words of what he leaves unuttered, and the form
'Let me do *a*' serves for this (*Freedom and Reason*, p. 55). It is significant that
he later maintains that in making moral judgments, i.e. in saying that one
ought to do *a*, one is 'prescribing to oneself', (op. cit., p. 73). In other words,
what he leaves unuttered is an imperative.

the close relation between the two. The chief reason for stressing the difference is that an imperative, order or command, is something that can be obeyed or disobeyed, followed or not followed; suggestions, proposals, etc., which we may lump together under the label 'hortations', on the other hand are accepted, agreed to, fallen in with, or rejected, disagreed with, and so on. It is of some importance that we do not speak of accepting or agreeing with a command or imperative nor of disobeying a suggestion. I do not think the importance of this distinction is mitigated by the fact that we also speak of 'following' both orders and advice; after all, we also speak of 'following' arguments, suspects, musical scores, etc. It is worth noting that as in the case of imperatives, grammar can be a poor guide as to whether a given location is or is not a hortation. Thus we often make suggestions and proposals by using an interrogative form of speech, for instance 'Why don't you do it this way?' We often speak like this to suggest that it should be done this way – but of course also to find out information about the *modus operandi*.

Now it might be argued that I am overstating my case, if it be admitted that I have a case at all, on the ground that many philosophers have held that even in the strongest 'action-guiding' use of language, namely imperatives, it is possible for an individual to utter an imperative to himself, if you like, to give himself an order. ('Possible' here refers, of course, to the logical intelligibility of applying the concept in this way, not to the undoubted factual possibility of an individual talking aloud to himself.) Philosophers who hold this view are not resting their case upon the linguistic fact that in many languages the imperative mood has a use in the first person singular. It is pretty clear, for example, that this sort of consideration was not in the mind of Wittgenstein when he said: 'A human being can encourage himself, give himself orders, obey, blame and punish himself; he can ask himself a question and answer it. So we could imagine human beings who spoke only in monologue, who accompanied their activities by talking to themselves'.[1] Doubtless it is possible for something like giving oneself an order to take place, and two possible kinds of cases

[1] *Philosophical Investigations*, p. 88.

N   H.A.

occur to me. One may remind oneself of a firm intention in the
face of danger or temptation; but if this were genuinely comparable with an imperative as it might be addressed to another
person, then it would make logical sense to talk of the possibility
of disobeying it – but it certainly would not make sense for a
man to say 'I disobeyed myself' rather than, for example, 'I
changed my mind', 'I gave in to temptation', etc. The second
example of what appears to be an individual giving himself an
order is when he addresses it to a group of which he himself is a
member. We might say that when the platoon commander
orders the platoon to advance, he also *inter alia* orders himself to
advance because he is part of the platoon. I think the main point
here is that the platoon as such is the object of the command and
it is a contingent fact that the man who gives the command is a
member of it. (But suppose, after giving the order to advance,
the commander stayed behind? Would he be court-martialled
for disobeying orders, and if not, why not?) The notion of
falling into temptation provides a clue to a partial explanation
of how the mistake of believing in orders to oneself came to be
made. There is a *prima facie* psychological or phenomenological
plausibility in describing the experience of temptation in this
way, that is, as if there were two selves warring together; hence
it is natural enough to describe the experience in terms
appropriate to a dialogue between persons. There are, of course,
many historical antecedents for this view. Thus, if like Plato,
we regard thought as a dialogue of the soul with itself, it is easy
to conceive practical deliberation in this light; and although
the notion of a moral imperative was, so far as I know, foreign
to Plato, it is notorious that he bifurcated, or rather trifurcated,
the self.

A similar situation exists in Kant's ethics; for him the concept
of the imperative is of supreme importance, doubtless owing
largely to his background of Pietism with its emphasis on
Divine Commands as revealing the moral law. For Kant it is
precisely because we consist of both practical reason and
inclinations – that is, because we are in effect divided in two –
that morality presents itself to us in the form of an imperative,
and I suggest that it is this dichotomy in the self which makes
it seem plausible to Kant to describe our moral experience in

terms of an imperative, a notion really at home only in inter-personal communication.

I have claimed that the importance of the imperative form of expression has been exaggerated; I would now like to draw attention to another type of action-guiding locution which is at least as important in this context, and which so far as I know has been unaccountably neglected by philosophers. I refer to suggestions, proposals, etc., that are made by a speaker to an audience which does not exclude himself, thus 'Shall we do so and so?', 'Let us do such and such'. In some languages, sug-gestions of this kind are conveyed by employing the first person plural of the imperative mood; in some others there is a special mood for the purpose – I am told that Hebrew is one of these – and the mood is called by grammarians the co-hortative, to distinguish it from exhortations that are addressed exclusively to persons other than the speaker.

If philosophers are concerned, as many of them claim to be, with the clarification of language as it is used to influence action, then they ought to recognise the importance of co-hortative types of expression because failure to do so can lead, as I think it has done, to a type of individualism that is false to the facts, that is, to life as it is lived. Practical deliberation is not primarily or essentially a matter for the isolated individual, it is very often a co-operative or group affair, and so is decision also. If this is so, then when in due course the deliberation and the action are subjected to evaluation as sensible or foolish, moral or immoral, the critic of practice can neither regard himself as set over against his fellow-men as if they constituted his subject matter, nor on the other hand is he concerned with thought and action for which he alone is responsible. I am not here advocating anything like a form of collectivism, but merely making a plea for a more realistic account of practical delibera-tion and decision.

Although group decisions, and indeed the whole co-hortative employment of language generally, are morally neutral, it is nevertheless the case that the current tendency to ignore in philosophy these phenomena that are familiar enough in ordinary life, brings into moral philosophy, which purports to be an analysis of action-guiding language, a certain moral outlook, with the result that the analysis is not as neutral or 'standpointless' as is claimed. The moral attitude in question can be characterised in only very general terms. It represents, as I have said, a form of individualism, according to which the moral agent functions in a kind of vacuum. That is to say, although the interests and desires of others may, and probably will, enter into his practical deliberations, they can do so only as raw material, so to speak, in the formulation of the decision about what he is to do. When he is not acting off his own bat, his concern with the actions of others is represented as attempts to influence them either by persuasion or by the stronger technique of imperative language. The individualist account depicts a somewhat tiresome and priggish fellow, whose concern is either with his own actions or with meddling with the affairs of other people. This applies also to the individualist account of the agent considered as critic, for here again the conception of the evaluation of actions other than his own is that of an individual presented with a set of data for his consideration, rather as if he were engaged in the contemplation of a work of art. The element of importance that is left out of the individualist view is the fact that many deliberations and decisions are made by groups of which the agent and critic is himself a member, and hence these can be neither described nor evaluated as if they were the responsibility either of a single agent or by others independent of him and set over against him. This view is not only untrue to the facts of experience but it results in the failure to recognise the practical and moral importance of co-operativeness.

If one claims to detect and diagnose a mistake in philosophy, one is, I think, under an obligation to offer some sort of account of why undoubtedly acute and able persons came to make it. I venture some tentative suggestions on this point. Most writers on moral philosophy are professional teachers, and are in a didactic and authoritarian relation to their pupils; I do not mean by this that they are regarded either by themselves or their pupils as moral authorities, but that they are able to insist on certain acts being carried out – the essay must be handed in next week – these references need to be checked, etc. These teachers are then called upon to grade and evaluate these same essays and examination papers, and indeed the man himself when it comes to the writing of references, etc. Small wonder then, that when writing their general accounts of practical deliberation and the evaluation of actions, these same persons should find the notions of advice, instruction and admonition looming so large, and the assessment of individuals interpreted as the judging of a presented and objective subject matter. It is true, of course, that the moral philosophers I have referred to are often engaged in group deliberations and decisions with their colleagues on various committees, etc.; it is not clear to me why these experiences have so little influence on their general philosophical theories.

PART II

In the second part of this lecture, I would like to raise some questions concerning the notion of meaning as it is applied to expressions of the kind that we have considered. I shall be concerned not only with imperatives as ordinarily understood, but also with requests, suggestions, proposals, etc., and I call all of these 'directives', because they all have the purpose of influencing action, whether positively or negatively, in various ways. As we have seen, the notion of obedience or disobedience is in place in respect only of those directives which have an imperative force, and so here we need a more general expression. For this purpose I borrow the verb 'to satisfy', defining it roughly as follows; a given directive is satisfied if the action specified, whether positively or negatively, is or is not performed.[1] Thus the positive directive 'Let's go to the pictures' is satisfied if in fact we go to the pictures, and the negative directive which may be seen on the railway station at York, 'Please help to keep this station tidy by not feeding the pigeons' is satisfied by those good citizens who are not in fact feeding the pigeons. (I may say in passing, that some definite reference to action seems to be essential; it is not sufficient to say, as some

[1] I must mention here two articles by Ernest Sosa, 'On Practical Inference and the Logic of Imperatives', and 'The Logic of Imperatives' in *Theoria*, vol. xxxii, part 3 (1966). In these he employs the concepts of 'directive' and 'satisfy' in a way similar to that which I outline. Unfortunately the two articles appeared too late for me to profit by them.

theorists have done, that a directive is satisfied if, after its promulgation, the proposition describing the state of affairs desiderated becomes true, for this reason. Suppose at the right time I address the sun and say 'Sun, arise!' and sure enough, up it comes, thus making true the proposition 'The sun rises' – it would be ridiculous to say, as this definition would require, that the sun has obeyed me or satisfied the directive.)

An important general feature of directives is that it is logically inappropriate to deny or contradict utterances of them, although we can obey or disobey an imperative, meet or refuse to meet a request, fall in with or reject a suggestion, and so on. The reason is obvious enough; in these locations nothing is being asserted, and hence there is nothing to deny. It may be thought that this is not a clear or genuine distinction, on the ground that we can speak of 'agreeing with' both assertions and directives. But here another distinction must be noted, viz. between two senses of the word 'agree'; in respect of an assertion one can agree or disagree that so and so is the case, and in respect of a directive one agrees or fails to agree to do some act or other.

In the remainder of these remarks I make some tentative and unsystematic comments on the question of whether it is possible to formulate a general criterion of meaning for directives. The issue arises for two reasons. It would be rash to assume that the dangers of talking nonsense in these forms of speech are less than those attending the indicative use of language, where the problem of meaning has rightly attracted a great deal of attention. Secondly, because directives do not assert, appeal to any version of the verification principle is obviously out of place[1] – not that I would defend it as an account of the meaning of indicative statements anyway.

It is probable, of course, that no general or blanket criterion of meaning for directives can be given, and we are nowadays rightly suspicious of a search for unifying formulae of this kind. Nevertheless, provided that we do not insist *a priori* that there

---

[1] A doctrine both obscure and extravagant to the effect that interrogatives and imperatives can be prescribed as true or false may be found in an article by H. S. Leonard, 'Interrogatives, Imperatives, Truth, Falsity and Lies', in *Philosophy of Science*, vol. 26 (1959).

must be an adequate general criterion, it may not be a waste of time to consider whether anything worth while can be said on the topic in general terms. I am going to assume that as far as meaning is concerned, there is no difference between imperatives and the other types of directive; in other words, if it is meaningless to order someone to do X, it is also meaningless to suggest or ask that he does it, and similarly if it makes sense to order him to do X. This seems to be intuitively all right, but needed to be made explicit.

It is natural to approach the problem in a way similar to that in which the verificationist interprets the meaning of indicative sentences, and say that a meaningful directive is one that is capable of being satisfied, while a meaningless one cannot. This is clearly inadequate as it stands, because although all meaningless directives are unsatisfiable, there are many unsatisfiable directives that are perfectly meaningful in any ordinary or acceptable sense of the phrase. Many of these, although not all, are unsatisfiable for contingent empirical reasons, for example 'Restore the hair of this bald man'. Influenced by the familiar distinction between verifiability in principle and verifiability in practice, we may be inclined to modify the formula by saying that in the case of meaningful directives a method of satisfaction can be specified, and that in the case of meaningless ones this cannot be done. There are a number of difficulties here, one of which is in the notion of a method; it would surely be a serious misapplication of the word if one were to say that the act of shutting the door constituted a method of satisfying the directive 'Shut the door!'. Leaving out the word 'method', we might interpret the meaning of a directive in terms of what it is to understand it, and this in turn as the ability to describe the way of acting – or not acting – which would constitute the satisfaction of the directive. (I do not think that there is here an analogy with falsifiability in the case of indicatives, for to fail to satisfy a directive would be either to do nothing, or to perform any one of an infinite number of other possible acts.)

On the face of it, the formula is a plausible account of directives concerned with overt action, but a difficulty arises in connection with mental activity. I may say 'Add up these figures in your head'. This is a perfectly intelligible instruction, but it would be exceedingly difficult to give a description of what this activity consists in, as anything separable from blurting out the total; furthermore, adding up the figures is not the same as giving the total, both because I could add them up without stating the sum, and also because I could give the (correct) answer without calculating but by guessing. Perhaps all that one can say here is that certain activities are such that the only test of whether they occur or have occurred, is that the end-product, in this case the answer, emerges or would emerge under certain conditions; they are not occurrently witnessable and indeed it would be hard to make sense of the supposition that they could be.

Other non-overt activities may appear to present a puzzle. These do not have an end-product, yet may be the subject of quite intelligible directives, e.g. 'Try to imagine (in the sense of 'form an image of') the Eiffel Tower'. In order to give a meaning to this, it is not necessary to form a general theory about the nature of the imagination, but rather to state the criteria by which to test any claim to have imagined the Tower. There is nothing particularly recondite here; all that we need to know is whether the individual can give a reasonably accurate description of the Tower or, if you like, of the way it looks. My tentative conclusion, then, is that the meaning of a directive is to be described in terms of the criteria by means of which we determine whether or not it has been satisfied, and that these criteria are very various.

In the final section of this paper I propose to say something about various non-empirical reasons why directives can be unsatisfiable. The same point could also be put by saying that some actions are logically impossible. This seems *prima facie* to be very queer because the notions of logical possibility and impossibility are normally confined to propositions, and so it does not appear to make sense to talk of logically possible or impossible actions. However, there is no doubt that some actions cannot be performed for reasons that are not empirical, but *a priori* and logical in character. Another objection might be that the notion of logical impossibility is so closely tied up with its opposite, logical necessity, that it seems hardly intelligible to separate the two – and yet to speak of logically necessary actions is palpable nonsense. Although some actions are necessary – e.g. eating – they are so for empirical and contingent reasons, and to the degree that they are necessary and forced on us, so are we less inclined to give them the name of actions in the ordinary sense. However, it is not only propositions that can be logically absurd, certain concepts are in the same boat, and certain directives are *a priori* meaningless because they refer, or purport to refer, to an action which is conceptually nonsensical.[1] Some examples are as follows:

(i) Consider the directive 'Take a bus to next week!' This is logically impossible to satisfy, because one cannot attach sense (or at any rate I cannot) to the notion of travelling in time. A less obvious, though I think similar, instance is the Biblical injunction, 'Be ye perfect, even as your Father in Heaven is perfect',[2] not, be it noted, perfect in the way appropriate to a finite part of the Creation, but 'as your Father in Heaven is perfect'. Orthodox theological concepts being defined in the way that they are, this directive appears to be in principle incapable of being satisfied.

(ii) Unsatisfiability may be due to lack of specification in the directive; in this way 'Complete the expansion of pi' and 'Name the largest integer' are unsatisfiable, as will be clear if we compare them with 'Expand pi to 500 places' and 'Name a large integer'.

(iii) Directives concerned with proving or establishing propositions of various kinds raise issues of their own. If the proposition is logically absurd, so also is the directive that it be proved – e.g. 'Prove that all concertos are oblong'. A similar consideration would apply to a directive concerning a logical contradiction, e.g. 'Prove that some bachelors are married'. One may also say *a priori* that a directive to prove a proposition that is empirically false is meaningless, e.g. 'Prove that wood is harder than iron'. Although these cases are in important ways different, the meaninglessness of the directive in each instance derives from the logical grammar of 'prove'; this is an achievement verb, and although there are different ways of failing,

[1] I am grateful to Mr K. W. Mills for making this point clear to me.
[2] Matt. 5. 48.

they have in common the fact that they are not successes. (There is in law a somewhat specialised sense of 'prove' in which it means roughly 'establish beyond reasonable doubt', and in this context it appears that it might make sense to talk of proving a false proposition, if on the evidence it would be unreasonable to doubt it. Thus a gangster who has committed a hold-up in New York may say to his lawyer 'Prove to the court that I was in Miami' and I think that this is logically if not morally defensible, because here 'to prove' means 'to give good grounds for believing' and one can give good grounds for believing something which is in fact false. There is more to it than this, though, because a *post facto* demonstration of the falsity of the proposition would overthrow any claim to have proved it, even though 'reasonable doubt' had been excluded.)

CONCLUSION

The question that I have been discussing in the latter part of this paper is the very general one 'Is it possible to set out a criterion of meaning for directive statements?' and the answer that I proposed was also a very general one, and you may think too much so to be of much interest, namely that a directive is meaningful if it is possible to describe what would count as satisfying it. Since different sorts of directives are satisfied in different sorts of ways, some requiring an overt action and others not, for example, no general account can be given of what satisfying a directive consists in. To paraphrase, every sort of directive has its own sort of grammar.

One final point. There seem to be important exceptions even to the very general formula that I have advanced; these are concerned with proof in mathematics. If one is asked to trisect an angle or square the circle one is being asked to do something which can be shown to be *a priori* impossible, not because the proposition to be proved is meaningless or self-contradictory, nor on account of lack of specificity in the problem, but because the rules of proving exclude the operation of proof. We know exactly where we want to get to, but we cannot get there. I conclude, therefore, that the formula must be used with caution and without dogmatism. Whether it could be restated so as to cover these awkward mathematical examples is a question I have to leave to those who know something about mathematics, which I do not.[1]

[1] The preparation of this paper was assisted by a grant from Durham University.

11

ETHICS AND LANGUAGE

G. J. Warnock

In a broadcast talk delivered in 1956, the late J. L. Austin began by outlining to his listeners his now well-known concept of 'the performative utterance and its infelicities'; and at the end of that first section of his talk he made this comment: 'That equips us, we may suppose, with two shining new tools to crack the crib of reality maybe. It also equips us – it always does – with two shining new skids under our metaphysical feet'.[1] In this talk I intend to illustrate a particular respect in which, in moral philosophy, the partial pessimism of Austin's comment has proved abundantly justified. I shall try to show how in this field one shining new tool has led in fact to the skidding of moral philosophers' feet – how one bright idea (an idea, as it happens, very closely akin to that which Austin himself was discussing) has led some influential theorists off in the wrong direction, and the rest of us back in the end, with rather little gained, to a position not far from that of our predecessors of about a hundred years ago. This dismal story, I should in justice make clear at the outset, is not that of the whole of moral philosophy, not even of moral philosophy in English; I shall be tracing only one out of several concurrent lines of thought, but the line which I shall trace will be, I think, readily recognised as having been, and perhaps as still being, more conspicuous than most.

One way (not the only way) of launching my story is to

[1] Austin, 'Performative Utterances', in his *Philosophical Papers* (1961), p. 228.

consider the way in which, some thirty years ago, the moral theory of 'intuitionism' was occasioning well-justified discontent. It was felt, with good reason, that the doctrines of intuitionism made the concepts of morality seem both mysterious and undiscussable. In that doctrine moral judgments, or at any rate the most fundamental moral judgments, were construed as simple assertions of moral fact. Very much as some things, for instance, are pink or blue, some things, it was supposed, are good or obligatory; just as we simply see that a thing is pink, we simply intuit that a thing is obligatory. Further, just as a person who can see does not need to have it explained to him what it is to be pink, and does not need to be shown by any argument that pink things are pink, just so there was supposed to be no question of explaining what it is for something to be obligatory, and no question of deploying any reasoning to show that what is said to be obligatory is indeed obligatory. In the one case we simply see; in the other we intuit.[1] That such doctrines should have occasioned discontent is not, of course, surprising. We know what seeing is; but do we really have any idea what 'intuiting' is? To learn that something is pink we need to look at it, not to reason; but is there really no room for reasoning in moral matters? Can it really be that there is practically nothing to be said? Furthermore, in what does the relevance of these supposed moral facts consist? That something is obligatory is supposed to be a reason, indeed a conclusive reason, for doing it; but why should this be so, if its being obligatory is a simple fact about it, like the fact that some flower in my garden is pink? I may know that some flower in my garden is pink, and find in that fact no reason for doing anything in particular; why then should it be the case, if it is the case, that to have knowledge of the fact that something is obligatory is somehow also to be apprised of a reason for doing it? In such doctrines too little is said, too much is left in undiscussable, *sui generis* obscurity.

Acknowledging, and not in the least disputing the justice of, the objection that I have here presented an ignoble caricature

---

[1] I have in mind here particularly the more extreme views of H. A. Prichard. Not all intuitionists went quite so far as he did, but it would be beside the present point to bring in the several variant forms of intuitionism.

of the views of serious men, let me briskly disregard it and proceed to present another. In what respect are we to say that intuitionist doctrine had gone wrong? No doubt there are a good many possibilities here – a good many points at which a theory of such bald simplicity might well be charged with failure to do justice to the state of the case. But there was one particular idea which, some thirty years ago, was very prominently pervasive in the philosophical air – the idea that there are diverse 'uses of language'; and it is to the criticism prompted by this general idea, by this 'shining new tool', that I wish on this occasion to direct attention. It was suggested, then, that perhaps the trouble, or at least part of the trouble, was that the intuitionists had failed to consider, and so had unwittingly misrepresented, that 'use of language' which is actually to be found in discourse on moral matters. Philosophers, it was suggested, have always been all too ready to assume, too often unconsciously, that there is only one, or only one interesting, use of language – namely, its use in making statements, in describing things, in saying something true or (possibly) false. Now certainly the intuitionists had evidently supposed that items of moral discourse were of this general kind; they had supposed that a grammatically indicative moral utterance simply made some kind of statement, truly or falsely, asserted or purported to assert some moral fact, and had at once become involved in hopeless difficulties as to the nature of these putative facts, as to the way in which they could be known or discovered, and as to their seemingly mysterious relevance to what people should or should not do. But we now see, it was said with a justified sense of enlightenment and liberation, that there are diverse uses of language; it is far from being the case, and a mere superstition to suppose, that the making of statements, the asserting of facts, is the only, or the only interesting, use there is; so why should we not drop the assumption the intuitionists made? Perhaps the 'use' of language, in discourse on moral matters, is not, or not mainly, to assert facts at all. Thus C. L. Stevenson was led to write, in 1937, that the 'major use [of ethical judgments] is not to indicate facts, but to create an influence'; the use of language we actually find here is not 'descriptive', but 'dynamic'; in saying to a hearer that such-

and-such is good, or right, or what he ought to do, I am not asserting either truly or falsely any fact at all, whether mysterious or otherwise, but seeking to influence his interests, his feelings, or, broadly, his attitudes. The resulting new theory, under the name of 'emotivism', was viewed by many as a great liberation, a notable advance. It seemed to rest firmly upon the bright (and for that matter perfectly correct) idea that there are various 'uses of language', and thereby to escape most satisfactorily from the mysteries, muddles, and mythology of intuitionism.

This, however, did not last. Ten years or so later it was beginning to be strongly maintained that, while of course there are diverse uses of language, and while very probably the intuitionists had misrepresented the use that is characteristic of moral discourse, yet emotivism itself had skidded in its particular way of undertaking to set matters right. In bringing into moral philosophy, in place of the old 'descriptive' prejudice, the notion of the 'emotive' or 'dynamic' use of language, had it not perhaps got hold of the wrong thing? It need not be doubted that such a use does actually exist; but is it the use that is really characteristic of moral discourse? There are three main grounds on which it was urged that it was not. First, it is perfectly clear that there are quite other regions of discourse in which this 'dynamic' use is clearly exemplified. It is a feature, and probably the essential, most central feature, of advertising slogans, or of propagandist political harangues, that in them language is used to 'create an influence'; the predominant aim here is not to inform, but to sway; words apt for the purpose in hand will be words with 'emotive meaning', and if any facts are alleged, or even truly asserted, this will really be incidental to the 'dynamic' business which is principally in view. It seems, then, that the emotivist theory of ethics either must hold the unappealing, and surely also unplausible, view that moral discourse is essentially no different from advertising or propaganda, or alternatively must concede that there is, in moral discourse, some feature besides its 'dynamic' use, some feature which the theory itself seems not to allow for, by which moral discourse can be distinguished from discourse in those other and less reputable modes. Second, is it actually true that moral discourse is always emotive, or dynamic? If I tell you quite coolly, even diffidently perhaps, that in my opinion your practices of tax-evasion are wrong, am I really, am I necessarily, attempting to work on your feelings, or indeed seeking in any way to 'influence your attitude'? 'I think it's wrong' is scarcely an utterance one would think of as emotively charged. Then, third, even when in some moral utterance my end is, as it sometimes really may be, 'dynamic' – even when I really am out to exert a bit of influence – is this the most important, the essential, feature of my utterance? Surely it is not. If I deliver, for example, a serious moral talk to some young persons on the evil of trafficking in drugs, it may be that I hope thereby to influence their attitudes; but what my words primarily offer them is, surely, guidance. Primarily, I tell them what line to take in that matter, and only consequentially, if at all, do I influence or move them towards taking that line. I am, so to speak, steering, not pushing.

In this way, then, it came to be felt that attention to the 'dynamic', or 'emotive', use of language did not really constitute the great advance in moral theory that it had once been taken for – by some, perhaps, that that notion had even done positive harm in opening its seductive primrose path to philosophical error. But if moral discourse is not, then, essentially 'emotive', what is it? We will scarcely be tempted to take up again, in these modern days, the old supposition, or superstition, that it is simply descriptive; but then of course we need not do so, since we know that there are lots of other uses of language to choose from. In picking the 'dynamic' use the emotivist theory had evidently put its money on the wrong thing, but no doubt we can find some other use that will turn out to be the right one.

The next idea, in fact, can be seen to emerge very naturally from reflection upon the sort of case last mentioned, the case of my serious talk to my group of young persons. I am therein, as we put it, steering, not pushing. I am offering to them advice or guidance, not merely administering some verbal prods. It could in fact be said correctly that, in discoursing as I do on the evils of drug-trafficking, I am essentially telling my audience something – but telling them what? Not (as an in-tuitionist would quietly have assumed) that something is the case: what I am really telling them, surely, is what to do, what line to take in their conduct, with respect to traffic in drugs. It may be that my discourse against drugs is actually un-solicited; but we may say nevertheless that, had it been the case that these young persons had confessed themselves worried about this business, and had put to me about it the practical question 'What shall we do?', then my discourse would have provided an answer to that question. May we not say, then, that the use of language in moral discourse is essentially such as to answer practical questions? Moral discourse is not indeed unique in this, since imperatives answer practical questions too; a possible answer to the question 'What shall I do?' would be, for example, 'Mow the lawn', or 'Sell all thou hast and give to the poor'. But at any rate a way of answering such a question would be to tell you what you ought to do, what would be the right thing. And thus, in the manner of Professor Hare, we may conclude that imperatives and moral discourse should be grouped together as species of 'prescriptive' discourse, of discourse the 'function' of which is to 'guide conduct'. The language of morals is not essentially, though it may be incidentally or deviantly, descriptive; nor is it always and essentially, though it may be on occasion, emotive; the best word for what it really is, is the word 'prescriptive'. This is the use of language which the language of morals crucially exemplifies.

Now the resulting moral theory, which is sometimes called nowadays 'prescriptivism', has in recent years been powerfully and persuasively stated, subtly elaborated, and most ingen-iously defended against a variety of objections. It has become too large and complex a structure to be satisfactorily surveyed in a couple of paragraphs; and thus, if I say that we have here yet another example of skids under the metaphysical feet, I cannot hope in the space here available to carry much convic-tion, unless, perhaps, to the already converted. But my point, though doubtless it could be made to stick only (if at all) by rather extensive and ramified argument, is in itself a very simple point: it is that the prescriptivist theory, like the emotivist theory upon which it was supposed to be an improve-ment, has picked on something which certainly does occur in moral discourse, but which, on the other hand, does not occur in all moral discourse; which, further, does not occur only in moral discourse; and which, further still, is not interestingly distinctive even of those tracts of moral discourse in which it does occur.

It is not very difficult, I believe, to see that this is so. Certainly it is true that, just as there may occur in moral discourse utterances which carry 'emotive meaning' and of which the intention or aim is to 'influence' their addressees, so there may occur in moral discourse utterances having what we may call 'prescriptive force'. For, sometimes, what is at issue in moral discourse is indeed some practical question: some person is considering the question what he should do; and it may then occur that he is offered, by way of an answer to his question, guidance or advice in some utterance or utterances carrying 'prescriptive force' – that is, which tell the question-raiser what he is to do. But it is plain that not all moral discourse is of this kind; it is not always the case that, when talk on moral matters is going on, there is one party engaged in considering a practical problem, and another in prescribing a course of action to him; moral discourse is not always addressed by one party to another, and about what that other party is currently, or in the near future, to do. My discourse may be about my own actions, not yours; about past actions, yours or mine, not present or prospective ones; about the actions of absent persons who are not parties in the conversation, or of dead persons for whom, now, it would be somewhat pointless to prescribe. The paradigm case of prescriptive speech is the case of advice; but, while of course the giving of moral advice or guidance does sometimes occur, it is plain that it is not always occurring when moral talk, or moral thinking, is going on. In talking and thinking on moral matters we do many other things, depending on what the particular topic may be, and on how and in what context the topic comes up for consideration. Sometimes what we say has prescriptive force, sometimes not.

Secondly, it is, I believe, even more evident that the occurrence of utterances having prescriptive force is not in any way peculiar to moral discourse. When one gives advice, when one tells someone what to do, it is not always moral advice that one gives; when one person consults another on a practical problem, it is not always a moral problem that he brings up. Even if the advice I offer is such as I would offer to any person in the same situation as my enquirer is, and even if the course of action which I prescribe to him is one that I myself would unhesitatingly adopt were I in his shoes, yet my advice may not be moral advice: for quite possibly his practical question is not a moral one, raises no moral issue. An utterance may well be prescriptive, even 'universally' prescriptive; it may, for the matter of that, be emotive as well; yet it may be concerned with no moral matters whatsoever, and not a specimen of moral discourse at all.

Thirdly, suppose that we have some utterance which is undoubtedly moral, and which does undoubtedly have pre-scriptive force; we have, let us say, a true specimen of moral advice. How interesting is it that such an utterance has pre-scriptive force? From the point of view of moral theory, I suggest, not very interesting. If our interest were in the philosophy of language, then indeed it might well be our main concern to consider what it is in such an utterance, or in the circumstances in which it occurs, which gives it prescriptive force – what it is that makes the issuing of that utterance the giving of advice. But it would seem that, if our interest is in moral philosophy, then we shall want to know, not how it is that that utterance is the giving of advice, but how it is that it is the giving of moral advice; and, even more interestingly, how if at all one could determine whether the moral advice so given was good advice or bad. No doubt, if a specimen of advice-giving is what we have got, it will be just as well to be clear that that is so; but this much scarcely impinges upon moral philosophy at all. That some specimen of discourse has pre-scriptive force is scarcely of more interest to a moral philosopher than would be, to a doctor, the information that some pill-shaped object is a chemical compound. He may be glad to know that it is; but for his particular purposes he needs to know more.[1]

---

[1] Let me say again here that I am fully, even painfully, aware that by some the last few paragraphs will be regarded as grossly unfair, or even as a foolish travesty. I do not (of course) share this view; but I think I under-stand it, and I believe that I could, given time, undermine its foundations.

Let me now, before turning into the home straight, briefly review the situation. We started from well-justified complaints made against Intuitionism, a body of doctrine which evidently supposed that moral judgments are statements, assert moral facts, or that moral discourse is essentially, as many would put it, 'descriptive'. Against this we set the bright (and correct, though vague) idea that there are diverse 'uses of language'; and we have now surveyed two moral theories which have sought to make use of this idea, the first holding that moral discourse is not descriptive but emotive, the second holding that it is neither descriptive nor emotive, but rather prescriptive. In each case we have suggested that the 'bright new tool', the liberating notion of the many uses of language, fulfilled Austin's warning by functioning actually as a skid under metaphysical feet – and doing so, in each case, in a curiously similar way, namely, by sliding moral theorists away from their proper subject-matter. Emotive meaning, the use of emotive language for 'dynamic' purposes, does actually occur and is, in its way, interesting; prescriptive force, the use of language for advising, for giving guidance on practical problems, does also occur and is, in its own way, interesting. But neither topic has very much to do with moral philosophy, for the reason that discourse on moral matters is only sometimes, not always and not uniquely and never very interestingly, exemplificatory either of emotive meaning or of prescriptive force. Each of these latter topics is something else again; and to confuse either with moral philosophy is, at best, unhelpful.

I come now, and finally, to a more recent and even more curious, though curiously similar, instance of skidding. It was one of Austin's major contributions to good order and philosophic discipline that he sought to introduce some much-needed clarity and distinctness into philosophical talk about the 'use' or 'uses' of language.[1] He thought rightly that the notion of 'use', though no doubt it had done good work in its day by, so to speak, loosening things up and widening the terms of discussion, had come in the end to breed new confusions by covering indiscriminately too many distinguishable, and too seldom distinguished, cases. The distinctions which he was mainly con-

---

[1] Particularly, of course, in his *How to Do Things with Words* (1962).

cerned to introduce, within the general notion of 'using' language, were those between, first, the act of saying something with a certain meaning, for example the sentence 'You're not allowed to do that'; second, the act of doing something in the saying of those words, as for example informing, forbidding, warning, or reprimanding; and third, the act of doing something by the saying of those words, as for example deterring, alarming, convincing, or offending. There are things besides these which might well be called 'uses of language', as for example reciting, making a noise or a joke; but Austin's main concern was with the above distinctions, with what he called locutionary, illocutionary, and perlocutionary acts. To ask what locutionary act a speaker performs is to raise one kind of question about his 'use' of language; to ask what illocutionary act, is to raise another kind; and what perlocutionary act, yet another kind again.

Here, then, we have an even shinier and sharper new tool; and, predictably enough, there seems some reason to apprehend that it may compass the downfall, or at least the distraction, of at least some moral philosophers. There was published in 1966 a book called *The Revolution in Ethical Theory*[1] which gives some substantial grounds for this apprehension.

The author of that book has, as he says, read Austin with attention, and has sought to apply his contributions in moral philosophy. Now up to a point things go well enough. In bald summary the author argues, making use of Austin's terminology, that recent moral theories, no doubt partly because of the fogginess of the idea of the many 'uses' of language, have sought to illuminate moral discourse by locating the perlocutionary object, or the illocutionary force, of discourse of that kind; they have sought to identify the perlocutionary act ('influencing'), or the illocutionary act ('prescribing') which moral discourse specifically exemplifies. But, as he rightly contends, such efforts have proved abortive, since the objects thus sought for actually do not exist – moral discourse has no one perlocutionary object, it exemplifies no one illocutionary act. In neither sense is there any single 'use' of language which is specially or uniquely characteristic of discourse on moral

[1] George C. Kerner (Oxford, Clarendon Press, 1966).

matters. So what is the remedy? The author's verdict on the position is, in effect, that recent moral theorists have not gone far enough. They have stuck at some one particular linguistic act, perlocutionary or illocutionary, and thus have neglected the very wide variety of other linguistic acts which discourse on moral matters also exemplifies. The remedy is to bring into account the whole breadth of this diversity; in his own words, 'a fully adequate ethical theory would analyse and systematise the whole variety of linguistic performances and commitments that are embedded in the use of moral language'. What is needed is more, much more, of the same.

But no: is it not quite clear, on a little reflection, that this author thus prescribes quite the wrong remedy for the disease – that he urges us, in fact, to go even further and further in the wrong direction? For the trouble is not only, as he suggests, that there is no single illocutionary act, no single perlocutionary object, which is specifically characteristic of moral discourse; it is also the case that if we consider the whole range, the whole and huge diversity, of all the illocutionary and perlocutionary acts, of 'linguistic performances', that actually occur in moral discourse, we find that all this is not distinctive of moral discourse either. For consider what our author says about 'You ought to do *Y*'. Certainly, he rightly says, this form of words may be used in prescribing; but not only in prescribing – 'it is also used for enunciating and subscribing to principles, placing demands, taking sides, licensing, advocating a course of action, transmitting authority, invoking sanctions, over-ruling, restricting, instructing, etc., etc.'. That is true, and worth saying; but then it should also be observed that no item in this list, nor yet the whole list taken together, has any particular connection with moral discourse – each, no doubt, is to be found there, but each and all may be found in many other settings as well. One could in fact talk minutely, even exhaustively perhaps, about every one of these 'linguistic performances' without even touching on morals at any point; analysis, that is, and systematisation of these might very well involve no mention of morals whatever, and might accordingly yield no ethical theory at all, let alone a 'fully adequate' ethical theory. It is particularly clear in this case, I think, what has gone wrong. Our author, understandably and indeed properly impressed by the bright new tool which Austin had forged for him, is resolved to put this tool to some philosophical use: there are, as Austin has now enabled us clearly to see, dozens and dozens of interestingly distinguishable speech-acts, of linguistic performances; so let our task be the analysis and systematisation of these. Well, let it be, by all means; but if so, let it also be recognised that what we shall be engaged in is the philosophy of language, and not in moral philosophy or anything like it. Advances on this front may, of course, prove serviceable for moral philosophy; but they will not be advances in moral philosophy, whose particular concerns might quite well remain wholly unmentioned in our arduous researches.

But, you may protest, can this really be correct? Consider again the form of words 'You ought to do *Y*'; and let us suppose these words to occur in discourse (not forgetting that they can play other roles) in such a way as to constitute the giving of advice, and specifically the giving of moral advice. Now if we exhaustively analyse and anatomise such a case, may we not hope to come up with – doubtless among other things – some interesting conclusions as to what moral advice is, what qualifies or entitles a person to be a moral adviser, even, perhaps, what it is for moral advice to be good advice or bad? If so, then it could not possibly be suggested that such study would not be contributory to moral philosophy; for what could be more vitally relevant to moral theory than, say, the ground of distinction between good and bad moral advice? This objection, however, is not at all to the purpose. For in so far as the particular bit of enquiry suggested might yield conclusions of some interest in moral philosophy, it is exactly not an enquiry into the 'linguistic performance'. The linguistic performance is simply the giving of advice; and the analysis of that, as a linguistic performance, will tell us, we may hope, what giving advice is, and how giving advice is to be distinguished from doing other things. But the giving of moral advice is not, or at any rate is not in any sense envisaged by Austin, a different 'linguistic performance' from the giving of advice in any other context or connection; and the giving of bad advice is, regrettably perhaps, the very same 'linguistic performance' as giving good. To raise these further questions is, accordingly, to abandon, to go beyond, the analysis of the linguistic perform- ance as such; it is, furthermore, to raise questions whose answers, were we able to find them, would have little to do with any linguistic performance in particular. For is it not to be anticipated that what makes moral advice moral will probably turn out to be exactly the same as what makes criticism, for instance, moral criticism, exhortation moral exhortation, a decision a moral decision, and so on? Expressions of advice, criticism, exhortation, and decision no doubt differ as linguistic performances, and their differences in that respect are of interest in the philosophy of language; but it is quite possible that what makes them, when they are, elements in moral discourse will be some respect in which they do not differ at all, and to which their differences as 'speech-acts' or as linguistic performances are totally irrelevant. Rather similarly, if I take a certain moral decision, advise you that you should also act as I have decided to do, and subsequently judge you unfavourably for failing to do so, it seems clear that what, if anything, makes my moral decision the right decision will be exactly the same thing as makes good advice my advice to you, and, subsequently, makes well-founded my unfavourable moral judgment of your failure to take it. What is of interest to moral philosophy is what, in such a case, the decision, the advice, and the critical judgment have in common; how they differ as linguistic performances is neither here nor there.

Thus I suggest, in conclusion, that our author of last year has drawn exactly the reverse of the correct conclusion from his enquiries. He has observed correctly that there is no single 'use of language', understanding thereby no single linguistic per- formance, which is specific to and characteristic of moral discourse. He has observed correctly that some influential recent theories have fatally erred in alleging that there is. He has further observed, again correctly, at Austin's prompting, that we find in moral discourse an immense diversity of lin- guistic performances – and, he might have observed, in fact exactly the same diversity as is to be found in discourse that is not moral discourse at all. But the conclusion to be properly drawn from these observations is exactly the reverse of the conclusion which he actually draws; it is that the analysis of linguistic performances has nothing in particular to contribute to moral philosophy. Such an analysis is an exercise in the philosophy of language – doubtless of absorbing interest, but what it will illuminate can only be respects in which moral discourse does not differ from discourse in general. What is of concern in moral philosophy is not to enquire how advice, say, is to be distinguished from exhortation; it is, in fact, exactly the reverse of this – to enquire, that is, what moral advice and moral exhortation, and for that matter moral judgment, criticism, resolution, or regret, have in common, what it is that makes them all instances of moral talking or thinking. What then may it be that all these things have in common? Surely what they all have in common is a certain kind of grounds. And thus we are led back again, sadder and perhaps a little wiser, to regard as the central question of moral philosophy that question which, among others, J. S. Mill set before us rather more than a century ago – the question, as he put it, 'concerning the foundation of morality'. If we have recently made no striking progress in answering this question, part of the explanation may lie in the fact that some of our most influential and able moral philosophers have attached their shiny new philosophical tools to their feet, and then unwittingly have skated away into another subject.

12

THINKING AND REFLECTING

Gilbert Ryle

JUST as there was a vogue at one time for identifying thinking either with mere processions or with more or less organised processions of images, so there is a vogue now for identifying thinking with something oddly called 'language', namely with more or less organised processions of bits of French or English, etc.

Both views are entirely wrong; wrong not because thinking ought instead to be identified with mere or organised processions or bits of something else instead, but because this very programme of identifying thinking with some procession or other is radically misguided. Certainly it is often the case, and nearly always just before we fall asleep, that the thought of something bobs up, and then the thought of another thing. But their serial bobbings-up do not constitute the thoughts as thoughts; and I am not pondering or calculating if only this is happening. I can be thinking when nothing of the sort is happening.

I am going to start off by considering what sort of characterisation we are giving when we say that someone, a tennis-player perhaps, is thinking what he is doing, or that he was for a few moments so *distrait*, vacant or somnolent that he was not thinking what he was doing. References to his thinking or not thinking what he is doing are obviously carried by our characterisation of him or of his play as cautious, alert, wild, cranky, impetuous, resourceful, experimental, unimaginative, cunning, stereotyped, amateurish, and so on.

At this point I can explain why in my title I use both the word 'thinking' and the word 'reflecting'. The tennis-player is thinking what he is doing, and Rodin's *le Penseur* is obviously thinking. But while we would happily describe *le Penseur* as musing, meditating, pondering, deliberating, ruminating, reflecting or being pensive, we would rather not so describe the tennis-player – save in the unoccupied intervals between rallies, games or sets. In these intervals, certainly, the tennis-player may do what *le Penseur* is doing; he may, while his racquet is idle, ponder either about his tennis-match or else about something else, like Gödel's theorem. But while he is engaged in the game, with his mind on the game, he looks and mostly is *un*reflective or *un*pensive. We should not naturally class him as a Thinker or a *Penseur* for what he is doing now. He is not in a brown study, nor even in a series of fleeting brown studies. He does not have to be called back to the flight of the tennis-ball, as *le Penseur* may have to be called back to the starting of a shower of rain or the momentary state of the traffic around him. *Le Penseur* is in some degree detached from what is going on around him; but the tennis-player's thinking almost consists in his whole and at least slightly schooled attention being given to, *inter alia*, the flight of the ball over the net, the position of his opponent, the strength of the wind, and so on. Both are absorbed, but the tennis-player's absorption is in his and his opponent's momentary playing, while *le Penseur*'s absorption is in something detached from the rock-squatting that he is momentarily doing, and the rain-drops that are momentarily wetting him. His quick and appropriate responses to what occurs around him on the tennis-court show that the player is concentrating. His non-responses to what occurs around him show, or help to show, that *le Penseur* is concentrating. There are things, like his strokes, eye-movements, foot-movements, etc., which the tennis-player is here and now doing that he could not do, as he does them, without concentrating. They are well-timed or mistimed, concerted, wary, etc. Yet it seems that *le Penseur* is doing nothing, nothing that can be characterised as well-timed or mistimed, concerted, wary or, generally, more or less attentive, except just tackling his problem. If he is visibly doing anything, like sitting still, breathing or scratching his cheek, he is not giving his mind to doing these things. He is detached, disengaged, 'absent' from all such doings. I am, with a good deal of arbitrariness and imprecision, going for this occasion to reserve the verb 'reflecting' for the thus disengaged thinking of *le Penseur*. There will assuredly be some half-way-house cases of thinking which have some of the engagement of the tennis-player and some of the disengagement of *le Penseur*. A person doing something fairly deliberately, e.g. playing bowls or talking to his solicitor, may be in this half-way house.

We are, of course, too sophisticated to suppose that because a verb is an active, tensed verb, in a sentence the nominative to which designates a person, therefore the person is being said to be performing an action, or doing something. The verbs to 'perish', 'inherit', 'sleep', 'resemble', 'outlive', 'succumb', 'know', 'possess' and 'forget' are conspicuous cases of active, sometimes transitive, tensed verbs which we could not be even tempted into treating as verbs of doing. I want to draw your attention to a special class, a pretty fluffy-edged class, of active, tensed verbs which we could easily be tempted into mistakenly treating as verbs of doing. I am going metaphorically to label them 'adverbial verbs', though this label is not to be taken very seriously. For one thing, I shall use the label to cover a wide range of things, with very little in common save a certain negative thing. Consider the active tensed verb 'hurry'. If told that someone is hurrying, we have not been told what he is doing, but only that he is doing whatever he is doing at an abnormally high speed. He may be hurriedly walking or typing or reading or humming or eating, and so on indefinitely. The command 'Hurry' is only the beginning of a command; it cannot yet, context apart, be obeyed or disobeyed. I label the verb 'to hurry' an 'adverbial verb', partly because any completed sentence containing it could be paraphrased by a sentence containing a proper verb of doing qualified by the adverb 'hurriedly' or the phrase 'in a hurry'. I might put the point by saying that hurrying is not an autonomous action or activity, as walking, typing and eating are. The command 'walk', 'type' or 'eat' is an obeyable command, and not the less so for being pretty unspecific. If I then eat lobster or bread or shoe-leather, I am obeying the command to eat. But to obey or disobey the command to hurry, I must do some autonomous X, like eating or humming, etc., for there to be a hurried or an unhurried X-ing that tallies with or flouts the understood command, no matter whether the command is specific or unspecific. Trying, scamping, succeeding and failing are, in generically similar ways, not autonomous activities. There must be an X-ing, if there is to be successful or unsuccessful, difficult or easy, industrious or scamped X-ing. Taking care, or being careful, vigilant or wary is, for the same general reason, not an autonomous doing. The command 'mind out' (full stop) cannot be obeyed or disobeyed unless some complement is understood. Driving with care is not doing two things, as driving with a song is. I can stop driving and go on singing, or vice versa. I can do the one well and the other badly; the one obediently and the other disobediently. But I cannot stop driving and go on exercising traffic-care. In obeying your command to drive carefully, I am not conjointly obeying two commands, such that I might have disobeyed the first while obeying the second.

Now if a person spontaneously initiates or embarks on something – a remark, maybe – and if he does the thing with some degree of care to avoid and correct faults and failures, and if, finally, he learns something as he goes along from his failures and successes, difficulties and facilities, he can claim and we shall allow that he has been thinking what he was doing. Unlike the delirious man he meant at that moment to say something and not anything else; he tried, in some measure, to satisfy already learned requirements of grammatical correctness, politeness, intelligibility, pertinence, etc., and he tried not to repeat inadequacies and faults, and to exploit and improve on successes and adequacies. So he was to some extent giving his in some degree trained mind to what he was doing, and to that extent not giving his mind to extrinsic things. He was not uttering absent-mindedly, or just raving or nattering or saying things by rote. Some of this is sometimes put, in philosophical circles only, by saying that his activity, in this case that of contributing to a conversation, was 'rule-governed'. For there were, *inter alia*, ungrammaticalities, rudenesses and irrelevances that he avoided, corrected or withdrew because they were or would have been such faults. He qualifies as having been thinking what he was doing, namely making a contribution to a conversation, not because, besides the uttering that he was doing, there was another autonomous thing he was also doing and might have continued doing after his uttering had stopped. There was some degree of initiative, care and self-coaching in his talking. But none of these elements was an autonomous action or activity. None of them stood to his uttering as singing to driving, or even as the steering-wheel movements to the pedal movements of driving. His bits of uttering were not accompanied by, or interspersed with bits of something else that he was also doing; or if they were, as they often are, it was not for these accompaniments that he qualified as thinking what he was saying. There are no separate chronicles for him to give of the thinking without which his utterings would not have been conversing, any more than the hurried breakfaster can give us one chronicle of his breakfasting and another of his hurrying. We can ask whether the converser was conversing in English or in French or, if in a noisy factory, perhaps in gestures and grimaces. We cannot ask whether the required thinking that he did, namely thinking what to say, how and when to say it, and how and when not to say it, was in its turn conducted in Russian, German, gestures or images. There was no 'it' to have a separate turn of its own. Nor can we ask of a person who had been listening vigilantly whether he conducted his 'vigilating' in hand or eye-movements or in Norwegian. There was no separate 'it' to conduct. If we did employ my manufactured verb to 'vigilate' it would be an adverbial verb, replaceable by our familiar adverb 'vigilantly'. Of course if, unlike the absent-minded or delirious man, a person has been doing something, thinking what he was doing, usually he can afterwards, if adequately educated, tell us what he was trying to do, and what for, what made him apologise, hesitate or stop and start again and so on. But to grant this is not to grant that to have been thinking what he was doing, X-ing, say, he must have been doing something else as well, Y-ing, say, e.g. telling himself in his head things in indicative, imperative and optative English or French sentences; or, of course, picturing things in his mind's eye either. He may in fact have been doing some bits of such Y-ing but it was not for these that he qualifies as having been thinking what he was doing. Indeed it could be because he had been doing some such bits of *Y*-ing that he had not been thinking what he was doing, namely the *X*-ing – as the centipede found who tried to run while considering how to run. In short, the thinking of the non-absent-minded, non-delirious talker is not a separate act or procession of acts, or a separate procession of anythings. The verbs 'to think', 'give one's mind to', etc., as used of him in this context, are adverbial verbs, like my manufactured verb 'to vigilate'. His thinking is not an autonomous action or activity; nor a concurrent procession of autonomous anythings. Nor is his vigilating, which is, of course, just one element in his thinking what he is saying.

I have heard part of my point put in this way, which I deprecate. It is sometimes said that while thinking does indeed need some vehicle or other, still some philosophers are so stingy about the number of eligible vehicles, that they restrictively say that thinking needs for its vehicle only bits of English or French, etc.; or that it needs only images; or that it can get along only with either bits of English or French or with images. What they should do, it is suggested, is let in lots more kinds of vehicles, like the tennis-player's wrist and eye-movements, the conversationalist's tongue-movements and ear-prickings; the typist's finger-movements; and so on. I am rejecting this vehicle–passenger model altogether. Adverbial verbs are not verbs for autonomous doings, and so not of autonomous doings which, like bicycling and strumming, need some apparatus or other. Hurrying over breakfast does require eating, but not as its vehicle; rather, to put it coarsely, as an adverb needs some suitable verb or other. Pugnacity or cunning at tennis does require strokes, but not as distemper requires brickwork or woodwork, or as marmalade requires bread or toast. Wariness in rock-climbing or taste in Latin verse composition can indeed not get along without rocks or Latin words, but not because it is left stranded or hamstrung without them, but because without them there is no 'it'.

Before moving on, let me just mention that a great many verbs of doing which can function in completed commands are in themselves partly adverbial and partly not. The verb 'scrutinise' already carries the notion of 'carefully'; and the verb 'misspell' already carries the notion of 'incorrectly'. A person who is sprinting must be running, but also he must be hurrying; and if he is guzzling, while he must be eating, he cannot be eating daintily.

But now we come to what *le Penseur* is engaged in doing. For brevity I label what he is doing 'reflecting', though the label does not naturally cover a good many of the things that *le Penseur* might be doing, such as day-dreaming, brooding, going over in his head the previously memorised dates of the Kings of England or, of course, just pretending to be reflecting.

When we think in the abstract about thinking, it is usually reflecting, calculating, deliberating, etc., that we attend to. It is from their reflectings that we grade Plato and Euclid as Thinkers; we do not so grade Bradman, Chaplin and Tintoretto. By the plural noun 'thoughts' we ordinarily refer to what *le Penseur*'s reflectings either incorporate or else are going to terminate in, if they prosper. Indeed it is just because reflecting is what we start off by considering, that we later on feel a strong pressure to suppose that for the tennis-player to be thinking what he is doing, he must be sandwiching some fleeting stretches of reflecting between some stretches of running, racquet-swinging, and ball-watching. That is, because reflecting does, or does seem to, qualify as an autonomous activity, therefore such adverbial expressions as 'on purpose', 'vigilantly', 'carefully', 'cunningly', 'tentatively', 'experimentally', 'resolutely', etc., seem to need to be construed as signifying some extra autonomous things that the tennis-player must be privily doing, besides what we see him autonomously doing. Where no one thinks that the would-be train-catcher is engaged synchronously in sprinting and also in hurrying, we are all tempted to suppose that for the tennis-player to be using his wits, he must be both making muscular movements and also be doing lots of short, sharp bits of reflecting. I think what I aim to do, if I can, is to show that it is the notion of engaged thinking, like that of the tennis-player or the conversationalist, that is the basic notion, while that of disengaged thinking or reflecting, like that of *le Penseur*, is supervenient. The notions of being pensive and having thoughts do not explain, but need to be explained via the notion of intelligently *X*-ing, where '*X*' is not a verb of thinking.

When Plato says that in thinking the soul is debating with herself, he is grossly over-generalising, not merely from reflecting, but from one or two very special brands of reflecting, namely philosophical and perhaps also forensic reflecting. If, for example, *le Penseur* is engaged in trying to complete a limerick, or trying to recall a friend's telephone number, then, though he is certainly reflecting, he is certainly not, unless *per accidens* and *en passant*, debating with himself; and if he is, *per accidens* and *en passant*, doing a bit of debating with himself, the required limerick-ending or telephone number is not whatever, if anything, is settled by his internal debate. We are always thinking when we are internally or externally debating. We are not always debating when we are reflecting.

Sometimes philosophers and psychologists, speaking a bit less restrictively than Plato, say that in thinking, that is, what I am calling 'reflecting', the thinker must, whether in his head or *sotto voce* or aloud, be talking to himself, the coverage of their word 'talking' being a lot wider than that of the word 'debating'. For example, narrating is talking, but it is not debating. Nor is most preaching. These philosophers and psychologists put their point, sometimes, by saying that the thinker must be thinking 'in English' or 'in French', etc., or sometimes that he must be thinking 'in symbols', whatever they are.

Now there certainly are a lot of tasks on which *le Penseur* may be engaged, though he need not be, which, in one way or another, are or incorporate linguistic tasks. For example, he may be trying to compose a poem or an after-dinner speech, trying to translate a bit of Horace into English, preparing to lecture to laymen on a subject the technical terminology of which is strange to them, wondering whether to italicise or how to spell a word, and so on. Here his particular problem is the more or less difficult linguistic problem what to say and how to say or write it. He is having to think up suitable French or German phrases and sentences; and the better he is at French or German the easier it is for him to think these up. Now, he may be so good at French or German that his task is, most of the time, not difficult at all, and not even fairly easy, but

P

perfectly easy. Then we may, in praise or envy, say that, unlike us, he can think in French or German. He no more has to hunt for the right French or German words or phrases that he needs than we, most of the time, have to hunt for the English words or phrases that we need when talking to Englishmen. When engaged in certain *ex officio* linguistic tasks, he can find the required German words and phrases without any rummaging at all.

But though *le Penseur*'s task may be, it certainly need not be a poet's task, a translator's task, an after-dinner speaker's task, or a proof-corrector's task; he need not be wondering how to say or write something. His problem is, perhaps, a historian's, a mathematician's, a mechanic's, a chess-player's, a detective's or a philosopher's problem. It is not a problem of expression, though it may carry with it some problems of expression; and these may be easy, while it is baffling, or vice versa. Solving them is not solving it. If 'Smith can think in German' means that he ordinarily finds it perfectly easy to put into suitable German what he wants to put into German, then this says nothing at all about his philosophical, mathematical or Scotland Yard reflectings, but only about his trans-frontier communicational undertakings, namely that he is good at German. It does not entail that while tackling a philosophical problem he is saying things to himself in German or in his first language, English. The view that he must be doing so has to be grounded elsewhere. I am not saying that there are no such grounds for, *inter alia*, philosophical reflecting. I do in fact think that an unworded argument belongs where an unworded quatrain belongs – nowhere. But I am not following this up, for *le Penseur* may be reflecting, though neither arguing nor composing a poem, a speech or a repartee.

I have so far sharply contrasted thinking what one is doing, e.g. conversing or playing tennis, with reflecting, e.g. what *le Penseur* is occupied in; engaged thinking with disengaged thinking. *Le Penseur* is concentrating on something, but not on sitting where and as he is sitting, or on propping his chin on the hand on which it is propped. He is, metaphorically, miles away, as the tennis-player cannot be miles away and still be playing tennis. But still, though, from this detachedness or disengagedness, in strong contrast with the tennis-player's engaged thinking, *le Penseur*'s reflecting itself, no less than tennis-playing, does require such adverbial things as trying, testing, experimenting, practising, initiative, avoidance or correction of lapses, resistance to distractions, interest, patience, self-coaching, etc. Whatever *le Penseur* is engaged in that qualifies him as reflecting, he cannot, any more than the tennis-player, be absentmindedly or deliriously or infantilely engaged in it. He, like the tennis-player, cannot be asleep or vacant, nor even an absolute beginner. Both alike must be on the *qui vive*. *Le Penseur*, no less than the tennis-player, must be, in some degree, using here and now his at least partly trained wits. He cannot not be thinking what he is doing, i.e. not be *X*-ing vigilantly, pertinaciously, etc. So even disengaged thinking, i.e. reflecting, is also, like tennis-playing, a species of engaged thinking. The adverbial verb 'to think' is presupposed by the activity-verb 'to reflect'. But where the tennis-player must be using hits wits in, *inter alia*, moving his feet, eyeing the ball, swinging his racquet and so on, we seem now to be stumped to nominate any corresponding autonomous *X*-ing or *X*-ings such that *le Penseur* must be *X*-ing more or less exploratorily, tentatively, pertinaciously, pugnaciously, scrupulously or cannily. What is the *X*-ing that *le Penseur* is non-absent-mindedly, non-somnolently or nondeliriously doing which *if* done absent-mindedly or somnolently or deliriously would not then amount to pondering, calculating, etc.?

Surely part of what stumps us is our vain presumption that our bill needs to be filled by just one uniform and nominatable *X*-ing; but I am not therefore going to resort to the now overhallowed 'family likeness' device so long before reaching, what it is for, the last resort. But certainly let us remember from the start that *le Penseur* unquestionably qualifies as reflecting or pondering as well if he is in the throes of musical composition, as if he is trying to construct or destroy a philosophical or a Scotland Yard argument; or trying to find out whether the number 1,000,001 is a prime number; or trying to solve a chess-problem; or to recollect a telephone number; or to run through the alphabet backwards.

Notice here, what I hope may turn out to be relevant, that

adverbial verbs may pyramid. In this way. If I am eating my breakfast, you may tell me to hurry over my breakfast. If I obey you, I do so not by breakfasting, since I am doing that already, but by accelerating the rate of my breakfasting. I am then obediently hurrying over my breakfast. If I resent your command but dare not disobey it, then I am with reluctance obeying your command to hurry over my breakfast. I am reluctantly obediently hurriedly breakfasting. I am not reluctantly breakfasting, nor necessarily reluctantly hurrying over my breakfast; I am with reluctant obedience hurrying over my breakfast, though I might have cheerfully hurried over it if you had ordered me not to do so. And so on, in principle, indefinitely. Notice that none of these adverbs can get going unless the bottom one is attached to a non-adverbial verb or a partly non-adverbial verb, in this case 'breakfasting'. This is not meant as a reminder of a bit of school-grammar; rather it is intended to bring out a corollary to one of the many things that could be meant by calling one concept 'parasitic' on another. Obeying can be parasitic on hurrying, and this in its turn on breakfasting. 'Big fleas have little fleas. . . .' The notion of stealing is parasitic on the notion of owning; the notion of pretending to steal is parasitic on the notion of stealing; and the notion of rebelliously pretending to steal is parasitic on the notion of pretending to steal. And so on. When the intention with which an agent does X is ancillary to the intention with which he will or would do Y, we can say that his X-ing is an intention-parasite on his Y-ing. He has to have Y-ing in mind in order to have X-ing in mind; and he may have to have Z-ing in mind in order to have Y-ing in mind.

Now for a quite different though connected matter.

Strolling across a golf course, we see a lot of pairs and fours of golfers playing one hole after another in a regular sequence. But now we see a single golfer, with six golf balls in front of him, hitting each of them, one after another, towards one and the same green. He then goes and collects the balls, comes back to where he was before, and does it again. What is he doing? He is not playing golf. He has no opponent; he does not putt the balls into the hole; he lays the balls by hand on to the turf from which he is going to hit them. Obviously he is practising approach-shots. But what distinguishes a practice approach-shot from a real one? Several things. Negatively he is not trying to win a match since there is no match. Nor in practising is he both making approach-shots and also doing something else as well. Positively he performs each of his strokes as a piece of self-training. Training for what? Training for making approach-shots in matches to come. But he cannot be practising without, in some way, having in mind the non-practice approach-shots of future live matches. The 'thick' description of what he is engaged in requires reference to his thoughts, in some sense, of future non-practice approach-shots. These are what it is for. His activity of practising approach-shots is parasitic on that of making match-approach-shots. There are two points about practice-approach-shots that need to be brought out for future use:

1. The first point is that the 'thick' description of them contains a reference to his having in mind will-be or may-be match-approach shots. He will have practised in vain if his performance in these matches shows no improvement.

2. The second point is that the practice-shots are in some degree detached or disengaged from the conditions under which match-approach-shots have to be made. The practiser can play from where he likes; he can hit without having to wait for his turn; he need not even have a green to play for; a tree-stump in a field would do. He need have only a mashie with him. Indeed he might do without golf-balls and a mashie; dandelions and a walking stick might serve his turn. As his circumstance-dependence and apparatus-dependence decrease, so his practise-actions approximate more and more closely to being pure 'voluntaries', that is, things the doing of which is within his absolute initiative and option. I suggest already that his partial detachment from the circumstances and the apparatus of golf-matches points up the road to *le Penseur*'s total or nearly total detachment from what exists and is going on around him.

There are many activities other than practising which share with it these two cardinal features of intention-parasitism and circumstance-detachment. (*a*) The rehearsing actor is not acting, but rehearsing for acting. He is trying this morning to make himself word-perfect and gesture-perfect on 'the night'. He rehearses in vain today if he falters on 'the night'. He may rehearse in mufti; in his own room; without an audience, prompter or fellow-actors; in the dark. He is in high or low degree circumstance-detached and equipment-free in his rehearsing. Yet the 'thick' description of what he is doing, being in terms of what he is doing it for, must refer to theatre-performances which, if they occur, will not be circumstance-detached or equipment-free. (*b*) The cooking-instructor teaches the making of a plum-cake by demonstrating. He can, if he likes, demonstrate with salt instead of sugar, with a cold oven, with a ten-second pause for the baking-process, which in live cake-making would be an hour; and so on. His success or failure is the later production by his pupils of good or bad plum-cakes. If and when they do cake-making, they will do it under full kitchen-conditions. (*c*) The boy who tries to jump the flower-bed may be neither practising to improve nor demonstrating to his friends a technique, but just experimenting, just trying to find out whether he can jump it or not. He is vexed with the grown-up who gives him a helping shove, since this stops him from finding out what he wanted to find out. He, too, enjoys a measure of circumstance-detachment. He can choose for himself when to jump, and from which side to jump. He needs no spectators. He needs only his legs, the flower-bed and maybe a decent light. Indeed, he can find out if he can jump the three-foot-wide flower-bed without even a flower-bed, since he can measure out a three-foot distance anywhere on the lawn or in the drive that he likes and try to jump that. (*d*) Some actions are preparations for others, as clearing the throat for singing, or pumping up the bicycle tyres for going for a bicycle-ride. The singing or the bicycle-ride may not take place, but the preparatory action requires for its 'thick' description a reference to the intended or expected singing or cycling. Consequently, I might clear my throat to give the false impression that I was about to sing. This throat-clearing is not a pretence throat-clearing; it is a pretence throat-clearing-in-preparation-for-singing. Its 'thick' description requires a second-remove reference to singing. Obviously I can clear my throat for singing minus the accompanist whom I shall need for my singing.

(*e*) Jerking the leafless branch of the tree can be at once an experiment and a preparation. The would-be climber wants to find out if the branch is sound in order to pull himself up on it if it is sound, and not to do so if it is not. There is nothing to prevent the branch-jerking from being also a demonstration to a novice of one of the techniques of tree-climbing. The branch-tester may not be trying to climb the tree today. He wants to find out its strength for tomorrow's or for someday's tree-climbing, or for someone else's tree-climbing. Climbing the tree will require twenty minutes and suitable clothes. Testing the branch does not require all this time, or this clothing. (*f*) Pretending to *X* is not *X*-ing, but reference to *X*-ing has to enter into the 'thick' description of what the pretender is doing. If, what is often not the case, the pretending to *X* is an attempt to deceive, its success consists in the spectator thinking that the agent is *X*-ing or trying to *X*. He pretends in vain if the spectator is not taken in. Obviously the pretender to *X* may be free of some of the adjuncts required for *X*-ing. I can pretend to be rich without having a lot of money; or I can pretend to know Budapest without having been there. (*g*) Consider lastly the notion of waiting – waiting for a train perhaps. I wait in vain if the train does not arrive, or if I am on the wrong platform, or if I get into the wrong train. The 'thick' description of what I am doing on the platform requires mention of my should-be train-catching. Here there is no *X*-ing in particular that I must be positively doing in order to qualify as waiting. I may sit or stand or stroll, smoke or tackle a crossword puzzle, chat or hum or keep quiet. All that is required is that I do not do anything or go anywhere or remain anywhere that will prevent me catching the train. Waiting is abstaining from doings that conflict with the objective. So waiting requires no apparatus at all, and only the simple circumstance of remaining near where the train will come in and not going to sleep.

So maybe *le Penseur's* total detachment, disengagement or remoteness from what is going on around him is *in excelsis* akin to the practising golfer's independence of lots of golf-course adjuncts; or the cookery-instructor's independence of lots of kitchen adjuncts; or the commuter's independence of almost any adjuncts, save, roughly, the right platform. We all know from our own experience how reflecting may require experimenting, testing, rehearsing, practising, and plenty of sheer waiting.

Suppose that *le Penseur* is a composer who is trying to compose a Hungarian Rhapsody, whatever that is. Yesterday he sat at a piano, trying out notes and note-sequences on the keys. The piano notes that 'thinly' he produced, 'thickly' were cancellings, modifyings, assemblings, reassemblings, rehearsings, etc., for what future trumpeters and violinists will, hopefully, be playing. Today, owing to spring-cleaning in his home, he is sitting on a rock on the hillside, half-humming notes and note-sequences, cancelling and modifying them, rehearsing them, etc. Today, unlike yesterday, he uses no instrument and he has not even to worry lest he wakes the baby. Tomorrow, perhaps, he goes on composing his Rhapsody, and does this without even half-humming anything. He just 'hears in his head' his still tentative snatches and stretches of music. Now the note-sequences which he tries out, rejects, modifies, assembles, rehearses, etc., are almost totally circumstance-disengaged and totally equipment-free. They are his own 100 per cent. 'voluntaries'.

But if *le Penseur* is composing not music, but an after-dinner speech, then, whether or not he happens also to be absent-mindedly humming snatches of music, he must be producing, mostly from his own resources, candidate-words, phrases and sentences. But he is free to produce them aloud or *sotto voce* or in his head; or in ink on paper; or in 'mental' ink on 'mental' paper, or, etc. Obviously his production at a certain moment of some unbegun and unfinished phrase is not all that he is 'thickly' doing. He is experimentally and suspiciously trying out, so to speak 'on appro', and quite often rejecting a candidate for what he will be delivering in the Grand Hotel tomorrow night. Or perhaps he is rehearsing, for 'the night', a now accepted candidate for inclusion; or perhaps he is operating with it as a spring-board from which to move on to its yet uncomposed sequel; or maybe he is doing several or all of these things together. But whatever he is now trying to do, his intention is frustrated if tomorrow's dinner is cancelled: and what he is now tentatively and rehearsingly doing requires no external adjuncts, apparatus, materials or circumstances – or almost none, save perhaps a dictionary and an anthology of humorous anecdotes.

If *le Penseur* is trying to solve a chess-problem he need not be humming snatches of anything or producing any words or word-sequences. He may experimentally move and re-move pieces on the chessboard in front of him, unpressed by an opponent or a clock. Or he may, like me, only much more efficiently, be considering alternative moves of visualised chessmen on a visualised chessboard; or he may in imagination, in some other manner, be experimentally making alternative moves. But whichever he is at this moment 'thinly' doing, 'thickly' he is trying to check and mate in four moves.

I now suggest that *le Penseur*'s disengagement from what exists and is going on around him does not involve that he is not, like the tennis-player, thinking what he is doing; we have seen that of course he must be doing this. Rather what he is 'thinly' doing is completely or in high degree circumstance-detached and apparatus-free. What he is 'thinly' doing, e.g. humming under his breath short sequences of notes, is entirely or almost entirely within his own initiative and option. It is a pure or nearly pure 'voluntary'. He can produce what notes he likes, when he likes and in what order he likes. He has all the freedoms that the practiser of approach-shots has, and more besides. He does not need to have 100 per cent. circumstance-emancipation in order to qualify as reflecting. I should qualify as engaged in reflection were I trying to solve a chess-problem with my eyes visibly travelling over the page of the news-paper on which the problem was set; and the composer could be fingering the keys of a real piano and still qualify as being in the throes of composition, and so as being in a brown study. His pensiveness does not require total absence of visible or audible *X*-ing; but the *X*-ing must be very much his own '*ad lib.*'.

But more than this. Not only must *le Penseur* be 'thinly' doing something which enjoys some measure of circumstance-disengagement and therefore some measure of author's optionalness; but also what he is 'thinly' doing must have a 'thicker' description. What he is 'thinly' doing must be in one or more ways and at one or more removes an intention-parasite, as the rehearsing actor's gesturings are intention-parasites on his gesturings on 'the night'; or as the tree-climber's branch-jerkings are intention-parasites on his or his son's branch-trustings or mistrustings tomorrow. The philosopher who, 'thinly', is at this moment mouthing a sentence or sentence-torso may, 'thickly' be, so to speak, jerking a tempting premiss-branch for use, or else for non-use in an argument which is not yet ready, and this would-be argument itself may in its turn be wanted for the rebuttal of some caviller's criticism. Intention-parasites may pyramid. 'Big fleas have little fleas'.

I suggest, finally, that these elements of (*a*) circumstance-detachment, author-optionalness or *ad lib*-ness and (*b*) intention-parasitism, simple or multiple, are what philosophers are trying to get under control when they say, Procrusteanly, that reflecting is, for example, 'operating with symbols' or 'using language'; or that in thinking of Folly Bridge, when I am not there, I must, instead, have in my presence some sort of proxy or token for that congested bridge – as if the gap between the tennis-player and *le Penseur* needed to be filled by a new sort of circumstance or a new sort of apparatus, only sorts which are exempted from the grosser actualities. I suggest that the gap needs to be filled by intention-parasitic and author-optional doings, of which word-producing and sentence-producing are only one species among many, though a specially important species. But this is not the time to account for its special importance.

13

EXPRESSION

Richard Wollheim

WHETHER the word 'passion', as indicating the suffering or affection from without of a soul, is by now no more than a dead metaphor, surviving from an antique conception of the mind; whether, indeed, there is any way open to us of determining the passivity or otherwise of our inner life, apart, that is, from how it strikes us, from how we are prompted to describe it, are not questions that I can take up this evening. It is enough for my purpose that for much of the time our feelings, our emotions, our inclinations are as fluctuating or as imperious as if they were not totally under our control. We are elated: we are dejected: we get angry, and then our anger gives place to a feeling of absurdity: we remain in love with someone who is lost to us but whom we cannot renounce: we are interested in something, and suddenly we are bored, or frightened that we will be bored: we see a stranger, someone who is nothing to us, who is poor or crippled, and we feel guilt: someone does something wrong or foolish, and we are unaccountably transported by laughter, by 'sudden glory' as Hobbes called it, knowing what it was about, and then, as unaccountably, we are thrown down. Man is, in Montaigne's famous phrase, *une chose ondoyante*, a creature of inner change and fickleness.

As we pass through these alternating states, these moods and reverses, which make up our inner life, there are, roughly, three things that we can do about them. We can put them into words: we can manifest them in our actions: or we can keep them to ourselves. We can conceal them, or we can reveal them: and if we reveal them, we can do so in behaviour or in language. If later this evening we may find reason to modify this way of classifying the possibilities, in that it overlooks, on the one hand, differences, on the other hand, similarities, to which attention is necessary, nevertheless for the moment it will do.

It will do, if only because it has done for so many others. The assumption that in this classification we have the three fundamental ways in which man, or at any rate man as a social animal, can stand to his inner life, provides the normal or conventional background against which an account of expression is set. For if we take the two ways in which a man is said not to keep his feelings to himself, and the two media to which he then resorts, namely behaviour and language, we can then establish, corresponding to this distinction, a dichotomy between expression and what is indifferently called communication, description, assertion. Now it is within this dichotomy, or, to put it the other way round, by contrast to the notion of, say, assertion, that the notion of expression acquires its significance. In behaviour a man expresses his feelings: in language he asserts or describes them.

That is stage one of the conventional account of expression. But the account generally goes beyond this. For it is then recognised that just what is distinctive of the way in which we reveal our feelings when the medium is behaviour, can also be found when the medium of revelation is language. The case of interjections is customarily cited. The dichotomy between expression and assertion does not neatly correspond to the distinction between behaviour and language. For there can also be expressive language: or, to put it perhaps in a finer way, an expressive use of language. Nevertheless – and this is where stage two of the account is firmly grounded in stage one – the notion of expression remains derived from, or finds its paradigmatic instance in, the behaviour of a man in the grip of feeling: even if it is then, under the influence of the analogy between such a man's behaviour and what his language might be like, extended to his language, or to a fragment of his language. Language is regarded as expressive if and only if it displays certain characteristics that in the first instance pertain to behaviour.

The fundamental distinction between expressing and asserting or describing a feeling or emotion is a commonplace of
eighteenth-century criticism: there linked, as it is at the first
stage of the foregoing account, with the distinction between
behaviour and language. We find it, for instance, in Lessing's
Laocoon, where it is not unrelated to his famous principle of
division between the arts. 'It is a different impression', Lessing
writes, 'which is made by the narration of a man's cries from
that which is made by the cries themselves'.[1] For the subsequent
attempt to take up or collect this distinction, once firmly seized
in the contrast that behaviour and language by and large offer
one another, and transplant it inside one of the terms of this
contrast, thus making a division within language, our thoughts
most naturally turn to the work of I. A. Richards.[2] His distinction between the scientific and the emotive uses of language
was the first systematic attempt of our day to record the fact
that we can express as well as assert our feelings in language.
It was, of course, to Richards's work that the author of *Language,
Truth and Logic* was indebted when he framed the famous
emotive theory of ethics: a new account of language was
invoked in order to redress the balance against the old morality.

But what, we must now ask, are these peculiar or distinctive
characteristics of the way in which we reveal our feelings in
behaviour, such that when we find these same characteristics
recurring in our linguistic utterances, we feel it right to regard
them too as expressive? We need, it would seem, to look at
behaviour and how it stands to our inner life, or to that part
of it which it reveals, to find the answer to our question. But
there is a difficulty here, which, when taken care of, gives us
stage three of the conventional account of expression. And that
is that just as not all the occasions on which we reveal our
feelings in speech can be regarded as assertive or declaratory of
those feelings; in that our utterances may so approximate to the
way in which we reveal our feelings in behaviour that they are
better thought of as expressive: so now, there are occasions on
which we reveal our feelings in behaviour, but what we do is

[1] Gottfried Lessing, *Laocoon*, IV.
[2] C. K. Ogden and I. A. Richards, *The Meaning of Meaning* (London, 1923),
and I. A. Richards, *Principles of Literary Criticism* (London, 1924).

not to be thought of as expressive; in that our behaviour so approximates to the way in which we reveal our feelings in language that it is better classified as declaratory. The kind of thing that would be cited here is gesture or ritualised behaviour.

But the effect of this reservation, it might be thought, is now such as to close us up in so narrow a circle that there is no issue from it. For what have we been told, to date? First, that we assert or declare our feelings when we reveal them in language: except in certain circumstances. Secondly, that we express our feelings when we reveal them in behaviour: except in certain circumstances. Then, when we go on to ask, what are the circumstances that constitute the exceptions, we learn that they are, in the first case, when we express our feelings, and in the second case, when we assert our feelings. So we assert our feelings in language unless we express them, and we express our feelings in behaviour unless we assert them. And to assert our feelings is to reveal them as we do in language unless we happen to express them: and to express our feelings is to reveal them as we do in behaviour unless we happen to assert them.

But the situation is not really as bleak as this suggests. For this way of putting the matter depends on there being no method to hand of separating off the central from the deviant cases of either the behavioural or the linguistic mode of self-revelation. When the conventional account of expression took its second step, it had a method of distinguishing the two kinds of case within the linguistic mode: by reference, that is, to (respectively) divergence from, and similarity to, the unitary kind of case exhibited by the behavioural mode. But when at the third step the behavioural mode lost its unity, are we to take this as indicating that we now have no method of picking out a characteristically behavioural and a characteristically linguistic way of revealing our feelings?

I shall waste no time before saying that I think we definitely have such a method: though unfortunately I cannot here go on to defend my contention.

The most familiar way of introducing my point would be to begin with the contrast between language as something rule-governed and behaviour as something law-like, or, rather, at best something law-like: so that when we reveal our feelings in language, we should expect what we say to be connected with the feeling we reveal by means of a rule, whereas when we reveal our feelings in behaviour, we should expect what we do and the feeling to be connected as instances of a constant conjunction. That, at any rate, should account for the central cases in the two modes: and the deviant cases in each mode can then be identified by their approximation to the central cases of the other. If we now link this up with the dichotomy between assertion and expression, as we have so far gone along with it, we can now say: when I say 'I am angry', this is characteristically an assertion or declaration of my anger, in that what I say and my anger are joined by a rule: when I scowl or bite my lip, this is characteristically an expression, in that the scowl or biting of the lip and my anger instantiate a constant conjunction. We now add the two reservations: that if I scream out 'I am angry' or if I scowl in a charade or some kind of organised dumb-show, deviation will occur.

Recently an argument has been advanced against this classification: not so much as to the lines it draws, but (what is really more significant for our purposes this evening) as to the nomenclature it attaches to these lines, and all that that involves. More specifically, though it is undoubtedly right to distinguish between the different ways in which 'I am angry' and a scowl stand to the anger revealed, and indeed right to do so as I have done, this by itself doesn't give us an account of expression: or if it does, it doesn't give us the account in the interests of which it is usually invoked – for example, in this lecture. For it is not of the man who scowls and says nothing, but of the man who says 'I am angry', that we say that he expressed his anger. Expression is, in other words, where the conventional account would set up description or assertion or declaration.

True enough (the argument goes on), the word 'expression' is used in connection with the revelation of feeling in behaviour. A scowl, for instance, is a facial expression. We call it such. Nevertheless it is worth observing, a shade more closely, just how the word 'expression', more specifically the verb 'to express', is used in these cases. Of the man who scowls, we say that his scowl expressed anger, not that he expressed anger.

It is the expression, not the person, that expresses the feeling.

Professor Alston, from whom I derive this argument,[1] is rightly not insistent on its philosophical potential. 'It would be an act of folly', he says, 'to place too much reliance on the word "express" in this connection.' Nevertheless it is worth staying with the argument a little longer: to make three comments on it.

First, assuming the premiss of the argument to be correct, I want to make an observation which may do something to take away from what must seem to anyone brought up on the conventional account of expression, the totally unprepared-for character of the conclusion. To such a person it must seem incredible that a man's saying something can express something: except deviantly. For to him expression goes with behaviour, not with language. But expression of what?, we might ask: surely not expression of thoughts? No, it will be agreed, not expression of thoughts: we characteristically express our thoughts in words: it is our emotions, our feelings, our moods, that we characteristically express in behaviour. But once this is conceded, we are half-way, or some way, to removing the strangeness of the argument's conclusion. For at the core of every feeling is a thought. It is, for instance, a thought that by and large secures a feeling its object: it is a thought that gives to feeling much of its elaboration and refinement. So part of what justifies the usage 'He expressed his anger', said of the man who puts it into words, is that we may regard what he does as expressing the thought that gives his anger its distinctiveness or inner elaboration.

Secondly – and here I come to question the premiss of the argument – it is far from clear that just any utterance by a man of the form 'I am angry with X' justifies us in saying of that man that he expressed his anger with X. I suspect that certain further requirements are imposed upon the conditions of utterance; requirements, I would suggest, taken from either end of the spectrum of conditions in which I may say 'I am angry'. Roughly, it seems that the utterance must either verge upon the ceremonial use of language or else be highly impassioned or emotive in its overall character – and it is worth

[1] William S. Alston, 'Expressing', in *Philosophy in America*, ed. Max Black (London, 1965).

noting that these are precisely the two kinds of occasion when it has been held that language takes on much of the nature of behaviour.

Thirdly, it is worth noting that though 'He behaved angrily' does not entail 'He expressed his anger', the contrapositive would seem to hold. 'He didn't express his anger' or 'He expressed no anger' entails 'He didn't behave angrily' or 'He didn't exhibit his anger'. This suggests that the point is very narrowly verbal. Alternatively it may mean (as they like to say) that there is a great deal more work to be done here; of a largely unpromising kind, we might add.

However, to many it will seem that the cogent objections to the conventional account of expression come not from specifically linguistic considerations, like those Alston advances, but from a rather different area. For it will be felt that to understand by the expression of a feeling the piece of behaviour that is constantly – constantly, that is to say, as opposed to conventionally – conjoined with that feeling utterly fails to account for, or do justice to, one indubitable and highly important feature of expression: what we might call its appropriateness, or its physiognomic character. By this I mean the way expression seems so finely matched or adjusted to the inner state of which it is the outer correlate, that we can see the one in the other. Phenomenologists and Wittgenstein and Stuart Hampshire are all agreed that any philosophical account of perception that requires us to place physiognomy outside the pale of what we see is to that extent inadequate. And, indeed, if we continue to take ordinary language as our guide in these matters, the fact of physiognomic perception is most certainly reflected in the idioms and turns of common speech. We say of a scowl not merely that it expresses anger but that it is itself angry: a smile can be the expression of pleasure, and when it is, it is a pleased smile.

To spell out the argument: If a scowl is the expression of anger, simply because it is the constant correlate of anger, then, if something other than a scowl were the constant correlate of anger then that piece of behaviour, rather than a scowl, would express anger. Any constant conjunction could be other than it is. Therefore any (or almost any) other piece of behaviour

could be the expression of anger. Therefore it cannot be that
we see anger in a scowl unless we are prepared to say that we
can see anger in any other (or almost any other) piece of
behaviour. In point of fact, however, we see anger in a scowl
and such-like things to the exclusion of all other pieces of
behaviour. Therefore, the understanding of expression, or the
expression of feeling, in terms of constant conjunction is false:
at least in that it is not the whole truth.

I want to consider a number of objections to or comments on
this argument.[1] If we imagine them for a moment laid out
according to the part of the argument to which they relate, I
shall then take them in the inverse order.

The first comment would be that the argument ignores the
well-established cultural relativity of expression. Since this
contention is very large, and not perhaps all that easy to
interpret, I shall put it aside: using only as much of it as comes
out in the remaining comments.

Secondly, it might be said that the argument is wrong to
suggest that the constant conjunction theory of expression
requires that we are able to see, that we can see, anger in every
other piece of behaviour that could be correlated with anger.
All it requires is that we should be able to see, that we could
see, anger in any particular piece of behaviour were it actually,
that is in point of fact, correlated with anger. If it is now retorted
that this comes to the same, for if we can see some characteristic
of a piece of behaviour in one connection, when the behaviour
enters into one specific correlation, then we must also be able
to see it in another connection, for either the piece of behaviour
has that characteristic or it hasn't, this retort would exhibit
very well precisely what is wrong with the original argument.
For it treats physiognomic properties as though they were
physical characteristics either had or not had by something,
and if had, then there to be seen. In reality, however, physiognomic properties are, or are close to, what Wittgenstein in the
second part of the *Philosophical Investigations*[2] called aspects:

[1] Cf. My 'On Expression and Expressionism', *Revue Internationale de
Philosophie*, nos. 68–9 (1964), fascs. 2–3.

[2] Ludwig Wittgenstein, *Philosophical Investigations* (Oxford, 1953), Part II,
xi.

whose existence, it might be said, depends upon their being seen, rather than, as the argument suggests, vice versa.

Thirdly, with this last comment in mind, it may now seem less implausible than the argument suggests to hold that we could see anger in any piece of behaviour: for this means only that we should see it were that behaviour correlated with anger. And if we now think that there are many pieces of behaviour that we just could not imagine ourselves seeing as angry, the explanation for this may be that we cannot, or perhaps just do not, imagine their being correlated with anger. Of course if we do not or cannot imagine the correlation, the physiognomic perception will remain inconceivable. And there is a further difficulty here, to which perhaps insufficient attention is paid in the philosophical discussion of imagination: the difficulty of what it is to imagine something like a correlation, for is not imagination ordinarily thought of as being, like perception, intractably particular in its operation?

Nevertheless, a problem remains. For if it is dogmatic to assert that we could never see anger in any piece of behaviour except that actually correlated with anger, it seems equally unwarranted to assert, without further demonstration, that there is no piece of behaviour that we could not see as angry were it correlated with anger. For this seems to suggest that physiognomic perception, the seeing of anger in a bodily gesture or movement, is nothing over and above bare intellectual awareness, the awareness that anger and the bodily gesture or movement in question are correlated. Physiognomic perception must be more than that. So perhaps there is more to the argument than we have given it credit for.

This brings us to the last, the most important, comment that I have to make. And that is that the supposition, said to be intrinsic to the constant conjunction theory of expression, to the effect that any piece of behaviour could come to be the expression of, say, anger, needs to be taken seriously. And in the argument before us it noticeably is not. It is not, because of a slipperiness in the way in which the notion of behaviour, of a piece of behaviour, is handled.

For when we are asked to suppose that, say, a smile rather than a scowl might become the expression of anger, through becoming its correlate, the words 'scowl' and 'smile' as they occur in this supposition are not intended simply to pick out differing ways in which the face might be pulled or might crease: they do not refer just to the lie of the face, as we might call it. For that by itself is not expression. A particular lie of the face expresses a feeling when and only when it comes about as the result of something that we do. A frown expresses anger when we frown: a smile pleasure when we smile. To put the matter the other way round: even as things stand we can smile or scowl in a purely configurational sense, in that our face can become dishevelled in this or that way, and thus express nothing. As, for instance, foolish parents discover when a baby 'smiles' with wind. It is precisely because the baby doesn't smile, though there is a smile on its face, that no constant conjunction is upset.

And having got only so far, we may pause for a moment. For we may already have in our possession a small bit – as we shall see later, it is no more than a small bit – of the reason why we feel that we can see anger in a scowl: where by 'scowl', we mean simply what I have called a particular lie of the face. For in seeing the scowl we are immediately made aware of the activity whereby it came into being. And from the activity we are led, a stage further back, to the feeling. The activity is a bridge which we may traverse in our imagination from face to feeling. In *Feeling and Expression* Professor Stuart Hampshire made great use of this idea.[1] Indeed slightly transposed, it became crucial to his philosophical account of how we come to acquire knowledge of other minds. The transposition, which may have somewhat obscured this similarity, was that, instead of the imaginative reconstruction of the scowl to which I make reference, Hampshire introduced the far more overt method of mimicry or imitation. We come to learn the feelings or sentiments of others through an inner mimicry of their natural expression, he argues: thereby reviving a late nineteenth-century view of the matter.[2] Neither in his terms nor in my terms, would I go as far as Hampshire goes: he being undoubtedly influenced here by the view, to which he subscribed

[1] Stuart Hampshire, *Feeling and Expression* (London, 1961).
[2] The main proponent of this view was Karl Groos.

at this stage, of the inner life as the residue or shadow of once open, now inhibited, behaviour. Nevertheless, the distinction made here between the two sides of expression, activity and trace as we might think of them, certainly has its bearing upon our knowledge of others; if only indirectly, through helping us to understand physiognomic perception.

Let us now return to the main argument. I have maintained that the supposition that a different piece of behaviour might be correlated with anger from that which now expresses it, is not exhausted by the thought that when we are angry a smile, say, might appear on our face. For this seems compatible with the supposition that when we are angry, we should scowl and a smile should appear on our face: equally, with the supposition that when we are angry, a smile should appear on our face from nowhere, or absent-mindedly. The supposition, taken seriously, as I have been insisting that it should be taken, seems to be to some such effect as that when we are angry, we should smile. We may later have to revive this formulation, but it will do for a start.

But now we have a difficulty: and that, of course, is to understand what is meant here by 'smiling'. It is naturally no part of my case to suggest that 'smile' must mean 'produce such-and-such a lie of the face'. But the trouble is that what looks like the other way in which we can understand the word 'smile', the other leg on which the meaning of the word rests, is not available to us either. For this other way of understanding 'smile' is where to smile is to express pleasure. Put more generally, having isolated things that we do with our body or parts of our body both from the feelings that they express and from the bodily modifications in which they issue, it now seems impossible to identify them without making reference to at least one of these things. Yet the supposition of a change in correlations of feeling and behaviour seems to require that we refer to neither.

The precise nature of the difficulty must be firmly grasped. For nothing has been said to suggest that we could not express our inner states other than as we do: which is all to the good, since any such suggestion would be empirically false. The difficulty is rather that, as things stand, we seem to have no way of indicating how we would express ourselves differently: since the terms that we use to identify or pick out the expressive activities seem so firmly rooted in the two circumjacent conditions from which, for the purpose of this argument, we need to detach them.

I now have a suggestion as to how we might extricate ourselves from this impasse, which will roughly occupy us for the rest of this lecture. I suggest that we turn to a rather different kind of activity from either smiling or scowling, but which has this in common with those activities: that it is regarded, and surely rightly, as expressive. I am referring to the activities upon which the visual arts repose: for instance, painting. Whether all painting is expressive or not, or whether the expressiveness of painting is a distinctively modern conception, I shall leave undiscussed. In our culture, in the context of the late bourgeois world, painting is certainly a mode of expression. But now we must ask in the light of all that has already been said, How can this be? How can painting be expressive, when it seems so contrived, so sophisticated and self-conscious an affair, so remote from the movements of the mind and the body?

We are not yet in a position to answer this question. To our existing account of the matter, we need to add another element before we can take in this further aspect of expression. And that is the tendency, operative in us (we are to believe) from the earliest experiences, to find objects in the outer world that seem to match, or correspond with, what we experience inwardly. This tendency is particularly sharp or poignant for us when we are in the grip of a strong feeling, but it is never long out of operation. A broken tree or tower will represent for us the sense of power or strength laid waste: the blue of the distant sky suddenly realises a feeling, a lost feeling perhaps, of happiness. The objects, of course, have originated quite independently of us: they are parts of the environment, which we in some broad sense appropriate, because they have this special resonance for us. Once again we find a reflection of this phenomenon in ordinary speech. For the correspondence between inner feeling and outer object leads us to characterise the object in the language of feeling. The landscape is cheerful, the sky is grim, the estuary is melancholy. And indeed it is only a piece of theory, an epistemological presupposition, that leads us to think that there is available a neutral description drained of emotion that fits the original perception we have of such objects. I shall call this tendency, following a famous nineteenth-century usage, the finding of 'correspondences'.

Now, it is upon this foundation that the function of painting as an expressive activity in part depends. Not wholly, but in part. For the concept of expression in painting, properly understood, would seem to lie at the intersection of two constituent notions. One notion, which is where painting joins itself most obviously with scowling or smiling, is that of a bodily activity – in this case, more specifically, a manual activity – whose variations coincide with variations of inner state. If we find this thought surprising, this is of course only because we are not painters. To put the matter the other way round: the manual activity of painting acquires expressiveness in this sense only when the activity itself has become habitual. It is, in other words, only in the hands of painters that painting is expression. It is useful to recall that we do not have a more general phenomenon than this that we are called upon to explain.

The other notion constituent of the concept of expression in painting is formed upon what I have called 'correspondence'. There is, however, now a difference. I have introduced the notion of correspondence by reference to the selection or isolation of natural objects as matching our feelings. We are now to envisage that these matching objects are made, not selected. So we bring into being, where previously we discovered, correlates to our inner states.

Of course we cannot simply think of this as an extension of the original notion and imagine that there will not also be differences that accrue to the notion when it is extended in this way. As a minimum there will be aspects of the notion that were so unproblematic in the original context as to escape detection, and that only rise to prominence in the new context. The thinker who has most powerfully drawn our attention to the difficulties that arise when we pass from natural correspondences to the deliberate construction or assemblage of elements in the interests of expression is, of course, Professor Ernst Gombrich. That part of his argument which bears directly upon

the present issue may be summarised as follows: When in nature
we find something that corresponds to an inner feeling, what
we do is that we select something out of a pre-existent range
of elements as being the closest match to that state. It is the
selection – that is, the picking out of one object rather than
another – that gives the notion of match or closeness its
significance: but just because the range out of which the
selection is made is pre-existent, we do not need to insist on
this point. When, however, we turn to the bringing into being
of expressive elements, the range, which can no longer be
equated simply with the bounty of nature, needs explicit
formulation. Unless the repertoire, as the range is called in this
context, is defined and known, we cannot talk of anything
being selected in preference to anything else, and hence
expression becomes a vacuous notion.[1]

The details of this argument deserve careful attention. But
not here this evening. For you will recall that I invoked this
further notion of correspondence, only so as ultimately to throw
light upon expression taken in a more general sense than that
of artistic expression. I chose to introduce this notion in the
context of art, for there the gap between the bringing into being
of an element that corresponds to a certain inner state and the
inner state itself is so wide that I can survey the phenomenon
in comfort: but that does not mean that I need examine the
mechanism by which such elements are brought into being in
the area of art, in any detail. So I shall now turn back to my
main subject this evening – the expression of feelings in
behaviour – and see how the account I have given can be
enriched by the notion of correspondence.

At first sight it might seem surprising that it could be. For
we seem to find no application for the notion. We cannot, say,
equate painting out of anger with scowling, and the angry
painting that we thereby paint with the scowl that results,
without total absurdity: as though we might start to scowl, and
then observe the scowl, and then experience dissatisfaction with
the scowl as it is, and so scowl a little differently, and eventually
get the scowl we want. Of course this conception is absurd: but

[1] E. H. Gombrich, *Art and Illusion* (London, 1960), ch. 12, and *Meditations on a Hobby Horse* (London, 1963), *passim*.

that is because it overlooks the narrowness of the gap between the activity and the trace, not because it conceives of a gap at all. Accordingly, to arrive at a less absurd, at a more realistic, conception, what we have to do is to imagine the process spread out across time and barely obtruding into consciousness. We postulate, that is, merely some kind of negative feed-back that occurs from perception or thought to the expressive activity, which ultimately brings about a change in what I have earlier on called 'the life of the face'.

If we can accept this insertion of the new element into the account of the expression of feeling in behaviour, we may now return to the impasse into which our examination of the constant conjunction theory of expression led us. For that theory seemed to require us to suppose that any particular feeling could find expression in any other piece of behaviour than that in which it does, were that piece of behaviour to be correlated with it. So, for instance, anger could be expressed by smiling rather than by scowling. But the difficulty we had in understanding this supposition was how words like 'scowling' or 'smiling' were to be taken. For it seemed inadequate to define them in terms of a certain lie of the face: and it seemed inviting self-contradiction to define them in terms of the feeling that they currently express. But now perhaps we have a third way open to us of taking them, directly derivative from the foregoing discussion. On this reading, to scowl would be 'to produce an angry lie of the face': to smile would be 'to produce a happy lie of the face'. In other words, smiling and scowling would be intentional verbs having as their aims the bringing about of something in so far as it fell under a certain description.

How does this help us? More specifically, does it or does it not make it possible for us to understand the supposition that is allegedly implicit in the constant conjunction theory of expression? That is, we could express our inner states other than as we do. The answer is, I think, that it does: on a certain assumption. I shall first of all try to show how it does, and then turn and look at the assumption.

At the outset it must be said that the way in which physiognomic change is made intelligible is not by equating this, as I earlier suggested we should, with the possibility that a man might, say, be angry and smile. For if we employ this new intentional notion of expression, then it is clear that a man could not be angry and smile. Or rather he could be angry and smile: but in such an eventuality his smile would not be the expression of his anger. He might be angry and smile, just as he might be angry and cough.

However, though a man could never express his anger other than by scowling, nevertheless there might be physiognomic change in this way: that the configuration on his face might be different. The man might be angry, and scowl, and the lie of his face might be that which currently appears on the face of a man who smiles.

But this, it will be said, is surely just the possibility that I rejected earlier on in the lecture. I considered that physiognomic change was not achieved simply when, say, a smile in the sense of a lie of the face appeared on the face of an angry man. I said it was also necessary that the man should smile. And now I appear to have abandoned that claim.

I think, however, that the new intentional notion of expression should allow us to see how that claim can be abandoned and yet the spirit that animated it be retained. For what we are now to insist upon in the case of the man who is angry and expresses this in a smiling lie of the face is that he should see the lie of the face as angry and should bring it about just because he does. What I was insistent upon was activity, and this element of activity is now adequately safeguarded. The difference between my original claim and the present formulation is that, since the activity is now identified intentionally, the appropriate word for the activity is not 'smile' but 'scowl'.

I said just now that this attempt to make sense of the notion of physiognomic change rests upon a certain assumption. And the assumption is that there is a basis for physiognomic perception independent of the constant conjunctions that hold between behaviour and inner state. For if there was no such independence, then the lies of the face that any man would see as angry would be those, and just those, which appear on the faces of angry men. So we could not appeal to his attempt to assume an angry face as any kind of explanation of the deviant or unorthodox way in which he might express his anger. But I think that the phenomenon of correspondences does seem to suggest that in man there is some independent base of physiognomic perception.

One way in which the suggestion can come to seem absurd is if we assume that if there is such a basis, it could be of any breadth: that if our physiognomic perception is not totally derived from our familiarity with the correlations of inner state and behaviour, then we should in principle be able to see, even as things stand, any phenomenon in any emotional light. The argument from parody is a much-used weapon in the philosophy of mind. It is not only use that accounts for its bluntness.

I am very conscious that at this stage my argument displays a yawning gap. Even if I cannot close this gap, I should like at least to bridge it. The gap originates in my assertion that an inner state is expressed when and only when there is activity: again, that only if I do something, can someone else see my feelings in my behaviour. This, it will be said, is manifestly false. Do we not indisputably see embarrassment in a confused countenance?

Well, let me first make a concession. I am prepared to concede that an activity should be insisted on only where there is a possible activity. It is only when I can bring about a certain lie of the face that the lie of the face is not expressive if it merely appears. But having said this, I must now ask how much I have conceded. More specifically, how do I determine when there is and when there isn't an activity? Why, for instance, is laughing an activity and blushing, presumably, not?

Part of this question must lie enmeshed in the question with which I began this lecture: where much the same issue was raised concerning our inner states and the determination of their activity. I wish, however, to lay aside as much of my question as cannot be dealt with independently of those highly 'inward' issues.

Here I would like to suggest simply three criteria of an activity. They are, it will be apparent, criteria for only a weak sense of activity: nevertheless it is one we use. First, that it can be inhibited. I can stop laughing at will, anyhow on occasions: but I cannot stop myself blushing. The Empress Eugénie, it is said, had herself bled so that she should not blush at her husband's stories. But this is not the kind of case I have in mind. To define direct inhibition, or stopping oneself doing something in the requisite sense, has its difficulties. But one requirement would be that there should not be some identifiable thing that we do, of which in turn we could ask whether it can be inhibited or not, in order to bring about the desired inhibition. We stop ourselves: we do not do something so as to stop ourselves.

Secondly, I would suggest that another requirement of an activity is that it should not be identifiable solely by reference to a bodily change: like, say, a hiccough. In order to tell, for instance, whether a man is smiling, where this is an activity, we must take into account the whole of, or a large part of, the rest of what he is doing and of what is happening to him. And as the description of this changes, so likewise our attribution of activity changes.

And, thirdly, I would suggest that an activity is something for which we can always cite beliefs in explanation or justification.[1] If we find something funny, and are amused, and laugh, the laughter it seems expresses the amusement, only if we can cite the belief, interchangeably with the emotion, as the reason for our laughter. This is perhaps what philosophers like Dewey have had in mind when they insisted that all expression was not just expression of emotion but expression of a particular emotion.[2] For when we cite the belief it is to the effect not simply that there is something or other that is funny, but that some particular thing is funny. I have brought you to one of those many points where we can see so clearly the intersection of the various aspects of the human being that the philosophy of mind has traditionally taken delight in isolating. I can think of no better place to stop.

[1] Cf. Charles Darwin, *The Expression of the Emotions in Man and Animals* (London, 1872), chap. xiii.

[2] John Dewey, *Art as Experience* (London, 1934).

INDEX

3/68